HUMAN RIGHTS EDUCATION

HUMAN RIGHTS EDUCATION

Usha Ajithkumar
MA [Eng], MA [HR], MED, PGDHE, Dip. in Journalism,
Assistant Professor, Hansraj Jivandas College of Education,
Khar, Mumbai.

HPH
Himalaya Publishing House
MUMBAI • NEW DELHI • NAGPUR • BENGALURU • HYDERABAD • CHENNAI • PUNE • LUCKNOW • AHMEDABAD
• ERNAKULAM • BHUBANESWAR • INDORE • KOLKATA

First Edition: 2011

Published by : Mrs. Meena Pandey
for **HIMALAYA PUBLISHING HOUSE PVT. LTD.,**
"Ramdoot", Dr. Bhalerao Marg, Girgaon, **Mumbai - 400 004.**
Phone: 2386 01 70/2386 38 63, Fax: 022-2387 71 78
Email: himpub@vsnl.com, Website: www.himpub.com

Branch Offices:

New Delhi : "Pooja Apartments", 4-B, Murari Lal Street, Ansari Road, Darya Ganj, New Delhi - 110 002. Phone: 23270392, 23278631, Fax: 011-23256286

Nagpur : Kundanlal Chandak Industrial Estate, Ghat Road, Nagpur -440 018. Phone: 011-2738731/3296733, Telefax : 0712-2721215

Bengaluru : No. 16/1 (Old 12/1), 1st Floor, Next to Hotel Highlands, Madhava Nagar, Race Course Road, Bengaluru - 560 001. Phone : 080-22281541/22385461, Telefax: 080-22286611

Hyderabad : No. 3-4-184, Lingampally, Besides Raghavendra Swamy Matham, Kachiguda, Hyderabad - 500 027. Phone: 040-27560041, 27550139, Mobile: 09848130433

Chennai : No. 85/50, Bazullah Road, T. Nagar, Chennai - 600 017. Phone: 044-28144004/28144005

Pune : First Floor, "Laksha" Apartment, No. 527, Mehunpura, Shaniwarpeth, (Near Prabhat Theatre), Pune - 411 030. Phone: 020-24496323/24496333

Lucknow : Jai Baha Bhavan, Church Road, Near Manas Complex and Dr, Awasthi Clinic, Aliganj, Lucknow - 226 024 Phone: 0522-23393294068914, Mobile: 09305302158, 09415349385, 09389593752

Ahmedabad : 114, "SHAIL", 1st Floor, Opp. Madhu Sudan House, C.G. Road, Navrang Pura, Ahmedabad - 380 009. Phone: 079-26560126, Mobile: 09327324149, 09314679413

Ernakulam : 39/104 A, Lakshmi Apartment, Karikkamuri Cross Rd., Ernakulam, Cochin - 622011, Kerala. Phone: 0484-2378012, 2378016, Mobile: 09344199799

Bhubaneswar : 5 Station Square, Bhubaneswar - 751 001. Mobile: 9861046007, E-mail: orissa@himpub.com

Indore : Kesardeep Avenue Extension, 73, Narayan Bagh, Flat No. 302, IIIrd Floor, Near Humpty Dumpty School, Narayan Bagh, Indore (M.P.) - 452 007. Mobile: 09301386468

Kolkata : 108/4, Beliaghata Main Road, Near ID Hospital, Opp. SBI Bank, Kolkata - 700 010. Mobile: 09910440956

DTP by : HPH, Editorial Office, Bhandup (Pravin)

Printed by : Sachin Printers, Mumbai.

DEDICATED TO

THE LOTUS FEET OF

MY GURU SHRI SATYA SAI BABA

AND

MY SON SAISHIVA, MAY GOD BLESS YOU

Preface

I began to ask myself about the inspiration for writing this book. The United Nation's message is: Know your human rights. People who know their rights stand the best chance of realizing them. Knowledge of human rights is the best defence against their violation. Learning about one's rights builds respect for the rights of others and points the way to more tolerant and peaceful societies. Vast number of people are still unaware of their rights. While laws and institutions could in many cases defend them, people must first know where they may turn for help.

This book is for all educators who intend to know about human rights and how to impart it to their students. The main objective of this book is to impart knowledge and skill related to human rights education.

The book is divided into twelve chapters focusing on the concept of human rights and human rights education, important declarations, conventions and covenants on human rights, state of human rights in India, activities to impart human rights in the educational institutions.

It is fitting to close this preface by thanking the many people who made it possible for me to finish this book. My young son Saishiva was understanding about my many physical and mental absences from the usual activities of family life. He is a very important stimulus to my thinking. My brother Shri Krishnan Kutty, my nephew Ashish and niece Vaishnavi need a special mention.

USHA AJITHKUMAR

Brief Contents

Contents

1 Concept of Human Rights

A right means a claim or power to do something or, to have (acquire) and own something, that is considered to be necessary for an individual to live with dignity as a human being and a member of mankind. Such claims or powers are known as, 'Human Rights'.

Human rights are universal; they are the birthright of every member of the human family. No one has to earn or deserve human rights. Human rights are inalienable: you cannot lose these rights any more than you can cease to be a human being. Human rights are indivisible: you cannot be denied a right because someone decides that it is 'less important' or 'non-essential'. Human rights are independent: all human rights are part of a complementary frame-work because human rights are not granted by any human authority such as a monarch, government, or secular or religious authority, they are not the same as civil rights. Constitutional rights are granted to individuals by virtue of their citizenship or residence in a particular country whereas human rights are inherent and held as attributes of the human personality.

Supported by several international conventions and treaties (such as the United Nation's Universal Declaration of Human rights in 1948), these include cultural, economic, and political rights. Promulgation of these rights is not binding on any country, but they serve as a standard of concern for people and form the basis of many modern national constitutions. They were defined first by the UK philosopher John Locke (1632-1704) as absolute moral claims or entitlements to life, liberty, and property.

Definitions of Human Rights

(1) Justice M.H Beg – "Human Rights imply justice, equality and freedom from arbitrary and discriminatory treatment".

(2) Justice Nagendra Singh of International Court of Justice opined that respect for the human personality and its absolute worth, regardless of colour, race, sex are the very foundation of Human Rights.

(3) Justice Durga Das Basu — "Human rights are those minimal rights, which every individual must have against the State , or other public authority, by virtue of his being a member of human family, irrespective of caste, colour, creed, place of birth, sex, cultural differences, or any other consideration".

(4) Protection of Human Rights Act, 1993 has defined the term — "Human Rights means the rights relating to life, liberty, equality and dignity of the individual guaranteed by the constitution or embodied in the international covenants and enforced by courts in India".

Human rights are those rights that are necessary in order for us to live as human beings. Human rights give us dignity and equality. Human rights ensure that we all have adequate access to basic needs such as food and shelter. Human rights protect us from violence and abuse and work against ignorance and hatred. Human rights allow us to fully develop our human abilities. They protect our right to participate in society, to work and provide for ourselves, to practice our culture and speak our language, to live in peace and to be free from harm.

Human rights are both abstract and practical. They hold up the inspiring vision of a free, just, and peaceful world and set minimum standards for how both individuals and institutions should treat people. They also empower people to take action to demand and defend their rights and the rights of others.

Human Rights may be defined as:-

- universal legal guarantees,
- that belong to all human beings,
- and that protect individuals and/or groups
- from actions and omissions of the State and some non-State actors
- that affect fundamental human dignity.

Nature of Human Rights

(a) Human Rights refer to "fundamental human dignity"

It is generally true that all human beings would like to enjoy human rights fully (e.g. to food, to work, to life, to a fair trial, against torture), and that nobody would want to be deprived of them. These aspects of human well-being are valued to the extent of being considered fundamental to human dignity. They can be promoted (or jeopardized) by the exercise of power or authority, particularly by the State.

(b) Human Rights are universal (they belong to all human beings)

Human rights belong to all human beings simply because they are human. This is known as the **"universality"** of human rights. Historically, rights were considered the privilege of people of a certain race, gender, social origin or economic status – who would also view the use of State power as primarily intended for their own benefit. The principle of "universality" is thus linked to **"non-discrimination"**. Non-discrimination does not necessarily mean identical treatment: **those who are in a disadvantaged or marginalized position sometimes require special attention**, as treating equally what are unequal situations may reinforce existing marginalization.

(c) Human Rights are legal guarantees, against actions and omissions

Societies can identify with (see point a)), but at the same time it is *legal* in character. Human rights are more than principles or values related to human dignity, they are also (and especially) **a legal-framework of entitlements and obligations**. Whenever there is a right, there is a duty. Hence, with respect to a particular right there are **claim-holders and dutybearers**. Human rights create mainly obligations for the State, because the State is generally the most powerful actor of social relations, and therefore has the greatest influence on human rights. States accept their responsibilities as duty-bearers upon ratification of international human rights treaties, and through constitutional and legal provisions. In certain cases, international customary law may bind States even in the absence of ratification (e.g. prohibition of slavery and genocide).

As **legal norms**, Human Rights **specify a series of actions that need to be taken** (e.g. adopting legislation to protect a healthy environment, ensuring decent work conditions), **or that should not be taken at all** (e.g. torturing somebody, denying education on racial or gender grounds), in the exercise of power or authority. Unequal power relationships can also exist among individuals (e.g. a man and a woman, a mother and her child, an employer and an employee).

(d) Human Rights protect individuals and groups

Human rights may protect an individual, or a group of individuals (e.g. minorities, indigenous peoples). Although most human rights are "individual rights", many human rights are exercised collectively (e.g. the right to profess and practice one's religion), and some human rights are generally applied to collectives of people, rather than individuals (e.g. rights of minorities).

(e) **Human rights belong to everybody, simply because we are human**

Human rights are sometimes considered to be a form of 'natural law' by virtue of being self-evident, and universally applicable to all of humanity. Human rights are inherent to all people, without exception.

(f) **Human rights do NOT need to be earned or bought. Similarly, they are NOT a luxury or privileges that are dependent on whether conditions permit.**

They cannot be cast aside simply because they may be difficult to uphold or fulfill.

(g) **Human rights are inalienable**

No one has the right to deprive another of their rights. Everyone has the right to have their human rights respected, even if their nation does not recognize or respect them. Put another way, human rights are not dependent on whether a government or its laws respect them or not; they are either upheld or breached, but cannot be erased.

(h) **While each of us has rights, we also have responsibilities.**

Every government and individual has the responsibility to respect the rights of others. To highlight the importance of these principles, consider how the breaching of these principles leads to grave injustices. Consider slavery in the United States during the 1800's. The fact that the laws or policies of the time did not acknowledge that all people, including those who were enslaved, were entitled to be treated as equals, or that slavery was inhumane, does not mean that they did not have human rights. The slaves who were victimized by this cruelty had their rights grossly violated, and the government failed in its responsibility to respect their rights.

(i) **Human Rights are never absolute**

Human rights are those limited powers or claims, which are contributory to the common goods and which are recognized and guaranteed by the State, through its laws, to individual. Such claims or power are recognized by the State only to the extend they are essential for the full development for the human personality.

(j) **Human Rights are dynamic in nature**

The dimensions of human rights go on expanding with the socio-eco-cultural and political developments. Today, the right to be protected from starvation has been extended to include the right to food, which is adequate in quality as well as quantity.

World Conference on Human Rights, Vienna, 1993· In 1993, the UN-sponsored World Conference on Human Rights was held in Vienna. The following principles were highlighted in the Vienna Declaration:

All human rights are universal, indivisible, inter-dependent and inter-related. The international community must treat human rights globally in a fair and equal manner, on the same footing, and with the same emphasis. In other words, all human rights apply to all people, and all people are entitled to them. In addition, rights are all related to each other, and neglecting some while emphasizing others is not justified.

It is the duty of states, regardless of their political, economic and cultural systems, to promote and protect all human rights and fundamental freedoms. These duties have been clarified and grouped as follows:

- **Respect:** Governments must refrain from interfering with the enjoyment of human rights;
- **Protect:** Governments must protect human rights of citizens from being infringed by other parties; and,
- **Fulfill:** Governments must facilitate access to, and provide for the full realization of, all human rights. As you can see, human rights principles establish not only what governments must not do to their citizens, but also what they must provide and ensure.

There is recognition that not all states have the means to immediately provide for the fulfillment of all rights, and that full realization of all rights can only be achieved progressively. Bearing this in mind, the principle of 'progressive realization' was established, which allows states to implement human rights over time. The burden is placed on the state to demonstrate that it is making measurable progress toward the full realization of human rights, and the principle does not absolve states of their legal obligations under human rights law to take certain steps immediately and others as soon as possible. Finally, states may not use the 'progressive realization' principle as a pretext for non-compliance.

In real practice the human rights is the sum of all rights necessary to ensure our rights to be human and it is the duty of all people and government to create the conditions needed to exercise our right to be human.

Ways of Categorizing Human Rights

Human rights relate to numerous and diverse areas of human activity. This broad scope is reflected in the many ways that human rights are conceptualized and categorized. Categorization methods group rights with common issues together. Common themes stem from and are associated with each category, so understanding the distinctions made between categories can help you to become familiar with a wide variety of human rights issues. Each categorization method has different advantages and drawbacks, particularly in terms of what is emphasized. Bear in mind that although distinctions between human rights are made when they are categorized, it does not imply that any right or group of rights is more important than any other. As you can see, human rights relate to numerous and diverse areas of human activity. This broad scope is reflected in the many ways that human rights are conceptualized and categorized. Categorization methods group rights with common issues together. Common themes stem from and are associated with each category, so understanding the distinctions made between categories can help you to become familiar with a wide variety of human rights issues. Each categorization method has different advantages and drawbacks, particularly in terms of what is emphasized. Bear in mind that although distinctions between human rights are made when they are categorized, it does not imply that any right or group of rights is more important than any other.

(I) Generations of Rights

This conception of human rights is based on a historical context. Each 'generation' of rights was developed and codified at different periods of time, and reflects different emphases. The three instruments of the United Nations' 'International Bill of Rights' are separated along these lines, and this approach is perhaps the most common way that human rights are categorized.

First Generation Rights or Civil Political Rights: These rights are primarily fulfilled when the government does not interfere with citizens or take offensive action. These rights are meant to preserve basic freedoms and civil liberties, create fairness in the justice system, and allow us to participate in society to a full extent. The philosophical source of such rights is primarily the enlightenment, liberalism, and the democratic theories that span numerous time periods and cultures. Examples include the right to: free assembly; freedom of religion; free expression; freedom from unlawful detention; and, the right to vote/participate in public life.

In the modern context, these rights are still the main defence against abuses such as false imprisonment, denial of due process, and political oppression. In the Western world, these rights are often what first come to mind. This group of rights is sometimes viewed as a luxury, or an expression of western values, and therefore is seen as not necessarily applicable in some situations. This leads to an unjust denial of these rights to many people.

Second Generation Rights, or Economic, Social and Cultural Rights: These rights are primarily fulfilled through the provision of, and access to, certain basic services and fair treatment. These rights are meant to provide us with what we need and allow us to thrive as human beings. The concept that the government ought to provide certain economic and social services is a relatively recent historical development. These rights rose to prominence after World War II with the growing acceptance of the welfare state. Examples include the right to health; shelter; education; food; and, cultural expression. In the modern context there is increasing recognition that these rights are a core aspect of human rights, and their legal foundations are deepening. That said, there is still reluctance in some circles to accept them as equal to civil and political rights because economic, social, and cultural rights require a large role for the state. The inability of some nations to provide services, as well as the resistance to doing so, means that these rights are routinely denied.

Third Generation Rights or Collective Rights: These rights are called 'collective rights' because they apply to society as a whole, and reflect the need to address modern abuses that occur at the group level. Human rights suffer greatly when people are afflicted by war, pollution, poverty, ethnic marginalization, and so forth. This generation of rights has been developed in recent years through various declarations of the UN General Assembly, the African Charter of Human and People's Rights, various thematic human rights Conventions, and even certain domestic Constitutions. Examples include the right to: peace; a clean environment; development; and, rights of minority groups.

In a sense, this generation of rights most plainly reflects the interdependence among human rights. For example, the right to a clean environment safeguards health, economic sustainability, and security of the person, and the right to peace seeks to protect people from the violence, poverty, social disintegration, and misery that stems from warfare.

(II) Positive or Negative Rights

The term **'negative rights'** describes those rights that prevent something harmful from being done. The right to a fair trial, to be free from cruel punishment, or non-discrimination are all examples of such rights. The term **'positive rights'** on the other hand, describes the freedom to do something or to have access to something. The rights to free association or access to education would be considered positive rights.

(III) Provision, Protection, and Participation

A different way to categorize rights is to divide them into three broad thematic categories relating to how people interact with government and society, and *vice-versa*. These categories are:

Provision – The right to receive or have access to certain services, such as health-care, education, leisure, or care for the disabled, or to possess certain basic human needs, such as a name and nationality.

Protection – The right to be free from harmful acts such as cruelty, physical or mental abuse, arbitrary detention, and sexual exploitation.

Participation – The right to be heard and to participate in society, such as free speech, religion, culture, and language.

Rights Those are Difficult to Categorize

Some rights are not easily categorized. Examples include:

Rights to life and security of the person are two of the most basic and longstanding rights, and are found in numerous human rights codes. These rights are meant to protect people from such things as violence, intrusions on bodily and mental integrity, and torture or cruel and inhumane treatment. As such, these rights cannot really be classified as either civil or political rights, or economic, social, or cultural rights. This is not a hard and fast distinction, however, as these rights are often associated or included with the **right to liberty/freedom**, which protects people from injustices such as arbitrary detention and detention without trial. This right is associated with civil and political rights, and thus the rights to life and security of the person are sometimes associated with that category as well. The **right to equality and freedom from discrimination** applies to all rights, and therefore should be placed in its own category. For example, if the generation of rights system is used, then the right to equality applies to civil and political rights, to economic, social, and cultural rights, and to third generation rights. If people are denied free association, a civil-political right, because they are part of a certain religion, then their right to equality and non-discrimination is breached. If people are denied access to proper health care, an economic-social right, because they are women, then their right to equality and non-discrimination is breached. If people are deprived of the benefits of development, a third generation right, because they belong to a certain ethnic group, then their right to equality and non-discrimination is breached. Non-discrimination is integral to the true fulfillment of all forms of rights, and for that reason it is included in numerous human rights instruments with the clear language that the right to equality and non-discrimination applies to all rights under the purview of the document. Cultural rights have traditionally been grouped in with economic and social rights, but are also quite distinctive as they focus primarily on the right to participate in cultural life and practices.

Issues such as these lead some to categorize human rights in five or six groupings. The following is an example of such groupings:

- **Political Rights**, which would include the right to vote and participate in government;
- **Civil Rights**, which would include the right to freedom of opinion and expression;

- **Equality Rights**, which would include the right to be free from discrimination;
- **Economic Rights**, which would include the right to fair wages and safe working conditions;
- **Social Rights**, which would include the right to education and health care; and,
- **Cultural Rights**, which would include the right to speak one's native language.

Prioritizing of Categories of Rights

One of the longest and clearest debates concerning categories of human rights occurred during the Cold War. This debate was based on the ideological polarity of the time, with the Soviet Bloc and other socialist nations pitted against the West and other democracies. The socialist countries argued that economic, social, and cultural rights were most important, while the western nations argued that civil and political rights were. Since the end of the Cold War, the world has become more multi-polar, and/but the debate over categorization has not ended. Despite the principle that no right is more important than any other, many still advocate certain rights as more essential than others. For example, some believe that basic needs and rights related to them ought to be met first, while other believe that it is best to have individual freedoms and a strong democratic system. This ranking of rights is misguided. It is very important to remember that all rights have a tremendous impact on quality of life. In a number of nations the people are relatively free, yet many groups remain impoverished and marginalized. A denial of either group of rights has a serious human cost. Some nations, such as Canada, enjoy relatively high standards of both rights, and are considered some of the best nations in which to live. The denial of any right has serious impact on human well-being, and all people are entitled to all human rights.

Is it a Right or a Freedom?

As you may have noticed at this point, some human rights are phrased in terms of 'freedoms', while others are phrased in terms of 'rights'. 'Freedoms' usually refer to such things as **freedom** of expression, opinion, peaceful assembly, and religion. These are considered freedoms because they seek to preserve basic forms of individual liberty and ensure that we are free from interference or mistreatment when carrying out legitimate activity. These freedoms are a cornerstone of democracy, as they preserve the right to have opinions, discuss them freely with others, critique the government, and advocate solutions to issues. **Rights** refer to such aspects of life as the right to education, equal treatment before the law, rights upon arrest, or the right to peace. These are all rights because they are articulated in a way that ensures we have access to basic needs and potential for growth and fulfillment, that human dignity is upheld, and that highlights our entitlement to humane treatment. The Canadian Charter of Rights and Freedoms provides a useful example of how the distinction is made between **rights** and **freedoms**. Section 2 of the Charter is entitled 'fundamental freedoms', and includes such **freedoms as expression, religion, and association**. The rest of the Charter is expressed as **rights,** such as: **equality, mobility, voting, and language use**. The Charter also uses the term 'rights and freedoms' in a number of clauses. Human rights apply to so many varied aspects of human life that distinctions between rights and freedoms are inevitable. Different issues are associated with rights and freedoms with distinct origins and distinct areas of impact, and understanding the differences is important. At the same time, although the distinction can be made between rights and freedoms, they are best understood a State Compliance Some rights, such as many civil and political rights, are primarily upheld when the **state does not interfere with people's lives.** Other rights, such as economic and social rights, are **upheld through the provision of certain essentials.** The world's vast disparity in wealth and resources is essential to the human rights debate, as some nations are not equipped to meet many economic and social rights, and this is reflected in the arguments made about which rights ought to be fulfilled. The principle of **progressive realization** allows states room to progressively meet their obligations, but in practice many still do not. In addition, while the realization of civil and political rights requires non-interference and thus fewer resources by governments, this does not mean that countries are more likely to respect and value these rights. In fact, in many places, a great deal of resources are spent oppressing people's civil and political rights.

The Seven Core International Human Rights Treaties

Seven international human rights treaties are considered to be the 'core international human rights treaties', and elaborate on the rights set out in the UDHR. They are signed by states, thereby creating binding obligations. These seven include:

International Covenant on Civil and Political Rights (ICCPR) 1966.

International Covenant on Economic, Social, and Cultural Rights (ICESCR).

International Convention on the Elimination of All Forms of Racial Discrimination (CERD) 1965.

Convention on Elimination of All forms of Discrimination Against Women (CEDAW) 1979.

Convention Against Torture and Other Inhuman or Degrading Treatment or Punishment (CAT) 1984.

Convention on the Rights of the Child (CRC) 1989.

International Convention On the Protection of the Rights of All Migrant Workers and Members of their Families (ICRMW) 1990.

Each of these treaties has a committee of experts to monitor implementation of the treaty provisions. Some of the treaties are supplemented by optional protocols that give the committees power to deal with specific concerns and adjudicate complaints by individuals.

The sky is the limit. The scope of Human Rights encompasses the entire spectrum of human life of the right to live with dignity. No UN Charter or Constitution of any country defines the term Human Rights. They are only listed in the various UN Charters and Constitutions of a number of States. Their sweep is expanding continuously by the human rights organisations (HROs) and the Courts of law dealing with their enforcement.

The term Human Rights came into usage when on December I0, I948 the United Nations General Assembly adopted Universal Declaration of Human Rights (UDHR). The preamble of the Charter states inter alia 'whereas recognition of the inherent dignity and of the equal and inalienable rights of all members of the human family is the foundation of freedom, justice and peace in the world. Whereas it is essential, if man is not to be compelled to have recourse, as a last resort to rebellion against tyranny and oppression, that human rights should be protected by rule of law'.

Some Common Questions Regarding Human Rights

(1) Is the State the only duty-holder, or do non-State actors have duties as well?

As human rights are generally reflected in international treaties, and these are signed by States, the primary subject of human rights obligations is the State – and specifically its legislative, executive and judicial branches. National constitutions also create primarily human rights obligations on the State. Armed insurgent groups are bound by some human rights provisions (e.g. Geneva conventions on humanitarian law), and some other non-state actors are increasingly being considered directly/indirectly bound by human rights law, especially businesses (e.g. Global Compact). The human rights frame-work recognizes that individuals have duties to other individuals and to the communities in which they live: all people have the obligation to contribute to the realisation of human rights. Further-more, all human beings have the obligation to exercise their rights responsibly – that is, nobody should use human rights as a means to deny human rights to others. These obligations are generally set by national legislation. Therefore, the State should have both the will and the necessary capacities to respect, promote and fulfil its own obligations, and to ensure others within its territory do so as well. Indeed, the State is liable under international human rights law if it fails to take reasonable steps to prevent/stop certain abuses in the private sphere (e.g. domestic violence, workers' rights under ILO conventions). The application of a rights-based approach to development programming requires the consideration of duty-holders at different levels, including not only government (at national, regional and local levels),but also individuals and non-State actors.

(2) How are human rights enforced?

The international community has weak mechanisms of enforcement, although these usually exist at the national level. At the international level, UN mechanisms (special bodies created by human rights treaties, or special structures within the UN system) can exercise political pressure. The UN Security Council may decide on the use of force, and the recently created International Criminal Court provides certain mechanisms for judicial enforcement. Still, enforcement is largely a function of the State. Accountability for human rights can be demanded through different mechanisms, including not only the judiciary, but also public audits, independent commissions, parliamentary processes, etc.

(3) Is there a hierarchy of rights?

Human rights are interrelated and interdependent and there is no hierarchy of rights. For instance, inadequate health services or lack of education can affect a person's right to work. The exercise of the right to health may require an independent judiciary that enforces environmental legislation, and so on. All rights are an expression of human dignity, and thus no right can be denied on the grounds of realising other human rights first or instead. However, because human rights are inter-dependent, some priorities can be established in terms of pursuing specific human rights objectives – those that will have a positive impact on other human rights at large, without harming any human right in particular. Such prioritisation requires a careful assessment and analysis of specific situations, and therefore it varies depending on the context.

(4) What happens if the State has no resources?

Ensuring human rights for all human beings requires not only willingness, but also time and resources. The international human rights frame-work takes these later two constraints into consideration, recognizing that the State would be complying with its obligations as long as it *strives* to ensure that human rights are respected for all, within the State's available natural, human and financial resources – including resources coming from development co-operation. Some human rights guarantees can be immediately realised (such as non-discrimination). Other goals need to be achieved progressively (e.g. free primary education); in this case, the State is under the obligation to *prove maximum progress is made given the constraints it faces*. This requires adequate budget allocation and the elimination of corruption, but also adequate financial assistance and other forms of co-operation among States.

(5) What happens if human rights contradict cultural norms in a society?

As legal norms, human rights have traditionally contradicted some of the existing cultural values of societies, particularly on the distribution of privileges and punishments. Cultures are not static, they can change - and generally they do. Human Rights are legal norms that can guide certain changes in social, political and cultural arrangements; changes that are necessary to minimize abuses of power. Generally human rights protect the rights of groups to retain their own cultural, religious and social practices. Only some cultural practices contradict human rights. Indeed, claims of 'cultural relativism' are often used as a justification to deny human rights. The same countries whose governments denounce human rights as a 'Western' imposition may have vibrant human rights movements at the grassroots level. Denials of human rights also occur in Western societies. 'Relativist' discourses on human rights deny the possibility of universal norms on how human beings should be treated. Such discourses would affirm that, whereas human rights may be relevant for some countries and cultures, they are not necessarily so for others. However, this argument is flawed in the sense that there are no 'Chinese' or 'French' human beings; there are human beings, period (as opposed to, for instance, whales) and Chinese or French citizens or nationals. Indeed, nationalist, ethnic, or class interests can prevail over human rights only if human beings are no longer considered as such. 'Relativism' of human rights should then be assessed by those who have the right, not by those who are in the obligation to respond. It is however true that the human rights discourse has been largely dominated by the West, with the consequence that some dimensions (such as 'individual freedoms' and 'State obligations') are highlighted more than others (such as 'collective rights' or 'individual responsibilities'). This bias limits human rights effectiveness. In the view of it, the cultural debate can play a constructive role in human rights, rather than a destructive one. Because they highlight important dimensions for the realisation of human rights, active participation of non-Western cultures is essential to strengthen human rights – as shown by the drafting of the UN Declaration on Indigenous Peoples, or the African Charter on Human Rights and People's Rights.

(6) What happens if human rights contradict each other?

Human Rights are essentially conflictive, in two ways:

(1) They create a tension between the person who has the right, and the person or institution who holds the obligation. It is natural that the right-holder wants to maximize his/her right to the greatest extent, and the duty-bearer tries to minimize the scope of its obligations and responsibilities.

(2) Human rights may also contradict each other (e.g. an indigenous people's right to food may contradict a commercial fisherman's right to work). The challenge is to prevent that such contradictions eventually result in human rights denials, by reaching a compromise consistent with the human rights frame-work.

⌘❐⌘

2 History of Human Rights

The belief that everyone, by virtue of her or his humanity, is entitled to certain human rights is fairly new. Its roots, however, lie in earlier tradition and documents of many cultures; it took the catalyst of World War-II to propel human rights on to the global stage and into the global conscience.

Human Rights Time Line

- **1750 B.C.E.** - Code of Hammurabi, Babylonia
- **1200 - 300 B.C.E.** - Old Testament
- **551 - 479 B.C.E.** - Confucius - "Do unto others what you wish to do unto yourself."
- **40 - 100 C.E.** - New Testament
- **644 - 656 C.E.** - Koran (original text)
- **1215 A.D** - Magna Carta, England
- **1400** - Code of Nezahualcoyotl, Aztec
- **1648** - Treaty of Westphalia, Europe
- **1689** - English Bill of Rights, England
- **1776** - Declaration of Independence, United States
- **1787** - United States Constitution
- **1789** - French Declaration on the Rights of Man and the Citizen, France
- **1791** - United States Bill of Rights
- **1863** - Emancipation Proclamation, United States
- **1864, 1949** - Geneva Conventions, International Red Cross
- **1919** - League of Nations Covenant
- **1926** - Slavery Convention

- **1945** - United Nations Charter, San Francisco
- **1947** - Mohandas Gandhi uses non-violent protests leading India to independence.
- **1948** - Universal Declaration of Human Rights (December 10)
- American Declaration of the Rights and Duties of Man
- Genocide Convention
- **1950** - European Convention
- **1951** - Convention Relating to the Status of Refugees
- **1959** - Declaration on the Rights of Children
- **1961** - Amnesty International founded in London
- **1965** - International Convention on the Elimination of All Forms of Racial Discrimination
- **1966** - International Covenant on Civil and Political Rights
- International Covenant on Economic, Social, and Cultural Rights
- **1973** - International Convention on the Suppression and Punishment of the Crime of Apartheid
- **1979** - International Convention on the Elimination of Discrimination Against Women
- **1984** - International Convention Against Torture and Other Cruel, Inhumane, or Degrading Treatment or Punishment
- **1986** - African Charter on Human and People's Rights
- **1989** - International Convention on the Rights of the Child
- **1992** - Rigoberta Menchu receives the Nobel Peace Prize for her struggle for the rights of indigenous peoples in Guatemala and around the world.
- **1993** - Declaration on the Rights of Indigenous Peoples
- United Nations World Conference on Human Rights, Vienna, Austria
- **1999** - Worst Forms of Child Labor Convention
- **2000** - Optional Protocol to Convention on Rights of Child (Sale, Prostitution, Pornography)
- **2006** - Convention on Enforced Disappearance

Human Rights Time Line – Expanded Descriptions

The Code of Hammurabi-1750 B.C.E.

Hammurabi was a ruler of Babylonia—one of several rival Mesopotamian kingdoms—whose reign marked a golden age of Semitic culture. Hammurabi eventually conquered the other Mesopotamian kingdoms, and issued a law code 'to establish justice throughout Mesopotamia'.

Clay tablet records show that Hammurabi was a scrupulous, able administrator. His code—one of the earliest legal documents—influenced Near Eastern civilization for centuries. It consolidated earlier regulations (of the formal rival kingdoms Akkad and Sumer) on practical aspects of trade, labor, property, family, slavery, trade, and the 'eye for an eye, tooth for a tooth' punishment. The Code of Hammurabi survives in a stone column discovered in Iran in 1901 (now in Paris), and in clay tablet versions, probably originally posted to inform literate citizens of their rights.

Old Testament-1200-300 B.C.E.

Unlike most ancient people, who worshiped many gods, ancient Israelites worshiped one universal God. They saw history as an interaction between God and humanity, whose course depended on obedience to God's laws. The Hebrew Scriptures—39 books by many authors—recorded the law the Israelites believed their God gave them. Christians and Muslims also founded their ethics on the Hebrew Scriptures. Christians know it as the Old Testament. Muslims regard the first five books, the Torah, as divine scripture.

The Torah contains laws God is said to have given to the Hebrew prophets, beginning with the mosaic laws—the Ten Commandments—given to Moses on Mount Sinai. The mosaic laws commanded respect for life and the property of strangers as well as neighbors by establishing rights in terms of duties (the right to life, for example, was expressed in the commandment not to kill). The asylum tradition in churches and synagogues and the principle that one is innocent until proven guilty also originate in Jewish law.

Confucius-551-479 B.C.E.

Living in politically and socially turbulent times, Confucius was a philosopher who taught government and social reform. His philosophical teachings revolved around 'jen' or benevolence, which he expressed in twin sayings 'Do not do to others what you would not like yourself' and 'Do unto others what you wish to do unto yourself'. He believed that people should practice jen towards those below them in a social or spiritual hierarchy and that government should practice jen rather than use force. His own employment in government was troubled by disagreements with his superiors.

Confucius' teachings, collected in his Analects and spread by 3000 disciples, became a code of conduct and the basis of a traditional way of life that made him the most influential philosopher in Chinese history. Confucian teachings emphasizing the individual's responsibilities to the community remain influential to this day in China and other Asian countries.

New Testament-40-100 C.E.

Jesus' followers, scattered around the Roman Empire, wrote letters and accounts of his life, which were circulated among early Christian churches. These became the New Testament, in which Jesus is reported to have quoted the Old Testament: 'The Spirit of the Lord is in me...to preach good news to the poor. He has sent me to proclaim freedom for the prisoners and recovery of sight to the blind, to release the oppressed, to [invite all to God's kingdom].' He then claimed he fulfilled those words.

The New Testament says Jesus angered religious leaders by denouncing hypocrisy, healing the sick, and treating women, foreigners, and the poor with dignity. The Apostle Paul, who wrote some New Testament books in prison, said that among Jesus' followers, 'there is neither Jew nor Greek, slave nor free, male nor female.' The New Testament also says that Jesus taught that rights come together with responsibilities. He urged his followers to feed the hungry, clothe the naked, and forgive their enemies.

Magna Carta-1215

English nobles and clergy rallied against King John I's abuse of power—heavy taxation to finance expensive, unsuccessful wars, and his refusal to accept papal authority, which effectively kept churches closed for years. They subjected the King to the rule of law by enacting from him a 'great charter' of liberties.

Though King John I soon violated it, the Magna Carta eventually came to be cited widely, in defense of many liberties. The U.S. national and state constitutions contain ideas and even phrases directly traceable to it—for example, the concept of no taxation without representation. Clause 39, which stated that 'no free man shall be arrested or imprisoned...[or dispossessed] except by...lawful judgement,' became known as the right of habeas corpus, or due process of law.

Treaty of Westphalia-1648

For centuries after Augustine, the Roman Catholic Church was the unique Christian authority in Europe. However, the church became plagued by depravity and an inability to satisfy its followers' spiritual needs, and in the 1500's, a reform movement spread. This reformation and a Catholic Counter-Reformation, along with sovereignty disputes, racked most of Europe for a century.

These wars were finally ended by the Treaty of Westphalia (named for the region of Germany where it was signed). The Treaty led to the modern notion of national sovereignty by freeing state rulers from Catholic church jurisdiction. It allowed rulers to choose their subjects' religion, but put an end to the Reformation and the Counter-Reformation by specifying that rulers would forfeit their lands if they changed religions. The Treaty also took a step toward religious toleration by allowing Catholic or Protestant minorities in some states rights to private worship, liberty of conscience, and emigration.

English Bill of Rights-1689

James II, like several kings before him, thought the law inconvenient and often dispensed with it. For this his subjects overthrew him in 1688, and when Mary II and William III took the throne in 1689, Parliament passed a bill declaring that it would no longer tolerate royal interference in its affairs. The bill became part of the foundation of the English constitution, and in the following century, most English took pride in the freedom its provisions gave them from arbitrary government.

The bill forbade royalty to suspend law without Parliament's consent, specified free elections for members of Parliament, and declared that freedom of speech in Parliament was not to be questioned, in the courts or elsewhere. The bill also prohibited taxation or maintenance of an army in peacetime without Parliament's consent, excessive bail or fines, and cruel and unusual punishment.

United States Declaration of Independence-1776

Calling themselves the Continental Congress, representatives of Britain's 13 colonies first convened in 1774 to protest British policies. When they convened again after the American Revolution had begun, they voted for independence from Britain and adopted the Declaration of Independence, becoming the first government of the 13 United States. The Declaration had far- reaching and lasting influence on individual rights in Western civilization, inspiring rebellion against Spanish rule in South America and against monarchy in France.

Because of his literary skill, Thomas Jefferson was chosen to write the Declaration. Based largely on Locke's and Montesquieu's 'natural rights' theories, it listed the colonists' grievances against King George, accusing him of systematic tyranny; announced the colonies' separation from Great Britain; proclaimed the creation of the United States; and justified the revolution. The Congress rejected two passages, in which Jefferson searingly denounced the slave trade and defamed the English people.

United States Constitution and the Bill of Rights-1787

Faced with teetering economies and armed revolt, 12 of the new states sent delegates to rethink the 1781 constitution. At the convention, the delegates (in their 20's or 30's, but led by veterans James Madison and George Washington) centralized and strengthened the government while aiming to limit its power enough to guarantee individual liberty.

The 1781 constitution replaced the almost powerless Continental Congress with three branches of government and provided for checks and balances among them. Twenty-six amendments to the Constitution have established specific rights (the Bill of Rights, contributed by antifederalists including Jefferson, contains the first 10). Adaptable, as one justice remarked, 'to various crises of human affairs' through judicial reinterpretation, the Constitution is now the oldest in operation and one of the most influential documents in Western history.

Declaration of the Rights of Man and the Citizen-1789

Since the 1730's, economic decline and the ideas of the Enlightenment had been spreading in France simultaneously, and the success of the American Revolution had infused French reformers with hope. The Estates General (representatives of the clergy, nobility, and the commoners) wrote the Declaration to exemplify the thoughts of Enlightenment figures such as Voltaire, Montesquieu, the Encyclopedists, and Rousseau.

Though the reform efforts failed and France tumbled into revolution, the Declaration legacy eventually prevailed. It attacked the political and legal systems of the monarchy and defined the natural rights of men as 'liberty, property, security, and the right to resist oppression.' The Declaration replaced the system of aristocratic privileges that had existed under the monarchy with the principle of equality before the law.

Emancipation Proclamation-1863

The Civil War started in 1861 as a Northern struggle to keep the United States from breaking apart. Abolitionists were a minority; Abraham Lincoln did not champion slaves' moral claims to freedom and could never have been elected president on a platform of abolishing slavery. But once the Southern states seceded, the political purpose of accommodating slavery disappeared, and as deaths mounted and volunteering declined, pressure grew to enlist blacks. Just two years later, when Lincoln issued the Emancipation Proclamation, the North had transformed the war into a crusade to free Southern slaves.

Because it applied only to territories in Confederate possession—taking effect only as Northern lines advanced—the Proclamation at first freed no slaves at all.

Its importance lay in opening the door to black army enlistment—which shocked many and aided the North's victory—and to passage of the thirteenth amendment, which outlawed slavery nationwide in 1865.

Geneva Conventions-1864, 1949

Brought into being by the newly created International Red Cross, the Geneva Convention of 1864 was the first international law treaty governing the conduct of nations in wartime, and so marks the origin of modern humanitarian and human rights law. The Convention created provisions for the treatment of sick and wounded soldiers.

The Convention was revised and amended several times, and the current version, approved in 1949 after World War-II, comprises four separate conventions. The first and second deal with the care of the sick and wounded in land and maritime warfare; the third deals with the treatment of prisoners of war; and the fourth deals with the protection of civilians and non-combatants. Together, the four Geneva Conventions aim to ensure that human dignity is respected even during hostilities. Their provisions continue to be monitored and enforced by the International Committee of the Red Cross.

Mohandas Karamchand Gandhi-1869-1948

Gandhi began his career in South Africa, where he practiced law and agitated against racism directed at Indians. There he developed his tactics of non-violent confrontation based on the principle of respect for life; he called his strategy 'satyagraha' (truth force). Later, in India, after a massacre by the British, Gandhi led a series of satyagraha campaigns until India achieved independence in 1947. Gandhi's campaigns alternated with imprisonment. His 'constructive program' consisted of movements against class discrimination and for Muslim-Hindu unity, women's rights, and basic education.

Later called Mahatma (great soul), Gandhi was assassinated by a religious fanatic. His influence has been felt around the world—notably in South Africa and the United States, where major civil rights movements based on his ideas were later carried out.

The United Nations Charter-1945

The U.N. Charter was signed by 51 nations in the postwar climate of 1945. It established an international organisation dedicated to maintaining peace and security and to co-operation in solving economic, social, cultural, and humanitarian problems. Although it affirmed 'faith in fundamental human rights,' its signatories disagreed on the nature of these human rights. The first U.N.

conference therefore rejected a proposal to include protection of human rights as an article of the Charter.

The Charter gives the U.N. General Assembly and its Commission on Human Rights primary responsibility for promoting human rights. The Commission was instrumental in creating declarations and covenants on human rights, including civil, political, economic, social, and cultural rights. Although not legally enforceable, these documents are used to interpret the human rights provisions of the U.N. Charter.

Universal Declaration of Human Rights-1948

Because representatives at the U.N. conference in 1945 wrestled with reconciling their various conceptions of human rights, the clauses relating to human rights that were finally included in the U.N. Charter were very ambiguous. The U.N. assigned a Commission, with Eleanor Roosevelt as chairperson, to clarify the Charter's references to human rights. The result was a statement of universal goals concerning human rights and freedoms, which was adopted by the U.N. General Assembly in 1948. The Declaration is not legally binding, but its content has been incorporated into many national constitutions, and it has become a standard measure of human rights.

Debates over the priority of individuals' political and civil rights versus social and economic rights made drafting the Declaration a long and arduous process. Socialist nations supported primacy of the latter. Many of the eastern-bloc countries abstained from voting; Saudi Arabia objected to religious freedom; and South Africa objected to racial equality.

European Convention on Human Rights 1950 (ECHR)

Is an international treaty to protect human rights and fundamental freedoms in Europe. Drafted in 1950 by the then newly formed Council of Europe, the convention entered into force on 3 September 1953. All Council of Europe member states are party to the Convention and new members are expected to ratify the convention at the earliest opportunity.

The Convention established the European Court of Human Rights. Any person who feels his or her rights have been violated under the Convention by a state party can take a case to the Court. Judgments finding violations are binding on the States concerned and they are obliged to execute them. The Committee of Ministers of the Council of Europe monitors the execution of judgments, particularly to ensure payment of the amounts awarded by the Court to the applicants in compensation for the damage they have sustained. The establishment of a Court to protect individuals from human rights violations is an innovative feature for an international convention on human rights, as it gives the individual an active role on the international arena (traditionally, only states are considered actors in international law). The European Convention is still the only international human rights agreement providing such a high degree of individual protection. State parties can also take cases against other state parties to the Court, although this power is rarely used. The Convention has several protocols. For example, Protocol 13 prohibits the death penalty. The protocols accepted vary from State Party to State Party, though it is understood that state parties should be party to as many protocols as possible.

The Convention Relating to the Status of Refugees, 1951

It established the United Nations High Commissioner for Refugees (UNHCR) to deal with the resettlement of refugees and the residual refugees following World War-II. The protocol is a key legal document in defining refugees, their rights, and states' legal obligations.

Declaration on the Rights of Children, 1959

Children have the right to special protection because of their defencelessness against mistreatment. The first United Nations statement devoted exclusively to the rights of children was the Declaration on the Rights of the Child, adopted in 1959 The *Declaration of the Rights of the Child* is comprised of 10 principles that each and every child on this planet should be entitled. These rights are not extravagant; they are the very heart of human rights. They are the rights that most of us routinely take for granted every day, the rights that most of us have that we never think about having. For example, Principle 3 guarantees each child a name and a nation. Think about it: from the very first moment of birth, most of us are automatically citizens of a country, members of a family and a heritage. We have a name, which often implies an identity. But when children are abandoned, abused, used as objects of labor or victims of sex trafficking, these children have neither nation nor a name. For these children that which we are immersed in every day is non-existent.

Amnesty International founded in London, 1961

Founded in London in 1961, Amnesty International is a Nobel Prize-winning grassroots activist organisation with over 1.8 million members world-wide. Amnesty International undertakes research and action focused on preventing and ending grave abuses of the rights to physical and mental integrity, freedom of conscience and expression, and freedom from discrimination, within the context of its work to promote all human rights. Peter Benenson, the founder of Amnesty International, was 83. He was born into a world without the United

Nations. Not a single international human rights treaty was in existence. The Universal Declaration of Human Rights had yet to be written. There wasn't a single one of today's major human rights organisations on the political landscape. Civil society was yet to be born.

International Convention on the Elimination of All Forms of Racial Discrimination, 1965

The International Convention on the Elimination of All Forms of Racial Discrimination is one of the six core international human rights instruments and the only one focused exclusively on eliminating racial discrimination. Given that indigenous peoples have been and continue to be subject to multiple forms of discrimination, it is obviously of great relevance to indigenous peoples' rights. The Convention places **binding** obligations on the states that have ratified it – 162 as of June 2002 – and has been interpreted to provide strong protections for indigenous peoples.

International Covenant on Civil and Political Rights, 1966

International Covenant on Economic, Social, and Cultural Rights,1966

The **International Covenant on Civil and Political Rights** (**ICCPR**) is a multilateral *treaty* adopted by the *United Nations General Assembly* on December 16, 1966, and in force from March 23, 1976. It commits its parties to respect the *civil and political rights* of individuals, including the *right to life, freedom of religion, freedom of speech, freedom of assembly*, electoral rights and rights to due process and a fair trial. As of October 2009, the Covenant had 72 signatories and 165 parties.

The **International Covenant on Economic, Social and Cultural Rights** (ICESCR) is a multilateral *treaty* adopted by the *United Nations General Assembly* on December 16, 1966, and in force from January 3, 1976. It commits its parties to work toward the granting of *economic, social, and cultural rights* (ESCR) to individuals, including *labour rights* and rights to health, education, and an adequate standard of living. As of December, 2008, the Covenant had 160 parties. A further six countries had signed, but not yet ratified the Covenant.

The ICESCR is part of the *International Bill of Human Rights*, along with the *Universal Declaration of Human Rights* (UDHR) and the *International Covenant on Civil and Political Rights* (ICCPR), including the latter's *first* and *second* Optional Protocols.

International Convention on the Suppression and Punishment of the Crime of Apartheid, 1973

The States Parties to the present Convention declare that apartheid is a crime against humanity and that inhuman acts resulting from the policies and practices of apartheid and similar policies and practices of racial segregation and discrimination, as defined in article II of the Convention, are crimes violating the principles of international law, in particular the purposes and principles of the Charter of the United Nations, and constituting a serious threat to international peace and security. The States Parties to the present Convention declare criminal those organisations, institutions and individuals committing the crime of apartheid.

International Convention on the Elimination of Discrimination Against Women, 1979

CEDAW is an International Bill of Human Rights for Women which sets a holistic agenda for women's empowerment as equal and responsible citizens in their societies. It is the most important international instrument for the advancement of women's rights. In many ways, the Women's Convention is a unique one. Adopted by the UN General Assembly in 1979 and coming into force in 1981, CEDAW is today, one of the most widely endorsed human rights treaties in the history of the United Nations, ratified by 170 countries. The process has been catalyzed first and foremost by the will of nations, to give themselves a vision, for putting women at the centre of development. Successive UN Conferences and Conventions contributed, to the setting up of a normative framework, to convert this vision into reality.

International Convention Against Torture and Other Cruel, Inhumane, or Degrading Treatment or Punishment, 1984

The participating States will ensure that all individuals in detention or incarceration will be treated with humanity and with respect for the inherent dignity of the human person; observe the United Nations Standard Minimum Rules for the Treatment of Prisoners as well as the United Nations Code of Conduct for Law Enforcement Officials.

African Charter on Human and People's Rights, 1986

The African Charter on Human and Peoples' Rights 2 entered into force on the 21st October 1986 and was a significant step in the terms of the recognition and implementation of human rights in Africa. Not only does the Charter provide for the rights that should be guaranteed within African States, but it also facilitates the creation of a body, the African Commission on Human and Peoples' Rights, to monitor the implementation of the rights contained therein. The Charter includes many of the fundamental rights laid down in other international treaties and UN Charters, such as civil and political rights as well as economic, social and cultural rights. Article 22 should be highlighted in this respect as clear reference is made to the 'right to economic, social and cultural development' and a duty is placed upon State Parties to take all necessary measures to ensure the exercise of this right to development. Furthermore, the Charter also places particular obligations upon individuals, not merely the State Parties.

International Convention on the Rights of the Child, 1989

The *UN Convention on the Rights of the Child* is the most comprehensive human rights document ever adopted by the international community. Forty-two countries spent 10 years drafting the *Convention*. All but two countries in the world —the United States and Somalia — have ratified it. Built on varied legal systems and cultural traditions, the *Convention* is a universally agreed set of non-negotiable standards and obligations linking the child and fundamental human rights. Notably, the *Convention* is the first legally binding international instrument to incorporate the full range of human rights — civil, political, economic, social and cultural, and it is the most comprehensive treaty for the protection and support of children in existence today. The *Convention* is also the only international human rights treaty that gives NGOs an explicit role in monitoring its implementation.

Rigoberta Menchu receives the Nobel Peace Prize for her struggle for the rights of indigenous peoples in Guatemala and around the world, 1992

Rigoberta Menchu Tum was awarded the Nobel Peace Prize in 1992 in recognition of her work for social justice and ethno-cultural reconciliation work based on respect for the rights of indigenous peoples in her native Guatemala. She is the first indigenous person to receive the Nobel Peace Prize.

Rigoberta was born in 1959 to a poor Indian family in the highlands of Guatemala. Like many other countries in the Americas, Guatemala has experienced great tension between the descendants of European immigrants and the native Indian population. The Menchú family experienced extreme hardship as a result of their Mayan background.

In the 1970s and 1980s, Guatemala's repressive military dictatorship began a large-scale repression of Indian peoples. Before she was 21, Rigoberta's mother, father and brother were brutally tortured and murdered by the Guatemalan army.

Declaration on the Rights of Indigenous Peoples, 1993

The Declaration sets out the rights of indigenous peoples. The language of 'peoples' is important. Indigenous peoples do not want to be treated simply as numerical populations. They want recognition of their rights as distinct peoples, including the right to self-determination, and the right to control development of their societies.

United Nations World Conference on Human Rights, Vienna, Austria, 1993

The key result of the World Conference on Human Rights was the *Vienna Declaration and Programme of Action*, which was formulated late in the meeting and was adopted by consensus of 171 states on 25 June 1993. While one possible interpretation sees this document as a 'well crafted but empty exhortation', it did come to represent as much of a consensus as could be found on human rights in the early 1990s. And it did in fact set new marks in human rights work in several areas. It established the interdependence of democracy, economic development, and human rights. Specifically, it replaced the Cold War division of Civil and Political Rights (CPR) apart from Economic Social and Cultural Rights (ESCR) with the concept of rights being indivisible (you cannot take one type of rights without the other), interdependent (one set of rights needs the other to be realised), and inter-related (that all human rights relate to each other). It called for the creation of instruments to publicise and protect the rights of women, children, and indigenous peoples. It requested more funding for the *United Nations Center for Human Rights*. Most significantly, it called for a new office, the *United Nations High Commissioner for Human Rights*.

Worst Forms of Child Labor Convention, 1999

For the purposes of this Convention, the term 'the worst forms of child labour' comprises:

(a) All forms of slavery or practices similar to slavery, such as the sale and trafficking of children, debt bondage and serfdom and forced or compulsory labour, including forced or compulsory recruitment of children for use in armed conflict;

(b) The use, procuring or offering of a child for prostitution, for the production of pornography or for pornographic performances;

(c) The use, procuring or offering of a child for illicit activities, in particular for the production and trafficking of drugs as defined in the relevant international treaties;

(d) Work which, by its nature or the circumstances in which it is carried out, is likely to harm the health, safety or morals of children.

Optional Protocol to Convention on Rights of Child (Sale, Prostitution, Pornography, 2000)

For the purposes of the present Protocol:

(a) Sale of children means any act or transaction whereby a child is transferred by any person or group of persons to another for remuneration or any other consideration;

(b) Child prostitution means the use of a child in sexual activities for remuneration or any other form of consideration;

(c) Child pornography means any representation, by whatever means, of a child engaged in real or simulated explicit sexual activities or any representation of the sexual parts of a child for primarily sexual purposes.

Convention on Enforced Disappearance, 2006

For the purposes of this Convention, 'enforced disappearance' is considered to be the arrest, detention, abduction or any other form of deprivation of liberty by agents of the State or by persons or group No one shall be subjected to enforced disappearance.

No exceptional circumstances whatsoever, whether a state of war or a threat of war, internal political instability or any other public emergency, may be invoked as a justification for enforced disappearance.

⌘❒⌘

3 The Universal Declaration of Human Rights

The Creation of the Universal Declaration of Human Rights

The Universal Declaration of Human Rights (UDHR) is a milestone document in the history of human rights. In less than half a century, the Universal Declaration of Human Rights (the UDHR) has come to be regarded as possibly the single most important document created in the twentieth century and as the accepted world standard for human rights. The UDHR draws life-preserving messages from the past, and is seen as an essential foundation for building a world in which all human beings can, in the centuries to come, look forward to living in dignity and peace. Drafted by representatives with different legal and cultural backgrounds from all regions of the world, the Declaration was proclaimed by the United Nations General Assembly in Paris on 10 December 1948 General Assembly resolution 217 A (III) as a common standard of achievements for all peoples and all nations. It sets out, for the first time, fundamental human rights to be universally protected. The Universal Declaration of Human Rights is the primary international articulation of the fundamental and inalienable rights of all members of the human family. Adopted by the United Nations General Assembly on December 10, 1948, the UDHR represents the first comprehensive agreement among nations as to the specific rights and freedoms of all human beings.

A Critical Historical Moment

As the Second World War began to close; the world climate was ready for a great leap forward in the recognition and observance of human rights. When representatives of the four major powers met in 1944 at Dumbarton Oaks, a stately mansion in Georgetown, Washington DC, two world wars had been fought in less than 30 years, and cruelty almost beyond belief had been inflicted on members of the Jewish race in Europe and on prisoners of war in detention in Asia and Europe. An atomic bomb was about to be set off that would show what enormous destructive power humankind could unleash in targeting nations as well as individuals, often simply because they were members of a particular race or religion.

The leaders felt there must be a better way for the nations and peoples of the world to live together and sort out their problems and laid plans for establishing what was to become the United Nations.

In late 1945, leaders of the world's nations met in San Francisco to form the United Nations. Inspired by the great South African pre-apartheid leader Field-Marshall Smuts, they included in the preamble to the Charter of the UN, an important reference to human rights. (A preamble is an important introductory section of a legal document, and explains the background to it rather than being part of its operative provisions.) The relevant part of the preamble said:

"We the peoples of the United Nations [are] determined - ....to reaffirm faith in fundamental human rights, in the dignity and worth of the human person, in the equal rights of men and women and of nations large and small".

This reference to human rights was followed up by six references throughout the UN Charter's operative provisions to human rights and fundamental freedoms. In addition, largely as a result of pressure brought to bear on the political leaders by some 42 United States non-government organisations, Article 68 was included. It required the Economic and Social Ccuncil to set up commissions in the human rights and economic and social fields. The outcome was the establishment of a Commission on Human Rights. Thus, the Commission is one of the very few bodies to draw its authority directly from the Charter of the United Nations.

Producing the Framework for the International Bill of Rights

In April 1946, Mrs. Eleanor Roosevelt, widow of President Franklin Roosevelt of the United States was appointed to chair an interim group of 9 members. By June the interim body had suggested that the new Commission should make its first task the development as soon as possible of an international bill of human rights.

Later in the year, the new Commission of Human Rights of 18 members, again chaired by Mrs. Eleanor Roosevelt, was appointed, and included China's P.C.Chang, Frenchmen Rene Cassin and Dr. Charles Malik of Lebanon. The

Commission met for the first time in January 1947 and considered several critical issues. Its decisions have greatly influenced the human rights development since then, including action at national level. It concluded that it should work to develop first a declaration rather than a treaty. (An international declaration is a statement of importance, and has high moral and often political significance, and is more than a recommendation, but it is less than a treaty, which is binding in international law.) Perhaps most important of all, it decided that the declaration should contain both civil and political and also economic and social rights.

The Commission's view was that the declaration should be a relatively short, inspirational and energising document usable by common people. It should be the foundation and central document for the remainder of an international bill of human rights. It thus avoided the more difficult problems that had to be addressed when the binding treaty came up for consideration - just what role the state should have in enforcing the rights in its territory, and whether the mode of enforcing civil and political rights should be different from that for economic and social rights.

It was fortunate that the Commission made the decision to separate the formally legally binding covenant from the initial declaration. Although the declaration was endorsed in December 1948, the two covenants (the International Covenant on Civil and Political Rights and the International Covenant on Economic, Social and Cultural Rights) that emerged to define the obligations of each state were not ready for ratification (formal approval by the governments of the world) until 1966, some 18 years later.

Among others, these include civil and political rights such as the right not to be subjected to torture, to equality before the law, to a fair trial, to freedom of movement, to asylum and to freedom of thought, conscience, religion, opinion and expression. The rights outlined in the UDHR also include economic, social and cultural rights such as the right to food, clothing, housing and medical care, to social security, to work, to equal pay for equal work, to form trade unions and to education.

Originally intended as a 'common standard of achievement for all peoples and all nations', over the past fifty years the Universal Declaration has become a cornerstone of customary international law, and all governments are now bound to apply its principles. Because the Universal Declaration of Human Rights successfully encompasses legal, moral and philosophical beliefs held true by all peoples, it has become a living document which asserts its own elevating force on the events of our world.

The drafting of the Universal Declaration of Human Rights represented the first time in history that people from cultures throughout the world worked together to formulate a comprehensive and common vision of inalienable human rights.

In the UN General Assembly's Third Committee alone, there were 85 meetings held with a total of 1,400 separate votes taken on various issues concerning the drafting of the Declaration (this is after the Commission on Human Rights had completed its work!). For nearly three years, representatives of various nations labored to enumerate and articulate the specific rights and freedoms that had been more broadly guaranteed to all in the UN Charter.

Remembering that the world was embroiled in the ideological controversies of the Cold War, this was an incredibly complicated and difficult task. Yet the final document encompassed rights and freedoms given varying emphasis by both Western democratic and Communist countries. The Universal Declaration reflects different beliefs as to the philosophical basis of human rights and balances traditional civil and political rights with economic, social and cultural rights.

The drafters of the UDHR struggled through a multitude of sometimes subtle and sometimes stark differences in linguistic, cultural, political, and philosophical values. The world's major legal systems and legal philosophies were considered in stages of the debate as were, to varying degrees, the most widely practiced religious beliefs, including Buddhist, Christian, Confucian, Hindu, Islamic and Jewish traditions. Under the chairmanship of Eleanor Roosevelt, the Commission on Human Rights successfully reached a shared understanding of what constitutes the inalienable rights and freedoms of all human beings in every corner of the globe'.

An Inspriratíonal Document

The Commission then turned to formulating the declaration. It decided to name it the Universal Declaration of Human Rights (UDHR). The very name emphasises the UDHR was to set a standard of rights for all people everywhere - whether male or female, black or white, communist or capitalist, victor or vanquished, rich or poor, for members of a majority or a minority in the community. In the words of the first preamble to the UDHR, it was to reflect "recognition of the inherent dignity and equal and inalienable rights of all members of the human family "... and through that recognition provide "the foundation of freedom, justice and peace in the world".

Article 1 reflects the inspirational nature of the project. It was included only after much controversy about whether it was just stating the obvious, or whether it should be included in the preamble rather than the main text. It proclaims in ringing terms that "All human beings are born free and equal in dignity and rights. They are endowed with reason and conscience and should act towards one another in a spirit of brotherhood".

The reason for including it in the main text is to state firmly the basis of all human rights, the rationality of human persons and their obligation to deal fairly with everyone else, regardless of race, sex, wealth and so on. Article 7 follows up this theme by saying that all are to be equal before the law and have a right to protection against any form of discrimination.

Articles 3 and 27 are probably the core of the substantive provisions in the Declaration. They give every human being the rights to life, to liberty, to security of person (Art 3) and to an adequate standard of living (Art 27). The first three are core civil and political rights, the last an economic and social right. The right to an adequate standard of living is interesting in that it specifies as part of it the right to health and well-being not only of a person but of his or her family, and also the right to necessary food, clothing, housing and medical care, and the right to social security (also covered in Art 22).

Overarching all the particular rights are Articles 28 and 29. (There are 30 Articles in the Declaration, of which 17 could be regarded as relating to civil and political rights and 8 to economic and social rights). Articles 28 and 29 have not received much discussion, and have not been given legally binding force in the two Covenants. But they are explosive in their significance. Article 28 emphasises the responsibility of the whole international community for seeking and putting into place arrangements of both a civil and political and an economic and social kind that allow for the full realisation of human rights. It would be easy to ask questions about current arrangements or plans that hardly seem to do this, such as those relating to trade and investment arrangements and perhaps some of those planning to eradicate international crimes such as genocide and war crimes.

Article 30 is also of high importance, because it underlines the responsibility all people have to their community. Notice that the Article does not talk about the state. There is danger in claiming, as so many dictators and even democratic leaders have claimed, that people owe duties of an inalienable kind to the state. They do not. But they do have obligations to their fellow human beings, as Article 1 also emphasises.

Perhaps, looking back at the UDHR after half a century, the only significant lack is in the area of the environment. It can however be implied from rights such as the right to life and to an adequate standard of living.

Tribute should be payed to three different groups. Firstly, to Eleanor Roosevelt and her advisers, mainly from the US Department of State. Somehow, she was able to maintain a generally harmonious atmosphere during virtually the whole of the long meeting phase. Second, to the many prominent people who provided drafts to the Committee for its consideration. These included noted international lawyer, Professor Hersch Lauterpacht of Cambridge University, and British author H. G. Wells. There was also a draft based on work done in preparation for an American Declaration of the Rights and Duties of Man. Finally, there was the enormous work done by the secretariat, led by Professor J. P. Humphrey, that brought all this material together for the Commission to consider.

When the Commission finally took its vote on 18 June 1948, twelve of its fifteen members voted in favour. The Soviet Union, Byelorussia, the Ukraine and Yugoslavia (the Soviet bloc technically had only two members) abstained.

The draft then went to the Economic and Social Council, which did not change the text but arranged for it to go to the Third Committee of the UN General Assembly, where it struck difficulties. It was fortunate that the Committee's chairman at the time was Charles Malik. After no less than 81 long meetings, at which at least 168 amending resolutions were considered, the Committee, on 6 December 1948, at last reached agreement - just in time to be taken by the General Assembly before it concluded its meeting for the year.

On the evening of 10 December 1948, the General Assembly endorsed the text of the UDHR without amendment, only two days before it rose until the next year. There were no dissenting votes, but the six communist countries then members of the UN, and also Saudi Arabia and South Africa, abstained. The Assembly, in a rare gesture of appreciation, gave Mrs. Roosevelt a standing ovation.

The Growing Stature of the UDHR

So, just ahead of the advent of the Cold War and the consequent slowing down of many constructive developments, the Universal Declaration managed to emerge successfully from the complex and politically hazardous processes of the United Nations to become its human rights flagship. The Declaration had not managed at that time to achieve full recognition from the communist and certain middle eastern countries, but at least they had not voted against it.

Notwithstanding the initial difficulties and resistance, the Declaration has probably achieved a stature in the world that even the most optimistic of its founders in 1948 would not have expected. First, it has become accepted (often rather reluctantly, it is true) as an influential statement of standards, even by countries that are doubtful about the whole human rights enterprise. When countries such as Burma, Argentina, China and the former Yugoslavia feel bound to defend themselves when they are accused of being in breach of the UDHR, then it can be said to have achieved an important political and moral status.

Equally important, the UDHR has become almost an extension of the UN Charter. Although, the Charter has only a few articles that refer to human rights and fundamental freedoms, it is now usual to refer to the UDHR as setting out the content of those rights and freedoms. So it has become a part of the fabric of the UN itself, and is often referred to in resolutions of the UN General Assembly, and in its debates, for example in relation to the Declaration on the Granting of Independence to Colonial Countries and Peoples of 1960. At the human rights conference in Teheran in 1978, to mark the 30th anniversary of the UDHR, the representatives of 84 nations unanimously declared that the UDHR states a common understanding of the inalienable rights of all people and constitutes an obligation for the members of the international community.

Third, most if not all the provisions of the UDHR have almost certainly become a part of international customary law. The view is steadily growing among international lawyers that practice (always an important source of international law) includes not only acts such as observing rules about navigation at sea but also acts such as voting for resolutions at United Nations and other international gatherings. The very large and increasing number of ratifications of the two human rights Covenants, and the fact that the rights stated in the UDHR are commonly recognised as well founded in moral and good practice terms, means that there are now virtually unchallengeable grounds for asserting that the UDHR rights have become part of international customary law. That means that, unlike treaties, which only bind a country once it has accepted the treaty obligations, all countries in the world are bound, whatever their particular view may be. A country cannot repudiate international customary law, as it can a treaty obligation.

For these three reasons, those who boldly moved to form and then approve the provisions of the UDHR have left an abiding legacy for humankind that will rank with the great religious contributions of past centuries. The UDHR is an increasingly powerful instrument for the achievement of human dignity and peace for all.

Universal Declaration of Human Rights (1948)

Original text	Plain language version
Article 1	
All human beings are born free and equal in dignity and rights. They are endowed with reason and conscience and should act towards one another in a spirit of brotherhood.	When children are born, they are free and each should be treated in the same way. They have reason and conscience and should act towards one another in a friendly manner.
Article 2	
Everyone is entitled to all the rights and freedoms set forth in this Declaration, without distinction of any kind, such as race, colour, sex, language, religion,	Everyone can claim the following rights, despite - a different sex - a different skin colour

political or other opinion, national or social origin, property, birth or other status. Further more, no distinction shall be made on the basis of the political, jurisdictional or international status of the country or territory to which a person belongs, whether it be independent, trust, non-self-governing or under any other limitation of sovereignty.	- speaking a different language - thinking different things - believing in another religion - owning more or less - being born in another social group - coming from another country. It also makes no difference whether the country you live in is independent or not.
Article 3	
Everyone has the right to life, liberty and security of person.	You have the right to live, and to live in freedom and safety.
Article 4	
No one shall be held in slavery or servitude; slavery and the slave trade shall be prohibited in all their forms.	Nobody has the right to treat you as his or her slave and you should not make anyone your slave.
Article 5	
No one shall be subjected to torture or to cruel, inhuman or degrading treatment or punishment.	Nobody has the right to torture you.
Article 6	
Everyone has the right to recognition everywhere as a person before the law.	You should be legally protected in the same way everywhere, and like everyone else.
Article 7	
All are equal before the law and are entitled without any discrimination to equal protection of the law. All are entitled to equal protection against any discrimination in violation of this Declaration and against any incitement to such discrimination.	The law is the same for everyone; it should be applied in the same way to all.
Article 8	
Everyone has the right to an effective remedy by the competent national tribunals for acts violating the fundamental rights granted him by the constitution or by law.	You should be able to ask for legal help when the rights your country grants you are not respected.
Article 9	
No one shall be subjected to arbitrary arrest, detention or exile.	Nobody has the right to put you in prison, to keep you there, or to send you away from your country unjustly, or without a good reason.

Article 10	
Everyone is entitled in full equality to a fair and public hearing by an independent and impartial tribunal, in the determination of his rights and obligations and of any criminal charge against him.	If you must go on trial this should be done in public. The people who try you should not let themselves be influenced by others.
Article 11	
1. Everyone charged with a penal offence has the right to be presumed innocent until proved guilty according to law in a public trial at which he has had all the guarantees necessary for his defence. 2. No one shall be held guilty of any penal offence on account of any act or omission which did not constitute a penal offence, under national or international law, at the time when it was committed. Nor shall a heavier penalty be imposed than the one that was applicable at the time the penal offence was committed.	You should be considered innocent until it can be proved that you are guilty. If you are accused of a crime, you should always have the right to defend yourself. Nobody has the right to condemn you and punish you for something you have not done.
Article 12	
No one shall be subjected to arbitrary interference with his privacy, family, home or correspondence, nor to attacks upon his honour and reputation. Everyone has the right to the protection of the law against such interference or attacks.	You have the right to ask to be protected if someone tries to harm your good name, enter your house, open your letters, or bother you or your family without a good reason.
Article 13	
1. Everyone has the right to freedom of movement and residence within the borders of each State. 2. Everyone has the right to leave any country, including his own, and to return to his country.	You have the right to come and go as you wish within your country. You have the right to leave your country to go to another one; and you should be able to return to your country if you want.
Article 14	
1. Everyone has the right to seek and to enjoy in other countries asylum from persecution.	If someone hurts you, you have the right to go to another country and ask it to protect you. You lose this right if you

2. This right may not be invoked in the case of prosecutions genuinely arising from non-political crimes or from acts contrary to the purposes and principles of the United Nations.	have killed someone and if you yourself do not respect what is written here.
Article 15	
1. Everyone has the right to a nationality. 2. No one shall be arbitrarily deprived of his nationality nor denied the right to change his nationality.	You have the right to belong to a country and nobody can prevent you, without a good reason, from belonging to another country if you wish.
Article 16	
1. Men and women of full age, without any limitation due to race, nationality or religion, have the right to marry and to found a family. They are entitled to equal rights as to marriage, during marriage and at its dissolution. 2. Marriage shall be entered into only with the free and full consent of the intending spouses. 3. The family is the natural and fundamental group unit of society and is entitled to protection by society and the State.	As soon as a person is legally entitled, he or she has the right to marry and have a family. Neither the colour of your skin, nor the country you come from nor your religion should be impediments to doing this. Men and women have the same rights when they are married and also when they are separated. Nobody should force a person to marry. The Government of your country should protect your family and its members.
Article 17	
1. Everyone has the right to own property alone as well as in association with others. 2. No one shall be arbitrarily deprived of his property.	You have the right to own things and nobody has the right to take these from you without a good reason.
Article 18	
Everyone has the right to freedom of thought, conscience and religion; this right includes freedom to change his religion or belief, and freedom, either alone or in community with others Everyone has the right to freedom of thought, conscience and religion; this right includes freedom to change his	You have the right to profess your religion freely, to change it, and to practise it either on your own orwith other people.

religion or belief, and freedom, either alone or in community with others.	
Article 19	
Everyone has the right to freedom of opinion and expression; this right includes freedom to hold opinions without interference and to seek receive and impart information and ideas though any media and regardless of frontiers.	You have the right to think what you want, and to say what you like, and nobody should forbid you from doing so. You should be able to share your ideas – also with people from any other country.
Article 20	
1. Everyone has the right to freedom of peaceful assembly and association. 2. No one may be compelled to belong to an association.	You have the right to organise peaceful meetings or to take part in meetings in a peaceful way. It is wrong to force someone to belong to a group.
Article 21	
1. Everyone has the right to take part in the government of his country, directly or through freely chosen representatives. 2. Everyone has the right of equal access to public service in his country. 3. The will of the people shall be the basis of the authority of government; this will shall be expressed in periodic and genuine elections which shall be by universal and equal suffrage and shall be held by secrete vote or by equivalent free voting procedures.	You have the right to take part in your country's political affairs either by belonging to the Government yourself of by choosing politicians who have the same ideas as you. Governments should be voted for regularly and voting should be secret. You should get a vote and all votes should be equal. You also have the same right to join the public service as anyone else.
Article 22	
Everyone, as a member of society, has the right to social security and is entitled to realization, through national effort and international co-operation and in accordance with the organisation and resources of each State, of the economic, social and cultural rights indispensable for his dignity and the free development of his personality.	The society in which you live should help you to develop and to make the most of all the advantages (culture, work, social welfare) that are offered to you and to all the men and women in your country.
Article 23	
1. Everyone has the right to work, to free choice of employment, to just and favourable conditions of work and to protection against unemployment.	You have the right to work, to be free to choose your work, and to get a salary that allows you to live and support your family. If a man and a woman do the same work, they should get the same pay.

2. Everyone, without any discrimination, has the right to equal pay for equal work. 3. Everyone who works has the right to just and favourable remuneration ensuring for himself and his family an existence worthy of human dignity, and supplemented, if necessary, by other means of social protection. 4. Everyone has the right to form and to join trade unions for the protection of his interests.	All people who work have the right to join together to defend their interests.
Article 24	
Everyone has the right to rest and leisure, including reasonable limitation of working hours and periodic holidays with pay.	Each work day should not be too long, since everyone has the right to rest and should be able to take regular paid holidays.
Article 25	
1. Everyone has the right to a standard of living adequate for the health and well-being of himself and of his family, including foods, clothing, housing and medical care and necessary social services, and the right to security in the event of unemployment, sickness, disability, widowhood, old age or other lack of livelihood in circumstances beyond his control. 2. Motherhood and childhood are entitled to special care and assistance. All children, whether born in or out of wedlock, shall enjoy the same social protection.	You have the right to have whatever you need so that you and your family: do not fall ill; do not go hungry; have clothes and a house; and are helped if you are out of work, if you are ill, if you are old, if your wife or husband is dead, or if you do not earn a living for any other reason you cannot help. Both a mother who is going to have a baby and her baby should get special help. All children have the same rights, whether or not the mother is married.
Article 26	
1. Everyone has the right to education. Education shall be free, at least in the elementary and fundamental stages. Elementary education shall be compulsory. Technical and professional education shall be	You have the right to go to school and everyone should go to school. Primary schooling should be free. You should be able to learn a profession or continue your studies as far as you wish. At school, you should be able to develop all your talents and you should be taught to get

made generally available and higher education shall be equally accessible to all on the basis of merit. 2. Education shall be directed to the full development of the human personality and to the strengthening of respect for human rights and fundamental freedoms. It shall promote understanding,tolerance and friendship among all nations, racial or religious groups, and shall further the activities of the United Nations for the maintenance of peace. 3. Parents have a prior right to choose the kind of education that shall be given to their children.	on with others, whatever their race, their religion or the country they come from. Your parents have the right to choose how and what you will be taught at school.
Article 27	
1. Everyone has the right freely to participate in the cultural life of the community, to enjoy the arts and to share in scientific advancement and its benefits. 2. Everyone has the right to the protection of the moral and material interests resulting from any scientific, literary or artistic production of which he is the author.	You have the right to share in your community's arts and sciences, and in any good they do. Your works as an artist, a writer or a scientist should be protected, and you should be able to benefit from them.
Article 28	
Everyone is entitled to a social and international order in which the rights and freedoms set forth in this Declaration can be fully realised.	To make sure that your rights will be respected, there must be an 'order' that can protect them. This 'order' should be local and world-wide.
Article 29	
1. Everyone has duties to the community in which alone the free and full development of his personality is possible. 2. In the exercise of his rights and freedoms, everyone shall be subject only to such limitations as are determined by law solely for the purpose of securing due	You have duties towards the community within which your personality can fully develop. The law should guarantee human rights. It should allow everyone to respect others and to be respected.

recognition and respect for the rights and freedoms of others and of meeting the just requirements of morality, public order and the general welfare in a democratic society. 3. These rights and freedoms may in no case be exercised contrary to the purposes and principles of the United Nations.	
Article 30	
Nothing in this Declaration may be interpreted as implying for any State, group or person any right to engage in any activity or to perform any act aimed at the destruction of any of the rights and freedoms set forth herein.	No society and no human being in any part of the world should act in such a way as to destroy the rights that you have just been reading about.

⌘❐⌘

4 International Covenant on Civil and Political Rights

In 1947, the United Nations Commission on Human Rights decided to draft a treaty which would cast the principles recognised by the Universal Declaration of Human Rights in a form binding in international law on countries which become parties to it, The International Covenant on Civil and Political Rights (ICCPR).

ICCPR was presented to the General Assembly of the United Nations in 1954, and was finally adopted in 1966. The ICCPR did not come into operation internationally until March 1976. The ICCPR is now the major human rights document in the international community. It covers fundamental rights such as the right to life, liberty, freedom of conscience and thought, freedom of assembly and association, freedom of speech, and privacy. It also covers political rights, such as the right to vote, and legal rights, such as the right to equality before the law.

The ICCPR is an international treaty which binds the countries that are party to it. It is a fundamental principle of international law that when a country becomes a party to a treaty, it agrees to comply with the obligations imposed by it. International law is different from domestic law, however, because it relies on co-operation, rather than enforcement by means of an international police force or army. Although in certain circumstances the United Nations Charter allows the imposition of sanctions or military involvement in international disputes, in almost all cases international law relies on co-operation and international political pressure for its enforcement. In the case of the ICCPR, the treaty establishes a Human Rights Committee to oversee compliance with the treaty.

The Human Rights Committee

Part IV of the ICCPR establishes a Human Rights Committee, and specifies its members and functions. The Human Rights Committee is made up of 18 experts who are nominated by countries that are parties to the ICCPR, and are elected for terms of four years by the parties to the ICCPR. The Committee is required, under article 45 of the ICCPR, to submit an annual report of its activities to the UN General Assembly, through the UN Economic and Social Council.

Reports to the Committee by Parties to the ICCPR

Article 40 of the ICCPR requires parties to submit regular reports to the Human Rights Committee on the measures they have adopted to give effect to the rights recognised in the treaty. The Committee considers the report and may then question a representative of the relevant country to elicit further information. The Committee makes its own report and comments to the relevant country, which may include recommendations for further action by that country. The Committee may transmit this report to the Economic and Social Council of the United Nations, and by doing so exert wider international pressure if it considers a country's report to be unsatisfactory.

Disputes Between Parties to the ICCPR

Another mechanism for compliance is to be found in article 41 of the ICCPR. This article allows parties to the ICCPR to make complaints against each other if they consider the other party is not fulfilling its obligations under the ICCPR. Only parties which make a declaration accepting the application of article 41 may use this mechanism, or have it used against them.

The complaint may be referred to the Human Rights Committee, which may assist the parties to resolve the dispute, or if this is not possible, make a report of the facts, which also contains the submissions of the party. The Committee has no power to state its views on the merits of the dispute. If, however, the matter is referred to an *ad hoc* conciliation commission under article 42, then that Commission can express its views if conciliation is unsuccessful. It does not appear that articles 41 or 42 have ever been used.

Complaints by Individuals: The First Optional Protocol

A further mechanism for obtaining compliance with the ICCPR is contained in the First Optional Protocol. As its title suggests, it is optional for parties of the ICCPR to enter into the First Optional Protocol, but once they do so, they are bound by it. Of the 145 nations and self-governing colonies that have ratified the ICCPR, only 76 have ratified the First Optional Protocol. Countries that have ratified the ICCPR, but have not ratified the First Optional Protocol, include the United States of America, the United Kingdom and Japan.

Countries which have ratified the First Optional Protocol recognise the competence of the Human Rights Committee to receive and consider communications from individuals subject to the country's jurisdiction, who claim to be victims of a violation by the country of any of the rights set out in the ICCPR.

The composition of the Human Rights Committee, which considers these complaints, has been the subject of some controversy. The Human Rights Committee is comprised of members elected by all the parties to the ICCPR, but it is able to consider complaints under the First Optional Protocol, even though the Protocol has only been ratified by some of the parties to the ICCPR. This means that the current members of the Committee who come from the United Kingdom, Japan, Egypt and Jordan may consider complaints about other countries under the First Optional Protocol, when their own countries have not ratified it, and are not subject to it.

Procedures for Making Individual Complaints

There are a number of restrictions on the ability to bring a complaint to the Committee. First, a person may only make a complaint if they, individually, are a victim of the violation. Complaints cannot be made by a body representing a group which may be subject to discrimination.

Secondly, a complaint will only be admissible before the Committee once all domestic remedies have been exhausted. This means that in most cases the matter will have to have been appealed to the highest court in the country, before it can be brought before the Committee.

If, however, the domestic law does not provide any remedy at all, then the matter can be brought directly before the Committee.

Thirdly, the complaint must not be under consideration by any other international body.

Once an admissible complaint is made, the Committee receives and considers submissions made by both the complainant and the country about which the complaint is made. Both sides may make further submissions, commenting on the other's submission. The Committee then examines the submissions in closed meetings. No witnesses appear before the committee, and therefore there is no cross-examination. The whole proceeding is based on the written submissions. The Committee then determines its 'view' on the complaint, and forwards a copy of its view to the parties. The Committee's view is published in its Annual Report.

The entire process can be very time consuming, particularly if objections are taken to the admissibility of a complaint. It usually takes from two to five years between the initial lodgement of a complaint and the publication of the Committee's view.

Status of the Committee's 'View'

The Committee's view is not, of itself, binding upon countries that are parties to the ICCPR and First Optional Protocol. It is the country's obligations under the ICCPR which are binding upon it under international law, rather than the Committee's view. The Committee's view is, however, highly persuasive evidence that the country is in breach of these binding treaty obligations.

As can be seen from the above description, although the treaty obligations themselves are binding under international law, the method of enforcement is not one of compulsion. The method used by the Human Rights Committee to achieve compliance with the ICCPR is publication and consequential political embarrassment. If a United Nations body publicly declares its view that a country is in breach of its human rights obligations, the adverse publicity, particularly in an international forum, is often an effective sanction, particularly amongst nations that are concerned about their good name.

The official version of ICCPR is given below:

PART I

Article 1

1. All peoples have the right of self-determination. By virtue of that right they freely determine their political status and freely pursue their economic, social and cultural development.
2. All peoples may, for their own ends, freely dispose of their natural wealth and resources without prejudice to any obligations arising out of international economic co-operation, based upon the principle of mutual benefit, and international law. In no case may a people be deprived of its own means of subsistence.
3. The States Parties to the present Covenant, including those having responsibility for the administration of Non-Self-Governing and Trust Territories, shall promote the realization of the right of self-determination, and shall respect that right, in conformity with the provisions of the Charter of the United Nations.

PART II

Article 2

1. Each State Party to the present Covenant undertakes to respect and to ensure to all individuals within its territory and subject to its jurisdiction the rights recognized in the present Covenant, without distinction of any kind, such as race, colour, sex, language, religion, political or other opinion, national or social origin, property, birth or other status.
2. Where not already provided for by existing legislative or other measures, each State Party to the present Covenant undertakes to take the necessary steps, in accordance with its constitutional processes and with the provisions of the present Covenant, to adopt such laws or other measures as may be necessary to give effect to the rights recognized in the present Covenant.
3. Each State Party to the present Covenant undertakes:
   (a) To ensure that any person whose rights or freedoms as herein recognized are violated shall have an effective remedy, notwithstanding that the violation has been committed by persons acting in an official capacity;
   (b) To ensure that any person claiming such a remedy shall have his right thereto determined by competent judicial, administrative or legislative authorities, or by any other competent authority provided for by the legal system of the State, and to develop the possibilities of judicial remedy;
   (c) To ensure that the competent authorities shall enforce such remedies when granted.

Article 3

The States Parties to the present Covenant undertake to ensure the equal right of men and women to the enjoyment of all civil and political rights set forth in the present Covenant.

Article 4

1. In time of public emergency which threatens the life of the nation and the existence of which is officially proclaimed, the States Parties to the present Covenant may take measures derogating from their obligations under the present Covenant to the extent strictly required by the exigencies of the situation, provided that such measures are not inconsistent with their other obligations under international law and do not involve discrimination solely on the ground of race, colour, sex, language, religion or social origin.

2. No derogation from articles 6, 7, 8 (paragraphs I and 2), 11, 15, 16 and 18 may be made under this provision.
3. Any State Party to the present Covenant availing itself of the right of derogation shall immediately inform the other States Parties to the present Covenant, through the intermediary of the Secretary-General of the United Nations, of the provisions from which it has derogated and of the reasons by which it was actuated. A further communication shall be made, through the same intermediary, on the date on which it terminates such derogation.

Article 5

1. Nothing in the present Covenant may be interpreted as implying for any State, group or person any right to engage in any activity or perform any act aimed at the destruction of any of the rights and freedoms recognized herein or at their limitation to a greater extent than is provided for in the present Covenant.
2. There shall be no restriction upon or derogation from any of the fundamental human rights recognized or existing in any State Party to the present Covenant pursuant to law, conventions, regulations or custom on the pretext that the present Covenant does not recognize such rights or that it recognizes them to a lesser extent.

PART III

Article 6

1. Every human being has the inherent right to life. This right shall be protected by law. No one shall be arbitrarily deprived of his life.
2. In countries which have not abolished the death penalty, sentence of death may be imposed only for the most serious crimes in accordance with the law in force at the time of the commission of the crime and not contrary to the provisions of the present Covenant and to the Convention on the Prevention and Punishment of the Crime of Genocide. This penalty can only be carried out pursuant to a final judgement rendered by a competent court.
3. When deprivation of life constitutes the crime of genocide, it is understood that nothing in this article shall authorize any State Party to the present Covenant to derogate in any way from any obligation assumed under the provisions of the Convention on the Prevention and Punishment of the Crime of Genocide.

4. Anyone sentenced to death shall have the right to seek pardon or commutation of the sentence. Amnesty, pardon or commutation of the sentence of death may be granted in all cases.
5. Sentence of death shall not be imposed for crimes committed by persons below eighteen years of age and shall not be carried out on pregnant women.
6. Nothing in this article shall be invoked to delay or to prevent the abolition of capital punishment by any State Party to the present Covenant.

Article 7

No one shall be subjected to torture or to cruel, inhuman or degrading treatment or punishment. In particular, no one shall be subjected without his free consent to medical or scientific experimentation.

Article 8

1. No one shall be held in slavery; slavery and the slave-trade in all their forms shall be prohibited.
2. No one shall be held in servitude.
3. (a) No one shall be required to perform forced or compulsory labour;
   (b) Paragraph 3 (a) shall not be held to preclude, in countries where imprisonment with hard labour may be imposed as a punishment for a crime, the performance of hard labour in pursuance of a sentence to such punishment by a competent court;
   (c) For the purpose of this paragraph the term "forced or compulsory labour" shall not include:
      (i) Any work or service, not referred to in sub-paragraph (b), normally required of a person who is under detention in consequence of a lawful order of a court, or of a person during conditional release from such detention;
      (ii) Any service of a military character and, in countries where conscientious objection is recognized, any national service required by law of conscientious objectors;
      (iii) Any service exacted in cases of emergency or calamity threatening the life or well-being of the community;
      (iv) Any work or service which forms part of normal civil obligations.

Article 9

1. Everyone has the right to liberty and security of person. No one shall be subjected to arbitrary arrest or detention. No one shall be deprived of his

liberty except on such grounds and in accordance with such procedure as are established by law.

2. Anyone who is arrested shall be informed, at the time of arrest, of the reasons for his arrest and shall be promptly informed of any charges against him.
3. Anyone arrested or detained on a criminal charge shall be brought promptly before a judge or other officer authorized by law to exercise judicial power and shall be entitled to trial within a reasonable time or to release. It shall not be the general rule that persons awaiting trial shall be detained in custody, but release may be subject to guarantees to appear for trial, at any other stage of the judicial proceedings, and, should occasion arise, for execution of the judgement.
4. Anyone who is deprived of his liberty by arrest or detention shall be entitled to take proceedings before a court, in order that that court may decide without delay on the lawfulness of his detention and order his release if the detention is not lawful.
5. Anyone who has been the victim of unlawful arrest or detention shall have an enforceable right to compensation.

Article 10

1. All persons deprived of their liberty shall be treated with humanity and with respect for the inherent dignity of the human person.
2. (a) Accused persons shall, save in exceptional circumstances, be segregated from convicted persons and shall be subject to separate treatment appropriate to their status as unconvicted persons;
   (b) Accused juvenile persons shall be separated from adults and brought as speedily as possible for adjudication.
3. The penitentiary system shall comprise treatment of prisoners the essential aim of which shall be their reformation and social rehabilitation. Juvenile offenders shall be segregated from adults and be accorded treatment appropriate to their age and legal status.

Article 11

No one shall be imprisoned merely on the ground of inability to fulfil a contractual obligation.

Article 12

1. Everyone lawfully within the territory of a State shall, within that territory, have the right to liberty of movement and freedom to choose his residence.

2. Everyone shall be free to leave any country, including his own.
3. The above-mentioned rights shall not be subject to any restrictions except those which are provided by law, are necessary to protect national security, public order, public health or morals or the rights and freedoms of others, and are consistent with the other rights recognized in the present Covenant.
4. No one shall be arbitrarily deprived of the right to enter his own country.

Article 13

An alien lawfully in the territory of a State Party to the present Covenant may be expelled therefrom only in pursuance of a decision reached in accordance with law and shall, except where compelling reasons of national security otherwise require, be allowed to submit the reasons against his expulsion and to have his case reviewed by, and be represented for the purpose before, the competent authority or a person or persons especially designated by the competent authority.

Article 14

1. All persons shall be equal before the courts and tribunals. In the determination of any criminal charge against him, or of his rights and obligations in a suit at law, everyone shall be entitled to a fair and public hearing by a competent, independent and impartial tribunal established by law. The press and the public may be excluded from all or part of a trial for reasons of morals, public order or national security in a democratic society, or when the interest of the private lives of the parties so requires, or to the extent strictly necessary in the opinion of the court in special circumstances where publicity would prejudice the interests of justice; but any judgement rendered in a criminal case or in a suit at law shall be made public except where the interest of juvenile persons otherwise requires or the proceedings concern matrimonial disputes or the guardianship of children.
2. Everyone charged with a criminal offence shall have the right to be presumed innocent until proved guilty according to law.
3. In the determination of any criminal charge against him, everyone shall be entitled to the following minimum guarantees, in full equality:
   (a) To be informed promptly and in detail in a language which he understands of the nature and cause of the charge against him;
   (b) To have adequate time and facilities for the preparation of his defence and to communicate with counsel of his own choosing;

(c) To be tried without undue delay;

(d) To be tried in his presence, and to defend himself in person or through legal assistance of his own choosing; to be informed, if he does not have legal assistance, of this right; and to have legal assistance assigned to him, in any case where the interests of justice so require, and without payment by him in any such case if he does not have sufficient means to pay for it;

(e) To examine, or have examined, the witnesses against him and to obtain the attendance and examination of witnesses on his behalf under the same conditions as witnesses against him;

(f) To have the free assistance of an interpreter if he cannot understand or speak the language used in court;

(g) Not to be compelled to testify against himself or to confess guilt.

4. In the case of juvenile persons, the procedure shall be such as will take account of their age and the desirability of promoting their rehabilitation.

5. Everyone convicted of a crime shall have the right to his conviction and sentence being reviewed by a higher tribunal according to law.

6. When a person has by a final decision been convicted of a criminal offence and when subsequently his conviction has been reversed or he has been pardoned on the ground that a new or newly discovered fact shows conclusively that there has been a miscarriage of justice, the person who has suffered punishment as a result of such conviction shall be compensated according to law, unless it is proved that the non-disclosure of the unknown fact in time is wholly or partly attributable to him.

7. No one shall be liable to be tried or punished again for an offence for which he has already been finally convicted or acquitted in accordance with the law and penal procedure of each country.

Article 15

1. No one shall be held guilty of any criminal offence on account of any act or omission which did not constitute a criminal offence, under national or international law, at the time when it was committed. Nor shall a heavier penalty be imposed than the one that was applicable at the time when the criminal offence was committed. If, subsequent to the commission of the offence, provision is made by law for the imposition of the lighter penalty, the offender shall benefit thereby.

2. Nothing in this article shall prejudice the trial and punishment of any person for any act or omission which, at the time when it was committed, was criminal according to the general principles of law recognized by the community of nations.

Article 16

Everyone shall have the right to recognition everywhere as a person before the law.

Article 17

1. No one shall be subjected to arbitrary or unlawful interference with his privacy, family, home or correspondence, nor to unlawful attacks on his honour and reputation.
2. Everyone has the right to the protection of the law against such interference or attacks.

Article 18

1. Everyone shall have the right to freedom of thought, conscience and religion. This right shall include freedom to have or to adopt a religion or belief of his choice, and freedom, either individually or in community with others and in public or private, to manifest his religion or belief in worship, observance, practice and teaching.
2. No one shall be subject to coercion which would impair his freedom to have or to adopt a religion or belief of his choice.
3. Freedom to manifest one's religion or beliefs may be subject only to such limitations as are prescribed by law and are necessary to protect public safety, order, health, or morals or the fundamental rights and freedoms of others.
4. The States Parties to the present Covenant undertake to have respect for the liberty of parents and, when applicable, legal guardians to ensure the religious and moral education of their children in conformity with their own convictions.

Article 19

1. Everyone shall have the right to hold opinions without interference.
2. Everyone shall have the right to freedom of expression; this right shall include freedom to seek, receive and impart information and ideas of all kinds, regardless of frontiers, either orally, in writing or in print, in the form of art, or through any other media of his choice.
3. The exercise of the rights provided for in paragraph 2 of this article carries with it special duties and responsibilities. It may therefore be subject to certain restrictions, but these shall only be such as are provided by law and are necessary:

(a) For respect of the rights or reputations of others;

(b) For the protection of national security or of public order, or of public health or morals.

Article 20

1. Any propaganda for war shall be prohibited by law.
2. Any advocacy of national, racial or religious hatred that constitutes incitement to discrimination, hostility or violence shall be prohibited by law.

Article 21

The right of peaceful assembly shall be recognized. No restrictions may be placed on the exercise of this right other than those imposed in conformity with the law and which are necessary in a democratic society in the interests of national security or public safety, public order (ordre public), the protection of public health or morals or the protection of the rights and freedoms of others.

Article 22

1. Everyone shall have the right to freedom of association with others, including the right to form and join trade unions for the protection of his interests.
2. No restrictions may be placed on the exercise of this right other than those which are prescribed by law and which are necessary in a democratic society in the interests of national security or public safety, public order, the protection of public health or morals or the protection of the rights and freedoms of others. This article shall not prevent the imposition of lawful restrictions on members of the armed forces and of the police in their exercise of this right.
3. Nothing in this article shall authorize States Parties to the International Labour Organisation Convention of 1948 concerning Freedom of Association and Protection of the Right to Organise to take legislative measures which would prejudice, or to apply the law in such a manner as to prejudice, the guarantees provided for in that Convention.

Article 23

1. The family is the natural and fundamental group unit of society and is entitled to protection by society and the State.
2. The right of men and women of marriageable age to marry and to found a family shall be recognized.

3. No marriage shall be entered into without the free and full consent of the intending spouses.
4. States Parties to the present Covenant shall take appropriate steps to ensure equality of rights and responsibilities of spouses as to marriage, during marriage and at its dissolution. In the case of dissolution, provision shall be made for the necessary protection of any children.

Article 24

1. Every child shall have, without any discrimination as to race, colour, sex, language, religion, national or social origin, property or birth, the right to such measures of protection as are required by his status as a minor, on the part of his family, society and the State.
2. Every child shall be registered immediately after birth and shall have a name.
3. Every child has the right to acquire a nationality.

Article 25

Every citizen shall have the right and the opportunity, without any of the distinctions mentioned in article 2 and without unreasonable restrictions:

(a) To take part in the conduct of public affairs, directly or through freely chosen representatives;

(b) To vote and to be elected at genuine periodic elections which shall be by universal and equal suffrage and shall be held by secret ballot, guaranteeing the free expression of the will of the electors;

(c) To have access, on general terms of equality, to public service in his country.

Article 26

All persons are equal before the law and are entitled without any discrimination to the equal protection of the law. In this respect, the law shall prohibit any discrimination and guarantee to all persons equal and effective protection against discrimination on any ground such as race, colour, sex, language, religion, political or other opinion, national or social origin, property, birth or other status.

Article 27

In those States in which ethnic, religious or linguistic minorities exist, persons belonging to such minorities shall not be denied the right, in community with the other members of their group, to enjoy their own culture, to profess and practise their own religion, or to use their own language.

PART IV

Article 28

1. There shall be established a Human Rights Committee (hereafter referred to in the present Covenant as the Committee). It shall consist of eighteen members and shall carry out the functions hereinafter provided.
2. The Committee shall be composed of nationals of the States Parties to the present Covenant who shall be persons of high moral character and recognized competence in the field of human rights, consideration being given to the usefulness of the participation of some persons having legal experience.
3. The members of the Committee shall be elected and shall serve in their personal capacity.

Article 29

1. The members of the Committee shall be elected by secret ballot from a list of persons possessing the qualifications prescribed in article 28 and nominated for the purpose by the States Parties to the present Covenant.
2. Each State Party to the present Covenant may nominate not more than two persons. These persons shall be nationals of the nominating State.
3. A person shall be eligible for renomination.

Article 30

1. The initial election shall be held no later than six months after the date of the entry into force of the present Covenant.
2. At least four months before the date of each election to the Committee, other than an election to fill a vacancy declared in accordance with article 34, the Secretary-General of the United Nations shall address a written invitation to the States Parties to the present Covenant to submit their nominations for membership of the Committee within three months.
3. The Secretary-General of the United Nations shall prepare a list in alphabetical order of all the persons thus nominated, with an indication of the States Parties which have nominated them, and shall submit it to the States Parties to the present Covenant no later than one month before the date of each election.
4. Elections of the members of the Committee shall be held at a meeting of the States Parties to the present Covenant convened by the Secretary General of the United Nations at the Headquarters of the United Nations. At that meeting, for which two thirds of the States Parties to the present

Covenant shall constitute a quorum, the persons elected to the Committee shall be those nominees who obtain the largest number of votes and an absolute majority of the votes of the representatives of States Parties present and voting.

Article 31

1. The Committee may not include more than one national of the same State.
2. In the election of the Committee, consideration shall be given to equitable geographical distribution of membership and to the representation of the different forms of civilization and of the principal legal systems.

Article 32

1. The members of the Committee shall be elected for a term of four years. They shall be eligible for re-election if renominated. However, the terms of nine of the members elected at the first election shall expire at the end of two years; immediately after the first election, the names of these nine members shall be chosen by lot by the Chairman of the meeting referred to in article 30, paragraph 4.
2. Elections at the expiry of office shall be held in accordance with the preceding articles of this part of the present Covenant.

Article 33

1. If, in the unanimous opinion of the other members, a member of the Committee has ceased to carry out his functions for any cause other than absence of a temporary character, the Chairman of the Committee shall notify the Secretary-General of the United Nations, who shall then declare the seat of that member to be vacant.
2. In the event of the death or the resignation of a member of the Committee, the Chairman shall immediately notify the Secretary-General of the United Nations, who shall declare the seat vacant from the date of death or the date on which the resignation takes effect.

Article 34

1. When a vacancy is declared in accordance with article 33 and if the term of office of the member to be replaced does not expire within six months of the declaration of the vacancy, the Secretary-General of the United Nations shall notify each of the States Parties to the present Covenant, which may within two months submit nominations in accordance with article 29 for the purpose of filling the vacancy.

2. The Secretary-General of the United Nations shall prepare a list in alphabetical order of the persons thus nominated and shall submit it to the States Parties to the present Covenant. The election to fill the vacancy shall then take place in accordance with the relevant provisions of this part of the present Covenant.
3. A member of the Committee elected to fill a vacancy declared in accordance with article 33 shall hold office for the remainder of the term of the member who vacated the seat on the Committee under the provisions of that article.

Article 35

The members of the Committee shall, with the approval of the General Assembly of the United Nations, receive emoluments from United Nations resources on such terms and conditions as the General Assembly may decide, having regard to the importance of the Committee's responsibilities.

Article 36

The Secretary-General of the United Nations shall provide the necessary staff and facilities for the effective performance of the functions of the Committee under the present Covenant.

Article 37

1. The Secretary-General of the United Nations shall convene the initial meeting of the Committee at the Headquarters of the United Nations.
2. After its initial meeting, the Committee shall meet at such times as shall be provided in its rules of procedure.
3. The Committee shall normally meet at the Headquarters of the United Nations or at the United Nations Office at Geneva.

Article 38

Every member of the Committee shall, before taking up his duties, make a solemn declaration in open committee that he will perform his functions impartially and conscientiously.

Article 39

1. The Committee shall elect its officers for a term of two years. They may be re-elected.
2. The Committee shall establish its own rules of procedure, but these rules shall provide, *inter alia*, that:

(a) Twelve members shall constitute a quorum;

(b) Decisions of the Committee shall be made by a majority vote of the members present.

Article 40

1. The States Parties to the present Covenant undertake to submit reports on the measures they have adopted which give effect to the rights recognized herein and on the progress made in the enjoyment of those rights:

   (a) Within one year of the entry into force of the present Covenant for the States Parties concerned;

   (b) Thereafter whenever the Committee so requests.

2. All reports shall be submitted to the Secretary-General of the United Nations, who shall transmit them to the Committee for consideration. Reports shall indicate the factors and difficulties, if any, affecting the implementation of the present Covenant.

3. The Secretary-General of the United Nations may, after consultation with the Committee, transmit to the specialized agencies concerned copies of such parts of the reports as may fall within their field of competence.

4. The Committee shall study the reports submitted by the States Parties to the present Covenant. It shall transmit its reports, and such general comments as it may consider appropriate, to the States Parties. The Committee may also transmit to the Economic and Social Council these comments along with the copies of the reports it has received from States Parties to the present Covenant.

5. The States Parties to the present Covenant may submit to the Committee observations on any comments that may be made in accordance with paragraph 4 of this article.

Article 41

1. A State Party to the present Covenant may at any time declare under this article that it recognizes the competence of the Committee to receive and consider communications to the effect that a State Party claims that another State Party is not fulfilling its obligations under the present Covenant. Communications under this article may be received and considered only if submitted by a State Party which has made a declaration recognizing in regard to itself the competence of the Committee. No communication shall be received by the Committee if it concerns a State Party which has not made such a declaration. Communications received under this article shall be dealt with in accordance with the following procedure:

(a) If a State Party to the present Covenant considers that another State Party is not giving effect to the provisions of the present Covenant, it may, by written communication, bring the matter to the attention of that State Party. Within three months after the receipt of the communication the receiving State shall afford the State which sent the communication an explanation, or any other statement in writing clarifying the matter which should include, to the extent possible and pertinent, reference to domestic procedures and remedies taken, pending, or available in the matter;

(b) If the matter is not adjusted to the satisfaction of both States Parties concerned within six months after the receipt by the receiving State of the initial communication, either State shall have the right to refer the matter to the Committee, by notice given to the Committee and to the other State;

(c) The Committee shall deal with a matter referred to it only after it has ascertained that all available domestic remedies have been invoked and exhausted in the matter, in conformity with the generally recognized principles of international law. This shall not be the rule where the application of the remedies is unreasonably prolonged;

(d) The Committee shall hold closed meetings when examining communications under this article;

(e) Subject to the provisions of sub-paragraph (c), the Committee shall make available its good offices to the States Parties concerned with a view to a friendly solution of the matter on the basis of respect for human rights and fundamental freedoms as recognized in the present Covenant;

(f) In any matter referred to it, the Committee may call upon the States Parties concerned, referred to in sub-paragraph (b), to supply any relevant information;

(g) The States Parties concerned, referred to in sub-paragraph (b), shall have the right to be represented when the matter is being considered in the Committee and to make submissions orally and/or in writing;

(h) The Committee shall, within twelve months after the date of receipt of notice under sub-paragraph (b), submit a report:

   (i) If a solution within the terms of sub-paragraph (e) is reached, the Committee shall confine its report to a brief statement of the facts and of the solution reached;

   (ii) If a solution within the terms of sub-paragraph (e) is not reached, the Committee shall confine its report to a brief statement of the facts; the written submissions and record of the oral submissions made by the States Parties concerned shall be attached to the report. In every matter, the report shall be communicated to the States Parties concerned.

2. The provisions of this article shall come into force when ten States Parties to the present Covenant have made declarations under paragraph I of this article. Such declarations shall be deposited by the States Parties with the Secretary-General of the United Nations, who shall transmit copies thereof to the other States Parties. A declaration may be withdrawn at any time by notification to the Secretary-General. Such a withdrawal shall not prejudice the consideration of any matter which is the subject of a communication already transmitted under this article; no further communication by any State Party shall be received after the notification of withdrawal of the declaration has been received by the Secretary-General, unless the State Party concerned has made a new declaration.

Article 42

1. (a) If a matter referred to the Committee in accordance with article 41 is not resolved to the satisfaction of the States Parties concerned, the Committee may, with the prior consent of the States Parties concerned, appoint an *ad hoc* Conciliation Commission (hereinafter referred to as the Commission). The good offices of the Commission shall be made available to the States Parties concerned with a view to an amicable solution of the matter on the basis of respect for the present Covenant;

   (b) The Commission shall consist of five persons acceptable to the States Parties concerned. If the States Parties concerned fail to reach agreement within three months on all or part of the composition of the Commission, the members of the Commission concerning whom no agreement has been reached shall be elected by secret ballot by a two-thirds majority vote of the Committee from among its members.

2. The members of the Commission shall serve in their personal capacity. They shall not be nationals of the States Parties concerned, or of a State not Party to the present Covenant, or of a State Party which has not made a declaration under article 41.

3. The Commission shall elect its own Chairman and adopt its own rules of procedure.

4. The meetings of the Commission shall normally be held at the Headquarters of the United Nations or at the United Nations Office at Geneva. However, they may be held at such other convenient places as the Commission may determine in consultation with the Secretary-General of the United Nations and the States Parties concerned.

5. The secretariat provided in accordance with article 36 shall also service the commissions appointed under this article.
6. The information received and collated by the Committee shall be made available to the Commission and the Commission may call upon the States Parties concerned to supply any other relevant information.
7. When the Commission has fully considered the matter, but in any event not later than twelve months after having been seized of the matter, it shall submit to the Chairman of the Committee a report for communication to the States Parties concerned:
   (a) If the Commission is unable to complete its consideration of the matter within twelve months, it shall confine its report to a brief statement of the status of its consideration of the matter;
   (b) If an amicable solution to the matter on tie basis of respect for human rights as recognized in the present Covenant is reached, the Commission shall confine its report to a brief statement of the facts and of the solution reached;
   (c) If a solution within the terms of sub-paragraph (b) is not reached, the Commission's report shall embody its findings on all questions of fact relevant to the issues between the States Parties concerned, and its views on the possibilities of an amicable solution of the matter. This report shall also contain the written submissions and a record of the oral submissions made by the States Parties concerned;
   (d) If the Commission's report is submitted under sub-paragraph (c), the States Parties concerned shall, within three months of the receipt of the report, notify the Chairman of the Committee whether or not they accept the contents of the report of the Commission.
8. The provisions of this article are without prejudice to the responsibilities of the Committee under article 41.
9. The States Parties concerned shall share equally all the expenses of the members of the Commission in accordance with estimates to be provided by the Secretary-General of the United Nations.
10. The Secretary-General of the United Nations shall be empowered to pay the expenses of the members of the Commission, if necessary, before reimbursement by the States Parties concerned, in accordance with paragraph 9 of this article.

Article 43

The members of the Committee, and of the *ad hoc* conciliation commissions which may be appointed under article 42, shall be entitled to the facilities, privileges and immunities of experts on mission for the United Nations as laid down in the relevant sections of the Convention on the Privileges and Immunities of the United Nations.

Article 44

The provisions for the implementation of the present Covenant shall apply without prejudice to the procedures prescribed in the field of human rights by or under the constituent instruments and the conventions of the United Nations and of the specialized agencies and shall not prevent the States Parties to the present Covenant from having recourse to other procedures for settling a dispute in accordance with general or special international agreements in force between them.

Article 45

The Committee shall submit to the General Assembly of the United Nations, through the Economic and Social Council, an annual report on its activities.

PART V

Article 46

Nothing in the present Covenant shall be interpreted as impairing the provisions of the Charter of the United Nations and of the constitutions of the specialized agencies which define the respective responsibilities of the various organs of the United Nations and of the specialized agencies in regard to the matters dealt with in the present Covenant.

Article 47

Nothing in the present Covenant shall be interpreted as impairing the inherent right of all peoples to enjoy and utilize fully and freely their natural wealth and resources.

PART VI

Article 48

1. The present Covenant is open for signature by any State Member of the United Nations or member of any of its specialized agencies, by any State Party to the Statute of the International Court of Justice, and by any other State which has been invited by the General Assembly of the United Nations to become a Party to the present Covenant.
2. The present Covenant is subject to ratification. Instruments of ratification shall be deposited with the Secretary-General of the United Nations.

3. The present Covenant shall be open to accession by any State referred to in paragraph 1 of this article.
4. Accession shall be effected by the deposit of an instrument of accession with the Secretary-General of the United Nations.
5. The Secretary-General of the United Nations shall inform all States which have signed this Covenant or acceded to it of the deposit of each instrument of ratification or accession.

Article 49

1. The present Covenant shall enter into force three months after the date of the deposit with the Secretary-General of the United Nations of the thirty-fifth instrument of ratification or instrument of accession.
2. For each State ratifying the present Covenant or acceding to it after the deposit of the thirty-fifth instrument of ratification or instrument of accession, the present Covenant shall enter into force three months after the date of the deposit of its own instrument of ratification or instrument of accession.

Article 50

The provisions of the present Covenant shall extend to all parts of federal States without any limitations or exceptions.

Article 51

1. Any State Party to the present Covenant may propose an amendment and file it with the Secretary-General of the United Nations. The Secretary-General of the United Nations shall thereupon communicate any proposed amendments to the States Parties to the present Covenant with a request that they notify him whether they favour a conference of States Parties for the purpose of considering and voting upon the proposals. In the event that at least one third of the States Parties favours such a conference, the Secretary-General shall convene the conference under the auspices of the United Nations. Any amendment adopted by a majority of the States Parties present and voting at the conference shall be submitted to the General Assembly of the United Nations for approval.
2. Amendments shall come into force when they have been approved by the General Assembly of the United Nations and accepted by a two-thirds majority of the States Parties to the present Covenant in accordance with their respective constitutional processes.
3. When amendments come into force, they shall be binding on those States Parties which have accepted them, other States Parties still being bound

by the provisions of the present Covenant and any earlier amendment which they have accepted.

Article 52

1. Irrespective of the notifications made under article 48, paragraph 5, the Secretary-General of the United Nations shall inform all States referred to in paragraph I of the same article of the following particulars:
   (a) Signatures, ratifications and accessions under article 48;
   (b) The date of the entry into force of the present Covenant under article 49 and the date of the entry into force of any amendments under article 51.

Article 53

1. The present Covenant, of which the Chinese, English, French, Russian and Spanish texts are equally authentic, shall be deposited in the archives of the United Nations.
2. The Secretary-General of the United Nations shall transmit certified copies of the present Covenant to all States referred to in article 48.

International Covenant on Civil and Political Rights (ICCPR)

Unofficial Summary

Article 1

All peoples have the right of self-determination, including the right to determine their political status and freely pursue their economic, social and cultural development.

Article 2

Each State must respect and ensure to all people within its territory and jurisdiction all rights in this treaty without discrimination of any kind.

Article 3

The States undertake to ensure the equal right of men and women to the enjoyment of all rights in this treaty.

Article 4

Derogation from State obligations is to be strictly limited.

Article 5

Derogation from State obligations is to be strictly limited.

Article 6

Everyone has the right to life.

Article 7

No one shall be subjected to torture or cruel or degrading treatment or punishment.

Article 8

No one shall be held in slavery or servitude.

Article 9

Everyone has the right to liberty and security of person. No one shall be arrested or detained arbitrarily.

Article 10

Everyone deprived of liberty shall be treated with respect.

Article 11

No one shall be imprisoned merely for failing to pay a debt.

Article 12

Everyone has the right to freedom of movement and to leave and enter his own country.

Article 13

An alien lawfully in the territory of a State Party maybe expelled only in accordance with law.

Article 14

Everyone is equal before the law. Everyone has the right to a fair trial. Everyone has the right to be presumed innocent until proven guilty. No one may be compelled to testify against himself.

Article 15

No one shall be held guilty of a criminal offense when the act did not constitute a criminal offense at the time it was committed.

Article 16

Everyone has the right to be recognized every-where as a person before the law.

Article 17

Everyone has the right to privacy.

Article 18

Everyone has the right to freedom of thought, conscience and religion.

Article 19

Everyone has the right to freedom of opinion and expression.

Article 20

Propaganda for war shall be prohibited. Hate speech that constitutes incitement to discrimination or violence shall be prohibited.

Article 21

Everyone has the right to peaceful assembly.

Article 22

Everyone has the right to freedom of association, including the right to join a trade union.

Article 23

All adults have the right to marry and found a family. Women and men have equal rights to marry, within marriage, and at its dissolution.

Article 24

Every child shall have protection as required by his status as a minor, without discrimination of any kind. Every child has the right to a nationality.

Article 25

Every citizen has the right to take part in public affairs and to vote.

Article 26

Everyone is equal before the law and has the right to equal protection of the law, without discrimination of any kind.

Article 27

Ethnic, religious, or linguistic minorities shall not be denied the right to enjoy their own culture.

⌘❒⌘

5 International Covenant on Economic, Social and Cultural Rights

Introduction

Economic, social and cultural rights (ESCR) include the human right to work; the right to an adequate standard of living, including food, clothing, and housing; the right to physical and mental health; the right to social security; the right to a healthy environment; and the right to education.

Need for Protection of ESCR

Economic, Social and Cultural Rights are an important part of the international human rights law. They have been fully recognized by the international community and throughout international human rights law.

Although these rights have received less attention than civil and political rights, far more serious consideration than ever before is currently being devoted to them. The question is not whether these rights are basic human rights, but rather what entitlements they imply and the legal nature of the obligations of States to realize them. The fact is that civil and political rights and economic, social and cultural rights are indivisible and interdependent. Without realizing economic, social and cultural rights, there cannot be a meaningful enjoyment of civil and political rights.

Key International Instruments on ESCR and the Optional Protocol to the International Covenant on Economic, Social and Cultural Rights (ICESCR)

Various international instruments recognize economic, social and cultural rights as integral parts of the human rights frame-work. The first comprehensive international instrument encompassing both sets of rights *i.e.*, civil and political rights and the economic, social and cultural rights is the Universal Declaration of Human Rights (UDHR). The International Covenant on Economic, Social and Cultural Rights (ICESCR) remains the principal instrument on economic, social and cultural rights. It recognizes the right to self determination; equality for men and women; the right to work and favourable conditions of work; the right to form and join trade unions; the right to an adequate standard of living including adequate food, clothing and housing; the right to health and healthcare; the protection of the family; and the right to social security. As of November 2005, 149 countries have ratified the Covenant.

General Principles of ESCR and State Obligations to Promote, Protect and Fulfill

State parties are bound to ensure minimum human rights regardless of their resource constraints. For ESC rights, minimum core requirements include available foodstuffs for the population, essential primary healthcare, basic shelter and housing, and the most basic form of education. The Committee on Economic, Social and Cultural Rights elaborated on state obligations under General Comment 3: The Nature of State Parties Obligations

How do States Fulfill their Minimum Requirements?

Respect – the obligation to respect requires governments to refrain from interfering directly or indirectly with the enjoyment of ESCR

Protect – the obligation to protect requires governments to prevent third parties such as corporations, from interfering in any way with the enjoyment of ESCR

Fulfill – the obligation to fulfill requires governments to adopt the necessary measures to achieve the full realization of ESCR.

The Indian Context

The Indian Constitution recognizes economic, social and cultural rights as Directive Principles of State Policy which, unlike the guarantee of civil and political rights in the Indian Constitution, are not directly enforceable in the courts, but are intended to serve as guidance for government policy. The Indian law of economic, social and cultural rights has been developed incrementally by the courts, drawing on the Directive Principles as aids to interpretation of the civil and political rights which are justiciable under the Constitution, to elevate the status of the Directive Principles as constitutional rights. In particular, the Indian Supreme Court has adopted an expansive interpretation of the constitutional right to life, based on principles of human dignity, to protect certain economic and social rights, including the right to adequate nutrition, clothing and shelter, the right to medical facilities, the right to earn a livelihood, and environmental rights.

International Covenant on Economic, Social and Cultural Rights

Adopted and opened for signature, ratification and accession by General Assembly resolution 2200A (XXI) of 16 December 1966, entry into force 3 January 1976,

PART I

Article 1

1. All peoples have the right of self-determination. By virtue of that right they freely determine their political status and freely pursue their economic, social and cultural development.
2. All peoples may, for their own ends, freely dispose of their natural wealth and resources without prejudice to any obligations arising out of international economic co-operation, based upon the principle of mutual benefit, and international law. In no case may a people be deprived of its own means of subsistence.
3. The States Parties to the present Covenant, including those having responsibility for the administration of Non-Self-Governing and Trust Territories, shall promote the realization of the right of self-determination, and shall respect that right, in conformity with the provisions of the Charter of the United Nations.

PART II

Article 2

1. Each State Party to the present Covenant undertakes to take steps, individually and through international assistance and co-operation, especially economic and technical, to the maximum of its available resources, with a view to achieving progressively the full realization of the rights recognized in the present Covenant by all appropriate means, including particularly the adoption of legislative measures.

2. The States Parties to the present Covenant undertake to guarantee that the rights enunciated in the present Covenant will be exercised without discrimination of any kind as to race, colour, sex, language, religion, political or other opinion, national or social origin, property, birth or other status.
3. Developing countries, with due regard to human rights and their national economy, may determine to what extent they would guarantee the economic rights recognized in the present Covenant to non-nationals.

Article 3

The States Parties to the present Covenant undertake to ensure the equal right of men and women to the enjoyment of all economic, social and cultural rights set forth in the present Covenant.

Article 4

The States Parties to the present Covenant recognize that, in the enjoyment of those rights provided by the State in conformity with the present Covenant, the State may subject such rights only to such limitations as are determined by law only in so far as this may be compatible with the nature of these rights and solely for the purpose of promoting the general welfare in a democratic society.

Article 5

1. Nothing in the present Covenant may be interpreted as implying for any State, group or person any right to engage in any activity or to perform any act aimed at the destruction of any of the rights or freedoms recognized herein, or at their limitation to a greater extent than is provided for in the present Covenant.
2. No restriction upon or derogation from any of the fundamental human rights recognized or existing in any country in virtue of law, conventions, regulations or custom shall be admitted on the pretext that the present Covenant does not recognize such rights or that it recognizes them to a lesser extent.

PART III

Article 6

1. The States Parties to the present Covenant recognize the right to work, which includes the right of everyone to the opportunity to gain his living by work which he freely chooses or accepts, and will take appropriate steps to safeguard this right.

2. The steps to be taken by a State Party to the present Covenant to achieve the full realization of this right shall include technical and vocational guidance and training programmes, policies and techniques to achieve steady economic, social and cultural development and full and productive employment under conditions safeguarding fundamental political and economic freedoms to the individual.

Article 7

The States Parties to the present Covenant recognize the right of everyone to the enjoyment of just and favourable conditions of work which ensure, in particular:

(a) Remuneration which provides all workers, as a minimum, with:

(i) Fair wages and equal remuneration for work of equal value without distinction of any kind, in particular women being guaranteed conditions of work not inferior to those enjoyed by men, with equal pay for equal work;

(ii) A decent living for themselves and their families in accordance with the provisions of the present Covenant;

(b) Safe and healthy working conditions;

(c) Equal opportunity for everyone to be promoted in his employment to an appropriate higher level, subject to no considerations other than those of seniority and competence;

(d) Rest, leisure and reasonable limitation of working hours and periodic holidays with pay, as well as remuneration for public holidays.

Article 8

1. The States Parties to the present Covenant undertake to ensure:

(a) The right of everyone to form trade unions and join the trade union of his choice, subject only to the rules of the organisation concerned, for the promotion and protection of his economic and social interests. No restrictions may be placed on the exercise of this right other than those prescribed by law and which are necessary in a democratic society in the interests of national security or public order or for the protection of the rights and freedoms of others;

(b) The right of trade unions to establish national federations or confederations and the right of the latter to form or join international trade-union organisations;

(c) The right of trade unions to function freely subject to no limitations other than those prescribed by law and which are necessary in a democratic society in the interests of national security or public order or for the protection of the rights and freedoms of others;

(d) The right to strike, provided that it is exercised in conformity with the laws of the particular country.

2. This article shall not prevent the imposition of lawful restrictions on the exercise of these rights by members of the armed forces or of the police or of the administration of the State.
3. Nothing in this article shall authorize States Parties to the International Labour Organisation Convention of 1948 concerning Freedom of Association and Protection of the Right to Organise to take legislative measures which would prejudice, or apply the law in such a manner as would prejudice, the guarantees provided for in that Convention.

Article 9

The States Parties to the present Covenant recognize the right of everyone to social security, including social insurance.

Article 10

The States Parties to the present Covenant recognize that:

1. The widest possible protection and assistance should be accorded to the family, which is the natural and fundamental group unit of society, particularly for its establishment and while it is responsible for the care and education of dependent children. Marriage must be entered into with the free consent of the intending spouses.
2. Special protection should be accorded to mothers during a reasonable period before and after childbirth. During such period working mothers should be accorded paid leave or leave with adequate social security benefits.
3. Special measures of protection and assistance should be taken on behalf of all children and young persons without any discrimination for reasons of parentage or other conditions. Children and young persons should be protected from economic and social exploitation. Their employment in work harmful to their morals or health or dangerous to life or likely to hamper their normal development should be punishable by law. States should also set age limits below which the paid employment of child labour should be prohibited and punishable by law.

Article 11

1. The States Parties to the present Covenant recognize the right of everyone to an adequate standard of living for himself and his family, including

adequate food, clothing and housing, and to the continuous improvement of living conditions. The States Parties will take appropriate steps to ensure the realization of this right, recognizing to this effect the essential importance of international co-operation based on free consent.

2. The States Parties to the present Covenant, recognizing the fundamental right of everyone to be free from hunger, shall take, individually and through international co-operation, the measures, including specific programmes, which are needed:
   (a) To improve methods of production, conservation and distribution of food by making full use of technical and scientific knowledge, by disseminating knowledge of the principles of nutrition and by developing or reforming agrarian systems in such a way as to achieve the most efficient development and utilization of natural resources;
   (b) Taking into account the problems of both food-importing and food-exporting countries, to ensure an equitable distribution of world food supplies in relation to need.

Article 12

1. The States Parties to the present Covenant recognize the right of everyone to the enjoyment of the highest attainable standard of physical and mental health.
2. The steps to be taken by the States Parties to the present Covenant to achieve the full realization of this right shall include those necessary for:
   (a) The provision for the reduction of the still birth-rate and of infant mortality and for the healthy development of the child;
   (b) The improvement of all aspects of environmental and industrial hygiene;
   (c) The prevention, treatment and control of epidemic, endemic, occupational and other diseases;
   (d) The creation of conditions which would assure to all medical service and medical attention in the event of sickness.

Article 13

1. The States Parties to the present Covenant recognize the right of everyone to education. They agree that education shall be directed to the full development of the human personality and the sense of its dignity, and shall strengthen the respect for human rights and fundamental freedoms. They further agree that education shall enable all persons to participate effectively in a free society, promote understanding, tolerance and friendship among all nations and all racial, ethnic or religious groups,

and further the activities of the United Nations for the maintenance of peace.

2. The States Parties to the present Covenant recognize that, with a view to achieving the full realization of this right:
   (a) Primary education shall be compulsory and available free to all;
   (b) Secondary education in its different forms, including technical and vocational secondary education, shall be made generally available and accessible to all by every appropriate means, and in particular by the progressive introduction of free education;
   (c) Higher education shall be made equally accessible to all, on the basis of capacity, by every appropriate means, and in particular by the progressive introduction of free education;
   (d) Fundamental education shall be encouraged or intensified as far as possible for those persons who have not received or completed the whole period of their primary education;
   (e) The development of a system of schools at all levels shall be actively pursued, an adequate fellowship system shall be established, and the material conditions of teaching staff shall be continuously improved.
3. The States Parties to the present Covenant undertake to have respect for the liberty of parents and, when applicable, legal guardians to choose for their children schools, other than those established by the public authorities, which conform to such minimum educational standards as maybe laid down or approved by the State and to ensure the religious and moral education of their children in conformity with their own convictions.
4. No part of this article shall be construed so as to interfere with the liberty of individuals and bodies to establish and direct educational institutions, subject always to the observance of the principles set forth in paragraph I of this article and to the requirement that the education given in such institutions shall conform to such minimum standards as maybe laid down by the State.

Article 14.

Each State Party to the present Covenant which, at the time of becoming a Party, has not been able to secure in its metropolitan territory or other territories under its jurisdiction compulsory primary education, free of charge, undertakes, within two years, to work out and adopt a detailed plan of action for the progressive implementation, within a reasonable number of years, to be fixed in the plan, of the principle of compulsory education free of charge for all.

Article 15

1. The States Parties to the present Covenant recognize the right of everyone:
   (a) To take part in cultural life;
   (b) To enjoy the benefits of scientific progress and its applications;
   (c) To benefit from the protection of the moral and material interests resulting from any scientific, literary or artistic production of which he is the author.
2. The steps to be taken by the States Parties to the present Covenant to achieve the full realization of this right shall include those necessary for the conservation, the development and the diffusion of science and culture.
3. The States Parties to the present Covenant undertake to respect the freedom indispensable for scientific research and creative activity.
4. The States Parties to the present Covenant recognize the benefits to be derived from the encouragement and development of international contacts and co-operation in the scientific and cultural fields.

PART IV

Article 16

1. The States Parties to the present Covenant undertake to submit in conformity with this part of the Covenant reports on the measures which they have adopted and the progress made in achieving the observance of the rights recognized herein.
2. (a) All reports shall be submitted to the Secretary-General of the United Nations, who shall transmit copies to the Economic and Social Council for consideration in accordance with the provisions of the present Covenant;
   (b) The Secretary-General of the United Nations shall also transmit to the specialized agencies copies of the reports, or any relevant parts therefrom, from States Parties to the present Covenant which are also members of these specialized agencies in so far as these reports, or parts therefrom, relate to any matters which fall within the responsibilities of the said agencies in accordance with their constitutional instruments.

Article 17

1. The States Parties to the present Covenant shall furnish their reports in stages, in accordance with a programme to be established by the Economic and Social Council within one year of the entry into force of the present Covenant after consultation with the States Parties and the specialized agencies concerned.
2. Reports may indicate factors and difficulties affecting the degree of fulfilment of obligations under the present Covenant.
3. Where relevant information has previously been furnished to the United Nations or to any specialized agency by any State Party to the present Covenant, it will not be necessary to reproduce that information, but a precise reference to the information so furnished will suffice.

Article 18

Pursuant to its responsibilities under the Charter of the United Nations in the field of human rights and fundamental freedoms, the Economic and Social Council may make arrangements with the specialized agencies in respect of their reporting to it on the progress made in achieving the observance of the provisions of the present Covenant falling within the scope of their activities. These reports may include particulars of decisions and recommendations on such implementation adopted by their competent organs.

Article 19

The Economic and Social Council may transmit to the Commission on Human Rights for study and general recommendation or, as appropriate, for information the reports concerning human rights submitted by States in accordance with articles 16 and 17, and those concerning human rights submitted by the specialized agencies in accordance with article 18.

Article 20

The States Parties to the present Covenant and the specialized agencies concerned may submit comments to the Economic and Social Council on any general recommendation under article 19 or reference to such general recommendation in any report of the Commission on Human Rights or any documentation referred to therein.

Article 21

The Economic and Social Council may submit from time to time to the General Assembly reports with recommendations of a general nature and a summary of the information received from the States Parties to the present Covenant and the specialized agencies on the measures taken and the progress made in achieving general observance of the rights recognized in the present Covenant.

Article 22

The Economic and Social Council may bring to the attention of other organs of the United Nations, their subsidiary organs and specialized agencies concerned with furnishing technical assistance any matters arising out of the reports referred to in this part of the present Covenant which may assist such bodies in deciding, each within its field of competence, on the advisability of international measures likely to contribute to the effective progressive implementation of the present Covenant.

Article 23

The States Parties to the present Covenant agree that international action for the achievement of the rights recognized in the present Covenant includes such methods as the conclusion of conventions, the adoption of recommendations, the furnishing of technical assistance and the holding of regional meetings and technical meetings for the purpose of consultation and study organised in conjunction with the Governments concerned.

Article 24

Nothing in the present Covenant shall be interpreted as impairing the provisions of the Charter of the United Nations and of the constitutions of the specialized agencies which define the respective responsibilities of the various organs of the United Nations and of the specialized agencies in regard to the matters dealt with in the present Covenant.

Article 25

Nothing in the present Covenant shall be interpreted as impairing the inherent right of all peoples to enjoy and utilize fully and freely their natural wealth and resources.

PART V

Article 26

1. The present Covenant is open for signature by any State Member of the United Nations or member of any of its specialized agencies, by any

State Party to the Statute of the International Court of Justice, and by any other State which has been invited by the General Assembly of the United Nations to become a party to the present Covenant.

2. The present Covenant is subject to ratification. Instruments of ratification shall be deposited with the Secretary-General of the United Nations.
3. The present Covenant shall be open to accession by any State referred to in paragraph 1 of this article.
4. Accession shall be effected by the deposit of an instrument of accession with the Secretary-General of the United Nations.
5. The Secretary-General of the United Nations shall inform all States which have signed the present Covenant or acceded to it of the deposit of each instrument of ratification or accession.

Article 27

1. The present Covenant shall enter into force three months after the date of the deposit with the Secretary-General of the United Nations of the thirty-fifth instrument of ratification or instrument of accession.
2. For each State ratifying the present Covenant or acceding to it after the deposit of the thirty-fifth instrument of ratification or instrument of accession, the present Covenant shall enter into force three months after the date of the deposit of its own instrument of ratification or instrument of accession.

Article 28

The provisions of the present Covenant shall extend to all parts of federal States without any limitations or exceptions.

Article 29

1. Any State Party to the present Covenant may propose an amendment and file it with the Secretary-General of the United Nations. The Secretary-General shall there-upon communicate any proposed amendments to the States Parties to the present Covenant with a request that they notify him whether they favour a conference of States Parties for the purpose of considering and voting upon the proposals. In the event that at least one third of the States Parties favours such a conference, the Secretary-General shall convene the conference under the auspices of the United Nations. Any amendment adopted by a majority of the States Parties present and voting at the conference shall be submitted to the General Assembly of the United Nations for approval.

2. Amendments shall come into force when they have been approved by the General Assembly of the United Nations and accepted by a two-thirds majority of the States Parties to the present Covenant in accordance with their respective constitutional processes.
3. When amendments come into force they shall be binding on those States Parties which have accepted them, other States Parties still being bound by the provisions of the present Covenant and any earlier amendment which they have accepted.

Article 30

Irrespective of the notifications made under article 26, paragraph 5, the Secretary-General of the United Nations shall inform all States referred to in paragraph I of the same article of the following particulars:

(a) Signatures, ratifications and accessions under article 26;

(b) The date of the entry into force of the present Covenant under article 27, and the date of the entry into force of any amendments under article 29.

Article 31

1. The present Covenant, of which the Chinese, English, French, Russian and Spanish texts are equally authentic, shall be deposited in the archives of the United Nations.
2. The Secretary-General of the United Nations shall transmit certified copies of the present Covenant to all States referred to in article 26.

International Covenant on Economic, Social and Cultural Rights (ICESR)

Unofficial Summary

Article 1

All peoples have the right of self-determination, including the right to determine their political status and freely pursue their economic, social and cultural development.

Article 2

Each State Party undertakes to take steps to the maximum of its available resources to achieve progressively the full realization of the rights in this treaty. Everyone is entitled to the same rights without discrimination of any kind.

Article 3

The States undertake to ensure the equal right of men and women to the enjoyment of all rights in this treaty.

Article 4

Limitations maybe placed on these rights only if compatible with the nature of these rights and solely for the purpose of promoting the general welfare in a democratic society.

Article 5

No person, group or government has the right to destroy any of these rights.

Article 6

No person, group or government has the right to destroy any of these rights.

Article 7

Everyone has the right to just conditions of work; fair wages ensuring a decent living for himself and his family; equal pay for equal work; safe and healthy working conditions; equal opportunity for everyone to be promoted; rest and leisure.

Article 8

Everyone has the right to form and join trade unions, the right to strike.

Article 9

Everyone has the right to social security, including social insurance.

Article 10

Protection and assistance should be accorded to the family. Marriage must be entered into with the free consent of both spouses. Special protection should be provided to mothers. Special measures should be taken on behalf of children, without discrimination. Children and youth should be protected from economic exploitation. Their employment in dangerous or harmful work should be prohibited. There should be age limits below which child labor should be prohibited.

Article 11

Every-one has the right to an adequate standard of living for himself and his family, including adequate food, clothing and housing. Everyone has the right to be free from hunger.

Article 12

Every-one has the right to the enjoyment of the highest attainable standard of physical and mental health.

Article 13

Every-one has the right to education. Primary education should be compulsory and free to all.

Article 14

Those States where compulsory, free primary education is not available to all should work out a plan to provide such education.

Article 15

Every-one has the right to take part in cultural life; enjoy the benefits of scientific progress.

6 Systems for Protection of Human Rights

The United Nations (UN) has created a global structure for protecting human rights, based largely on its Charter, non-binding declarations, legally binding treaties and on various activities aimed at advancing democracy and human rights through-out the world.

The UN's system of human rights protection has three main components: first, it establishes international standards through its Charter, legally binding treaties, non-binding declarations, agreements, and documents; next, it mandates Special Rapporteurs and experts, and groups, such as working groups, committees and treaty bodies, to work in various manners for the promotion and protection of human rights; finally, it offers technical assistance through the Voluntary Fund for Advisory Services and Technical Assistance in the field of Human Rights.

Main Bodies of the United Nations

The United Nations is composed of six major bodies: the General Assembly, the Secretariat, the Security Council, the International Court of Justice, the Trusteeship Council and the Economic and Social Council. Although the United Nations was divided into these six spheres, they are of unequal size (some possess many subsidiary bodies and committees while others have very few), status (some are quite powerful while others have become almost obsolete), and relevance to human rights (some focus extensively on the issue while others bear little or no relevance for the protection and promotion of human rights).

[1] General Assembly

The General Assembly is the legislative body of the UN. It currently consists of 191 member states, all of which must take part in its sessions and none of which may have more than five representatives. The General Assembly has established Permanent Committees, such as the seven Main Committees, the Procedural Commissions and the Permanent Commissions, that meet between General Assembly sessions. It is also responsible for appointing the Secretary-General, upon recommendation from the Security Council, to a renewable five year term.

[2] Secretariat

The Secretariat is headed by the UN Secretary-General, who is recommended by the Security Council and then appointed to a five-year term by the General Assembly. It is in charge of carrying out programs designed by other branches of the United Nations, such as peace-keeping missions, international dispute mediation, and studying economic, cultural, human rights, or social trends. It also handles administrative details, such as speech and documents translations, UN news and information releases, and international conference co-ordinations. The Secretariat hosts around 9,000 staff members.

[3] Security Council

The Security Council possesses the power to draft resolutions providing for the use of force against states, with an emphasis on non-violent conflict resolution and preventative measures. In order to pass a resolution permitting the use of arms against a state, it must gain at least nine "yea" votes from its fifteen members with no vetoes. Only its permanent members hold veto power. Its composition was established in the UN Charter, and consists of five permanent members, China, France, Russia, the United Kingdom and the United States. Additionally, ten non-permanent members serve on the Council who are elected to two year terms. Non-members may participate in hearings and meetings, but may not vote. The Security Council is an important branch of the UN, developed for the maintenance of peace and security in the world.

[4] International Court of Justice

The International Court of Justice (ICJ), the judicial branch of the UN, is based in the Hague, the Netherlands, and was established in 1945 by the Charter of the United Nations. All states that have signed the UN Charter are members of the ICJ. Its jurisdiction extends to international conflicts, with the exception of political ones. Its responsibilities include: giving opinions on concrete topics; ruling on cases; and clarifying international legal norms.

The ICJ is the latest step in the continuing evolution of international courts. The first such court, Permanent Court of Arbitration, was founded in 1899 and still exists today. The Permanent Court of International Justice was created by the League of Nations and existed between 1922 and 1946. It served as the model on which the International Court of Justice is based.

[5] Economic and Social Council (ECOSOC)

The Economic and Social Council (ECOSOC) makes recommendations to the General Assembly on human rights issues. It reviews the reports submitted by the Commission on Human Rights and submits the amended versions to the General Assembly. ECOSOC is composed of 54 members serving three year terms; members meet twice a year. Additionally, it oversees several committees and commissions, such as the Commission on Human Rights, the Sub-Commission on the Promotion and Protection of Human Rights, the Commission on the Status of Women and the Commission on Crime Prevention and Criminal Justice, as well as UN specialized agencies, such as the International Labor Organisation (ILO) and the World Health Organisation (WHO).

[6] Trusteeship Council

This council was originally established to preside over the so-called "dependent areas" within the international Trusteeship System, under Article 75 of the UN Charter. However, the goals for and tasks of the Council have largely been fulfilled, and it is therefore now mostly obsolete. Currently, the Trusteeship Council only meets if and when a scenario requires it.

Charter-Based Mechanisms for Human Rights Protection and Promotion

The type of protection provided by the United Nations on issues of human rights is based on either Charter-based or treaty-based mechanisms. Those mechanisms based on the UN Charter include: the Universal Declaration of Human Rights; the Commission on Human Rights; and the Sub-Commission on the Promotion and Protection of Human Rights.

[1] Universal Declaration of Human Rights

The Universal Declaration of Human Rights (UDHR) is one of the first international documents to be based on the idea that rights are guaranteed to each human being. Most previous international declarations and treaties were based on the idea of positivism, whereby rights are only recognized once they have been set forth in national legislation. Like the UN itself, the UDHR was written with the aim of establishing world peace by promoting human rights. Originally, the UDHR brought together 58 distinct geographic, cultural and political backgrounds in the formation of one universal document. Although the UDHR is not legally binding it has created international human rights standards that are codified in various international treaties.

The Universal Declaration of Human Rights was drafted between January 1947 and December 1948. Its text was composed by the then eight-member Commission on Human Rights headed by Eleanor Roosevelt, and sought to include the whole spectrum of human rights: from cultural, social and economic to civil and political rights. Following over 1,400 votes modifying the document's text, the UN General Assembly unanimously passed the Declaration on December 10, 1948, with eight abstentions to the vote, coming from Belarus, Czechoslovakia, Poland, Saudi Arabia, South Africa, the Soviet Union, Ukraine, and Yugoslavia.

The UDHR consists of 30 articles specifying basic rights guaranteed to each individual. The first two articles establish the document's premise, that all humans share universal equality, and that this equality is based on the fundamental dignity bestowed upon humanity. This equality of human dignity translates to universality of human rights. Included in the notion of universality is the idea that these rights are automatically extended to everyone and may not be denied for any reason or because of any action an individual may commit.

Article 1 states: *"All human beings are born equal in dignity and rights. They are endowed with reason and conscience and should act towards one another in a spirit of brother-hood."*

Article 2 continues: *"Everyone is entitled to all the rights and freedoms set forth in this Declaration, without distinction of any kind such as race, colour, sex, language, religion, political or other opinion, national or social origin, property, birth or other status."*

Articles 3 through 21 specify civil and political rights. In these articles, rights set forth include the right to life, liberty, a fair trial, free speech, privacy, of personal security, and of movement, as well as freedom from slavery, torture, and arbitrary arrest.

Articles 22 through 27 provide for economic, social and cultural rights. These rights are specified as an indispensable aspect of an individual's life, being necessary for one's dignity and personal development, and include economic rights such as the right to social security, economic work-related rights, fair payment and leisure; social rights such as the right to an adequate standard of health, well-being and education; and cultural rights, such as the right to participate in cultural life.

Finally, Articles 28 through 30 establish a general frame-work to provide for the enjoyment of human rights: the recognition of the right to a social and international system that promotes human rights; a statement that humans have obligations to the community along with fundamental rights; and a reminder that no state or individual may utilize the Declaration to promote goals contrary to the mission or goals of the UN.

[2] Commission on Human Rights

Composed of 53 member states, the Commission on Human Rights is the Charter-based body that most directly deals with the area of human rights. It is assisted by the Sub-Commission on the Promotion and Protection of Human Rights, individual experts, representatives, and Special Rapporteurs. The Commission on Human Rights meets for six weeks each year in Geneva, although it may also meet in majority-endorsed "Special Sessions" in order to provide the most expeditious manner of dealing with human rights abuses. In evaluating a situation, the Commission may choose to monitor a situation itself or may request for an outside body to do so. Its jurisdiction of human rights protection was expanded by ECOSOC in the 1970s to include the entire globe.

From its inception, the Commission has influenced international human rights standards, working to set as well as to enforce rights standards. It helped author the Universal Declaration of Human Rights in 1948. Since then, it has formed standards relating to the right to development, civil and political rights, economic, social and cultural rights, the elimination of racial discrimination, torture, the rights of the child and the rights of human rights defenders.

Monitoring Human Rights

The Commission on Human Rights also devotes much time to monitoring the implementation of the standards it has set. It may turn to any number of permanent or special procedures when examining a specific area of human rights.

Articles 22 through 27 provide for economic, social and cultural rights. These rights are specified as an indispensable aspect of an individual's life, being necessary for one's dignity and personal development, and include economic rights such as the right to social security, economic work-related rights, fair payment and leisure; social rights such as the right to an adequate standard of health, well-being and education; and cultural rights, such as the right to participate in cultural life.

Finally, Articles 28 through 30 establish a general frame-work to provide for the enjoyment of human rights: the recognition of the right to a social and international system that promotes human rights; a statement that humans have obligations to the community along with fundamental rights; and a reminder that no state or individual may utilize the Declaration to promote goals contrary to the mission or goals of the UN.

The Commission on Human Rights also devotes much time to monitoring the implementation of the standards it has set. It may turn to any number of permanent or special procedures when examining a specific area of human rights. Its two permanent procedures are the 1503 Procedure and the 1235 Procedure; its special procedures include fact-finding missions, thematic mechanisms or mandates and advisory services.

The **1503 Procedure** is a confidential procedure named after ECOSCO Resolution 1503 by which it was established. It is activated when the Commission receives a communication about a consistent pattern of gross human rights violations. Violations considered under this procedure include genocide, apartheid, racial or ethnic discrimination, torture, forced mass migrations and mass imprisonment without a trial. The report of consistent gross human rights violations to the Commission may not be an anonymous one, yet does not require the consent of the state concerned for an investigation to take place. This regulation gives the Commission great leeway in deciding how to best approach a situation. Following its investigation, the Commission then decides what action to take. When a 1503 Procedure has failed to stop a human rights violation it has investigated, the Commission on Human Rights may invoke the **1235 Procedure** under which it can hold an annual public debate about the gross violations of human rights in question. If this also fails to adequately affect the situation, the Commission may move to have ECOSOC pass a resolution condemning the violators. This public condemnation tarnishes the reputation of the leaders in the state in question and discredits their legitimacy as political elites.

Among the special procedures available to the Commission on Human Rights, **fact-finding missions** are a useful tool. In a fact-finding mission, an expert or group of experts studies the human rights situation and looks for violations in a given state with the purpose of gathering information for a 1503 or a 1235 procedure. However, a fact-finding mission may only occur with the consent of the state whose human rights recored is being questioned. As of April 2003, 47 countries had extended standing invitations to the Thematic Special Procedures of the United Nations Commission on Human Rights to investigate human rights issues, meaning that the Commission may initiate a fact-finding mission to any one of those countries at any time. For all other nations, the Commission must first seek and gain approval before dispatching its experts to the country.

Another special procedure available to the Commission on Human Rights is a **thematic mechanism** or mandate. Working groups and/or Special Rapporteurs investigate human rights violations and the problems they have caused on a multi-state level. Recently, there has been an increase in the number of Special Rapporteurs investigating human rights issues.

Lastly, the Commission on Human Rights offers **advisory services** to nations that request it. The Commission provides educational and informational assistance to states in order to help them observe a high level of human rights protection. Additionally, the Commission on Human Rights may request assistance from the

Office of the High Commissioner for Human Rights in the form of seminars, training courses, and clinics as well as advice from experts.

[3] Sub-Commission on the Promotion and Protection of Human Rights

The Sub-Commission was established by the Commission on Human Rights at its first meeting in 1947, and was titled the Sub-Commission on Prevention of Discrimination and Protection of Minorities before a 1999 vote to change its name. It serves as the main subsidiary body to the Commission on Human Rights.

The Sub-Commission is comprised of 26 member experts acting independently, without affiliation to their state of origin, though they are elected by the Commission proportionally according to geographical population distribution. Presently, member experts are divided as follows: seven from Africa, six from Western Europe and other States, five from Asia, five from Latin America and three from Eastern Europe. Each member has one alternate; half the members and their alternates are elected every two years and each serves for a term of four years. The Sub-Commission meets for three weeks each year in Geneva; government officials, staff of UN specialized agencies and NGO observers may also attend their meetings.

The Sub-Commission's mission is to undertake studies under the guidance of the UDHR and to make recommendations to the Commission on Human Rights concerning the prevention of discrimination of any kind relating to human rights and fundamental freedoms and the protection of racial, national, religious and linguistic minorities. The Sub-Commission also undertakes work assigned to it by the Commission or ECOSOC, and distributes these assignments between its six working groups: the Working Group on Communications (which considers complaints regarding a consistent pattern of gross and verifiable violations of human rights within the scope of communications, together with any existing replies from governments), the Working Group on Contemporary Forms of Slavery, the Working Group on Indigenous Populations, the Working Group on Minorities, the Working Group on Administration of Justice and the Working Group on Transnational Corporations.

[4] High Commissioner for Human Rights

The position of the High Commissioner for Human Rights was established by the General Assembly of the United Nations in December 1993. The High Commissioner carries out the Secretary-General's 'good offices' duties relating to human rights, and is accountable to the Economic and Social Council as well as the Secretary-General. The Commissioner holds the principal position of promoting human rights and dealing with human rights activities in the UN, and must also maintain dialogue with all member states on the subject of human rights. Responsibilities of the High Commisioner include: crisis management; prevention and early warning of abuses; assistance to states in periods of political transition; promotion of substantive rights to governments; and co-ordination and rationalization of human rights programs.

The Commissioner is assisted by a Deputy to the United Nations High Commissioner for Human Rights, a staff for dealing with substantive issues, and an administrative staff. The Deputy, who assists the Commissioner in fulfilling assignments, is the Officer-In-Charge when the Commissioner is absent. The policies of the High Commissioner are implemented by the Office of the High Commissioner for Human Rights (OHCHR), is 'to protect and promote human rights for all.' OHCHR fulfills its goals through a variety of activities, including: emphasizing the significance of human rights globally and locally; providing education and resources regarding human rights; supporting human rights organs and treaty monitoring bodies; and responding to serious human rights violations.

Treaty-Based Mechanisms for Human Rights Protection and Promotion

International law takes precedence over the domestic law of a state. Thus, when a nation signs a treaty, it is pledging to adopt the provisions set forth within the treaty into the domestic law of a state. In this way, treaty-based mechanisms vary from Charter-based ones. Whereas the UN Charter's mechanisms are at times either not legally binding or require permission to be executed, treaties are backed by the norms regulating international law and are therefore legally binding.

International legal instruments take the form of a treaty (also called agreement, convention, protocol) which may be binding on the contracting states. When negotiations are completed, the text of a treaty is established as authentic and definitive and is 'signed' to that effect by the representatives of states. There are various means by which a state expresses its consent to be bound by a treaty. The most common are ratification or accession. A new treaty is 'ratified' by those states who have negotiated the instrument. A state which has not participated in the negotiations may, at a later stage, 'accede' to the treaty. The treaty enters into force when a pre-determined number of states have ratified or acceded to the treaty.

When a state ratifies or accedes to a treaty, that state may make reservations to one or more articles of the treaty, unless reservations are prohibited by the treaty. Reservations may normally be withdrawn at any time. In some countries, international treaties take precedence over national law; in others, a specific law may be required to give an international treaty, although ratified or acceded to, the force of a national law. Practically all states that have ratified or acceded to an international treaty must issue decrees, amend existing laws or introduce new legislation in order for the treaty to be fully effective on the national territory.

The UN currently has seven human rights treaties: the International Covenant on Economic, Social and Cultural Rights (ICESCR); the International Covenant on Civil and Political Rights (ICCPR); the International Convention on the Elimination of All Forms of Racial Discrimination (ICERD); the Convention on the Elimination of All Forms of Discrimination against Women (CEDAW); the Convention against Torture and Other Cruel, Inhuman or Degrading Treatment or Punishment (CAT); the Convention on the Rights of the Child (CRC); and the International Convention on the Protection of the Rights of All Migrant Workers and Members of their Families.

Each of these seven human rights treaties has a monitoring body, composed of independent experts who examine the reports that signatory nations submit under the treaty. These committees are also in charge of issuing 'concluding observations/comments', where they summarize their concerns about certain states and also give recommendations for the future.

Four of the treaty committees have mechanisms to deal directly with individual complaints of human rights violations under their respective treaties. These four bodies are: the Human Rights Committee, for the ICCPR; the Committee on the Elimination of Racial Discrimination, for the ICERD; the Committee on the Elimination of all forms of Discrimination against Women, for CEDAW; and the Committee against Torture, for CAT. Strict regulations exist regarding when an individual may formally issue a complaint to one of the monitoring bodies. All domestic options for settling the violation must have been previously exhausted. Additionally, the individual issuing the complaint must be under the jurisdiction of a state that is a party to the relevant treaty. No complaint may be made anonymously; it must come from either the victim, a representative of the victim, or, in rare circumstances in which it is impossible for either of these people to complain, a third, non-anonymous party may issue a complaint. The event in question must have occurred on or after the later date of either the treaty's entrance into force or the date the state in question signed the treaty.

[1] International Covenant on Economic, Social and Cultural Rights (ICESCR)

This International Covenant on Economic, Social and Cultural Rights (ICESCR) was adopted by the United Nations in 1966 and entered into force one decade later, in 1976. Along with the International Covenant on Civil and Political

Rights, the amount of time that it took the ICESCR to enter into force maybe partly attributed to the Cold War, in which Communist regimes, who advocated for economic, social and cultural rights, stood squarely against Western capitalist democracries, who embraced the civil and political rights codified in the International Covenant on Cival and Political Rights. The ICESCR is monitored by the Committee on Economic, Social and Cultural Rights.

Committee on Economic, Social and Cultural Rights

The Covenant itself did not provide for the creation of a monitoring body, so in the early days of ICESCR, states that had ratified the treaty reported to a working group of ECOSOC. In 1986, the Committee on Economic, Social and Cultural Rights (CESCR) took over the role as an independent expert committee to monitor the implementation of the Covenant. Currently, the Committee does not have a mechanism for processing individual complaints, although in 1996, CESCR sent to the Commission on Human Rights a draft of a proposed optional protocol that would provide for this kind of complaints procedure. It meets three times a year in Geneva.

[2] International Covenant on Civil and Political Rights (ICCPR)

The International Covenant on Civil and Political Rights, like the ICESCR, was adopted by the UN in 1966, but did not enter into force until 1976. Also like the ICESCR, the ICCPR saw a great deal of delay in its ratification due to the Cold War conflicts. These two treaties were signed separately because of the thought that political and civil rights could and must be guaranteed from the moment a nation signs on to the Covenant listing them, but that, while it was desirable for the same to be true of economic, social and cultural rights, it was not feasible. Implementation of social and economic rights was expected to take much time and thus could not be forced upon a nation merely because it has ratified the Covenant.

This application theory is recognized in the respective second articles of each Covenant: In Article 2, paragraph 1 of the ICCPR, the Covenant obliges a state "*...to respect and to ensure to all individuals...the rights recognized in the present Covenant.*" Meanwhile, a state "*undertakes to take steps...to the maximum of its available resources, with a view to achieving progressively the full realization of the rights recognized in the present Covenant...*", according to Article 2, paragraph 1 of the ICESCR. The ICCPR is monitored by the Human Rights Committee.

These two treaties account for most of the provisions listed under the Universal Declaration of Human Rights; further, they make the provisions binding for those nations who are parties to the covenants. The two covenants along with their optional protocols and the Universal Declaration of Human Rights are known as the International Bill of Human Rights.

Human Rights Committee

The Human Rights Committee was established to ensure that the rights listed under the ICCPR were protected. It is composed of 18 elected representatives, who serve four-year terms as independent and not representatives of their state of origin, and is based in Geneva. Its role is comprised of four main duties: to review reports submitted by states on their domestic actions taken to comply with the treaty; to consider information submitted from one member state accusing another member state of violating the treaty in some manner; to consider individuals' complaints against states that have signed the treaty, as well as reports written also by NGO; and to issue 'General Comments'.

Each member state of the ICCPR is required to submit a report to the Human Rights Committee each year 'on the measures they have adopted which give effect to the rights recognized herein and on the progress made in the enjoyment of those rights.' (ICCPR, Article 40). These reports must contain both a general and a specific component to them. The general aspect of the report must include data and statistics on the nations' frame-works in place that protect the rights listed in the treaty, whereas the report's specific aspect must include information addressing each article in the ICCPR as well as information about court rulings and the extent to which rights are being enjoyed in the member state.

Member states may report on other member states not abiding by the treaty's provisions. If such a circumstance were to arise, the report would first be sent to the offending state. Then, if it were not addressed adequately by the state, it could be sent to the Human Rights Committee for review. Despite the availability of this mechanism, it has never been utilized.

In the case of the ICCPR, the state in question must be a party to the treaty's optional protocol, which allows for the registering of individual complaints. If all these preconditions are met, the complaint proceeds through three stages: the registration of the complaint, an examination of whether or not the complaint satisfactorily meets the preconditions, and a communication on whether the complaint falls under the ICCPR and may therefore be given consideration. When the Human Rights Committee considers a complaint, the Committee will submit 'views' on the issue in an annual publication. Although these views may condemn a government or state sector, the Committee has no means of sanctioning the guilty party nor of enforcing its views.

[3] International Convention on the Elimination of All Forms of Racial Discrimination (ICERD)

The International Convention on the Elimination of All Forms of Racial Discrimination was adopted in 1965 and entered into force in 1969. It seeks to eliminate all forms of racial discriminations, and is monitored by the Committee on the Elimination of Racial Discrimination.

Committee on the Elimination of Racial Discrimination

The Committee on the Elimination of Racial Discrimination (CERD) exists to monitor state parties to the CERD. It has 18 independent experts who are elected to CERD by state parties to the Convention. They meet in Geneva each year for two three-week sessions.

CERD's four main duties are the same as Human Rights Committee's: to review reports submitted by states on their domestic actions taken to comply with the treaty; to consider information submitted from one member state accusing another member state of violating the treaty in some manner; to consider individuals' complaints against states that have signed the treaty; and to issue written 'General Comments'.

[4] Convention on the Elimination of All Forms of Discrimination against Women (CEDAW)

The Convention on the Elimination of All Forms of Discrimination against Women was adopted 1979 and entered into force in 1981. It focuses on the areas of education, employment, health, marriage, and the family as each area relates specifically to women. CEDAW calls for the elimination of discrimination against women within society as well as the adoption of legislation to further women's rights. It is monitored by the Committee on the Elimination of all forms of Discrimination against Women.

Committee on the Elimination of all forms of Discrimination against Women

The Committee on the Elimination of all forms of Discrimination against Women (the CEDAW Committee) monitors the CEDAW treaty. It consists of 23 independent experts who are elected by those states that are parties to the Convention. It is one of the four monitoring committees that may undertake confidential inquiries into individual complaints.

As the Committee on the Elimination of Racial Discrimination and the Human Rights Committee, the CEDAW Committee has four main duties: to review reports submitted by states on their domestic actions taken to comply with the treaty; to consider information submitted from one member state accusing another member state of violating the treaty in some manner; to consider individuals' complaints against states that have signed the treaty; and to issue Committee written 'General Comments' on each state's compliance with the treaty, taking into account reports written also by NGOs, to present to the Secretary General.

[5] Convention against Torture and Other Cruel, Inhuman or Degrading Treatment or Punishment (CAT)

The Convention against Torture and Other Cruel, Inhuman or Degrading Treatment or Punishment was adopted in 1984 and entered into force in1987. Among other provisions, it bans torture and rape as weapons during wartime. It is monitored by the Committee against Torture.

Committee against Torture

The Committee against Torture exists to monitor the Convention against Torture treaty. Its membership includes ten independent experts, elected by parties to the Convention. The Committee meets twice a year in Geneva for two to three weeks at a time, and submits an annual report to the UN General Assembly.

The Committee against Torture shares four of its five main duties with the Human Rights Committee, the Committee on the Elimination of Racial Discrimination, and the CEDAW Committee. Its mission includes: reviewing reports submitted by states on their domestic actions taken to comply with the treaty; considering information submitted from one member state accusing another member state of violating the treaty in some manner; considering individuals' complaints against states that have signed the treaty; issuing Committee written 'General Comments' on each state's compliance with the treaty, taking into account reports written also by NGOs, to present to the Secretary General. In addition to these four shared goals, CAT also investigates into allegations of general systematic forms of torture.

[6] Convention on the Rights of the Child (CRC)

The Convention on the Rights of the Child was adopted in November of 1989 and entered into force less than a year later, in September of 1990. It is the UN's most universally ratified human rights convention. It protects children from economic and sexual exploitation, among other things, and is monitored by the Committee on the Rights of the Child.

Committee on the Rights of the Child

The Committee on the Rights of the Child monitors the Convention on the Rights of the Child. While the Committee engages in many of the same practices as do other committees, there is no individual complaints mechanism associated with the Convention, nor is there one associated with either of its two optional protocols, the Optional Protocol to the Convention on the Rights of the Child on the sale of children, child prostitution and child pornography and the Optional Protocol to the Convention on the Rights of the Child on the involvement of children in armed conflict. However, the Committee still examines state reports submitted and makes general recommendations to the General Assembly on state parties and their compliance with the Convention.

[7] International Convention on the Protection of the Rights of All Migrant Workers and Members of their Families

The latest of the UN's human rights treaties, the International Convention on the Protection of the Rights of All Migrant Workers and Members of their Families, was adopted in 1990 and entered into force July 1, 2003. It is monitored by the Committee on the Protection of the Rights of All Migrant Workers and Members of their Families.

Committee on the Protection of the Rights of All Migrant Workers and Members of their Families

The Committee on the Protection of the Rights of All Migrant Workers and Members of Their Families monitors the treaty under the same name. It is composed of 10 members, and its roles are: to examine state reports submitted and to make general recommendations. Under the treaty, it will be possible to address individual complaints once a minimum of ten states have agreed to the practice.

Some UN Specialized Agencies

UNESCO – United Nations Educational, Scientific and Cultural Organisation

The creation of UNESCO is provided for in the UNESCO Constitution adopted at the UN Conference in November of 1945. UNESCO is to contribute to peace and security in the world by promoting collaboration among nations through education, science, culture and communication. One condition necessary for such development is a free flow of information and ideas. UNESCO also emphasizes the need for the protection of cultural heritage. UNESCO organises research and educational programs, at times sponsors them as well. One of the first aims of UNESCO was to fight illiteracy. An enormous amount of the research inspired by UNESCO concerns human rights: the socio-cultural conditions necessary for human rights realization, efforts to popularize human rights by bringing various nations and cultures closer to each other. Above all, by a wide range of educational activities, UNESCO aims to gradually even out the chances had by all people. The most important organ within UNESCO is the General Conference which adopts conventions, recommendations and declarations. The General Conference headquarters are in Paris. To begin with, UNESCO adopted over 25 declarations and conventions, *i.e.* on the right of each human being to a cultural identity and the obligation of the state to preserve cultural traditions.

UNICEF – The United Nations Children's Fund

UNICEF was established in accordance with the decision of the UN General Assembly in December 1946. The man who came up with the idea was a Pole, Ludwik Rajchman, one of the greatest experts on health care during the interwar period. Rajchman was the only representative from Eastern Europe in the secretariat of the League of Nations.

At first, the main function of UNICEF was to help children in countries devastated by the Second World War. In the fifties, UNICEF started to lend its assistance to developing nations who are still today the greatest recipients of UNICEF funds, such as programs of technical assistance in the field of health care for children (vaccinations, medicine and medical equipment, personnel training, etc.) UNICEF also assists in building up a socio- educational infrastructure, provides relief services and delivers food.

In 1990 the UN General Assembly drew up the UNICEF Strategy of Action for the nineties. Included are the following goals: to decrease infant mortality of children under five years old , radically reduce the frequency of respiratory illnesses and dysentery (primarily pneumonia and diarrhea). UNICEF is one of the more important organizations in the UN in providing aid. UNICEF also publishes impressive reports which show that children are the 'forgotten part' of humanity. Many preventative campaigns aimed at child prostitution and trafficking in children are also a part of UNICEF's work.

WHO – The World Health Organisation

Founded in 1946, WHO works towards the highest level of health care for the greatest number of people. WHO co-ordinates research in such fields as: epidemiology and immunology, environmental protection, genetics, drug and alcohol abuse, primary health care, education, preventative medicine, nutrition and food hygiene, and also publishes the findings of such research.

Technical assistance is aimed in two directions. The first is the improvement of sanitation and hygiene in developing countries. In many countries, WHO also is involved in the organisation of the health care system by helping build and equip medical facilities and by training medical personnel.

Since 1955, WHO has been conducting a global campaign to fight contagious diseases, such as tuberculosis, cholera, malaria and black small-pox. In 1984 WHO began a Global Program to Combat AIDS.

WHO also conducts global campaigns aimed at popularizing their activities, such as World Health Day (April 7), World No-Tobacco Day(May 31), World AIDS Day (December 1). A fundamental sphere of activity is prevention, thus the WHO distributes publications which propagate nutrition and a healthy lifestyle.

FAO – Food and Agriculture Organisation

Created in 1950, FAO's initial agenda was to inform, advise, and promote scientific research. In 1960, FAO adopted a program for technical assistance to assist development in under-developed countries. At the same time, FAO's initiative led to the creation of a Committee to Combat Hunger which co-ordinates the flow of food aid to Asian and African countries. Three years later, FAO along with the United Nations drew up the World Food Program (WFP) which with time became the most important institution within the UN structure conducting food relief operations.

FAO is above all involved in activities which aim to increase the output of farmlands, forests and fisheries, and to raise nutritional levels and standards of living. A long-term goal of the FAO is to eliminate famine areas and ensure a basic standard of nourishment for all human beings. Their research on new technologies of nutrition is highly advanced.

Furthermore, FAO is involved in publishing. Their texts on problems of nutrition, hunger, and farming as well as posters, films and other advertising materials are widely distributed.

ILO – The International Labour Organisation

The International Labour Organisation was established in 1919, under the Treaty of Versaille, as an autonomous institution associated with the League of Nations. It was given the task of raising world standards of life and work and its goal was to eliminate social injustice for working people every-where. ILO began by concentrating on standardizing the legislation of States-Parties via recommendations and conventions. The ILO's activities in this area are diverse and encompass such topics as: social policy, improvement of working conditions by initiating international labour standards, improvement of management techniques, collective bargaining, protection of children, women and special occupational categories, labour law, etc. The highest organ of the ILO is the General Conference, called to session once a year where it adopts conventions and recommendations.

It is important to point out that the ILO has an effective control mechanism for realizing its signed conventions, and that means that it has real influence on the realization of its recommendations. A Special Commission of Experts evaluates the differences between norms created by the ILO and regulations in force in States-Parties.

The Commission of Norm Application discusses specific cases and creates a list of states which are not respecting or applying the recommended provisions. In the case of a complaint submitted by one State-Party about another State-Party, an Investigative Commission is formed whose recommendations are legally binding for member states.

United Nations Volunteers (UNV)

The United Nations Volunteers programme was established in 1970 by the General Assembly in 1970 and is administered by the United Nations Development Programme (UNDP). It is funded by the UNDP and UN agencies, as well as by donations from governments.

Some 6,000 volunteers have taken part in the program since its beginning. Right now over 2,000 volunteers of over 100 nationalities are in the programme.

UNV is active in various sectors and employs specialists of 115 different occupations. The most need occupations are: nursing, farming, agronomy, electronics, statistics, economics, education, organisers of work for disabled persons. Volunteers are also involved in humanitarian relief work (*i.e.* in Iraq, Sudan and Honduras) in areas hit by armed conflict, natural disaster or hunger. Volunteers make up 10% of the UN civilian personnel employed in such cases.

UN volunteers are active in 130 countries: half of this number is in Africa, 1/3 in Pacific Asia, and the rest in Arab countries, and Central and South America.

Work as a UN volunteer can be a real adventure for young people; people more experienced professionally can even make it a way of life. The minimum age is 21, and there is no upper-age limit (there are seventy-year-old volunteers). In addition to the appropriate educational background and work experience, UN volunteers also need to have a particular motivation to perform this kind of work.

Work as a UN volunteer is not highly profitable; however, enormous moral satisfaction is to be gained by it. Furthermore, volunteers do not work without pay -they receive a living allowance, and numerous benefits such as free transportation, housing, medical care and can also bring their families with them.

⌘❐⌘

7 The State of Human Rights in India

The Constitutional goal of socio-economic justice has become mirage. Directive principles of state policy have been either observed in non-compliance or used to accumulate the authoritative powers. For millions of poor people, they are not more that 'decorative principles of state policy'. Every political party claims to be champion of the down trodden. But it is not even half-true as pathetic conditions of hungry, poor people hardly prick the conscience of our leaders and representatives. Let us discuss the issues under the following heads:

1. Caste Based Discrimination

Caste based discrimination is one of the most heinous forms of discrimination practiced by humans. Caste being a qualifying quotient in social life in India, attributed by birth and fortified by religious beliefs, once born into a particular caste, the stigmas and/or benefits continue till death. It is precisely for this reason that caste based discrimination is considered as a form of discrimination that haunts a person from cradle to grave.

The caste structure and the injunctions attached to it control the social life and define the role of an individual in India. One is born into it and dies with it. If born a member of a lower caste or an untouchable, you die the same. There is no way out. The concept of the caste system brings in stratification of society based on duties. It is a defining tool to cast obligatory duties on people as the result of birth, which cannot be taken away. On the surface, it seems to paint a picture of societal obligation and duty. In reality, it is used as an instrument of exploitation by the upper castes against the lower castes.

India has ratified the International Convention on the Elimination of All Forms of Racial Discrimination. The ratification of the convention and the obligations attached to it is in addition to the obligations by the state under the

Constitution and other domestic laws. However, in reality most of these obligations remain as sections and clauses in the domestic laws and fail to reach out to the Dalit communities across India. Caste based discrimination is worse than slavery. A person is born into the caste, whereas slavery is slightly different. A person may become a slave due to numerous circumstances. However, a slave may earn his or her freedom, whereas in the caste system there is no escape, because the only defining factor is birth or descent. Once born as an untouchable one remains an untouchable. Dr. B. R. Ambedkar who is also known as the father of Indian Constitution and also a Dalit by birth stated that untouchability based on caste is worse than slavery. "Neither slavery nor untouchability is a free social order. But if a distinction is made there is no doubt that there is distinction between the two. The test is whether education, virtue, happiness, culture and wealth is possible within slavery or within untouchability. Judged by this test, it is beyond controversy that slavery is hundred times better than untouchability. In slavery there is room for education, virtue, happiness, culture or wealth. In untouchability there is none" he said.

The avenues for those who are born into the lower caste are many in theory, however, in practice, none of these mechanisms work, especially if the person is poor. Dalits, 99% of them are poor with less than 1USD per day as their income. Oppression of the 160 to 180 million Dalits, who are viewed as being too low to even be part of the caste system, is one of the most repelling, but enduring, realities of the India. Equally oppressive is the violence perpetrated against them, especially the women. To be a Dalit today means having to live in a subhuman, degraded, insecure fashion: every hour, two Dalits are assaulted, every day, three Dalit women are raped, and two killed. In most parts of India, Dalits continue to be barred from entering Hindu temples or other holy places - although doing so is against the law. Their women are banned from wearing shoes in the presence of caste Hindus. Dalit children often suffer a form of apartheid at school by being made to sit at the back of the classroom.

Yet, the Dalits are resisting. In parts of the country, they are organising politically to demand their rights. A Dalit woman rules the largest state, Uttar Pradesh. However, breaking the barriers laid down by the Hindu caste system is an uphill struggle, especially when the government does little to uphold the law of the land that prohibits discrimination on account of descent.

The practice of caste based discrimination has been so much engraved into the social fabric that even legal deterrence could not make the slightest dent upon this evil practice. Out of those who suffer the worst from caste based discrimination are the rural poor who are still under the repression of the feudal landlords. In the absence of a comprehensive land reforms policy in India, in the rural villages in India the majority of the land is held by upper caste landlords who literally rule the villages as feudal lords. Most of the agricultural land holdings are with these landlords who force the Dalits to work for them for a pittance. Often wages are in the form of a meal for the family once a day. Once, the agricultural season is over the Dalits are left with no food or work.

Caste based discrimination is not limited to a particular region in India. Even academic curricula in schools downplay the practice of caste based discrimination. Evil practices associated with caste based discrimination are practiced across the country. For example, in the state of Tamil Nadu the Dalit community Arunthathiyar is forced to work as manual scavengers. Manual scavenging is prohibited in law in India. The government of India had declared that the practice of manual scavenging would be completely eradicated in the country by 2007.

The programme of liberation and rehabilitation of scavengers has three necessary components, which between them should have been sufficient to achieve the objective. These are: (1) Legislative back up to prohibit dry latrines and manual scavenging in the form of 'the Employment of Manual Scavengers' and Construction of Dry Latrines (Prohibition) Act. 1993; (2) an alternative to dry latrines in the form of low cost sanitation units for which loan and subsidy are provided under the 'Centrally Sponsored' Scheme of Low Cost Sanitation Scheme for Liberation of Scavengers'; and (3) the National Scheme for Liberation and Rehabilitation of Scavengers and their Dependents for training and rehabilitation in alternative occupations. There is a separate scheme of scholarships for children of families practicing unclean occupations under which children of families engaged in manual scavenging are eligible for pre-matric scholarships. Despite these provisions, the programme has not achieved success in removing the practice of manual scavenging. While government estimates suggest that there are about one million manual scavengers in India, 95 per cent of whom are women, unofficially the figures are much higher and all this, more than a decade since the Employment of Manual Scavengers and Construction of Dry Latrines (Prohibition) Act, 1993. Even the Indian Railways employs manual scavengers. According to a petition filed in the Supreme Court – in its recently announced Integrated Railways Modernization Plan (IRMP), the Indian Railway does not have the elimination of manual scavenging on its radar. The Tenth Five Year Plan, however, has mentioned the eradication of manual scavenging by 2007 as a goal.

In spite of all this most of the Indian states have not adopted the Act, and those who have adopted the law have not enforced its provisions to achieve the intended results. As a result of the complete failure by the state governments to implement the law within their jurisdiction, the practice of manual scavenging continues even as of today in India.

Discrimination based on birth and caste is condemnable. The government of India also in theory condemns this practice. There are a series of laws in India that not only prohibits caste based discrimination but also penalises such practices. Discrimination is prohibited in the Constitution of India. Untouchability, one of the worst practices of the caste system is specifically prohibited in the Constitution. Article 17 of the Constitution abolished untouchability and its practice in any form is forbidden. Article 25(2b) of the Constitution provides that Hindu religious institutions of a public character to be open to all classes and sections of Hindus.

The Protection of Civil Rights Act, 1955 and the Scheduled Castes and Scheduled Tribes (Prevention of Atrocities) Act 1989 criminalises certain acts against the members of the Scheduled Castes and Scheduled Tribes. The Bonded Labour System (Abolition) Act, 1976 provides for a special program for identifying bonded laborers, and for their liberation and rehabilitation. While this law does not specifically mention Scheduled Castes, it is significant to them because the majority of bonded laborers belong to the Scheduled Castes. The practice of requiring Dalits to clean/remove human feces by hand continues despite the prohibition of manual scavenging by the Employment of Manual Scavengers and Construction of Dry Latrines (Prohibition) Act, 1993.

The question is in spite of all these domestic laws and the legal frame-work in India, why is that caste based discrimination still continuing in India. For example the practice of untouchability is practiced widely in India. The answer probably lies in the fact how far these laws are practiced? Enacting a law is one thing, but implementing the law is a completely different game. In India, the implementation of the laws and the mechanisms available to implement the laws has somehow failed to meet the challenge. The implementation of the domestic laws have failed to that extent that even registering a complaint based on these laws calling for an action from the authorities itself is a difficult task. Where implementation fails, the law fails and thus the evil practice of caste based discrimination continues. The failure of implementation of laws however is not limited to caste based discrimination.

Of the series of issues that arise due to the practice of caste based discrimination, the most important is the denial of right to food to the members of the lower caste. The milieu of overwhelming corruption spread throughout India not only perpetuates the practice, but also hampers development. The denial of development is not however limited to the lower caste but also affects the entire country. Even government assisted programmes like the Food For Work Programme and the National Rural Employment Guarantee Act, 2005 fails to deliver result due to caste based discrimination and widespread corruption.

2. Policing and Custodial Torture

India is hardly different from any of its neighbors. To the outside world, India is a democracy marching ahead with sustainable development. In fact, within India democratic values have suffered a major dent due to non-democratic approaches in governance. A true democracy is where basic guarantees are assured for the protection of persons and property, and where life is free from fear and repression.

The mere existence of a Constitution and the possibility to cast a vote once in awhile is not what democracy means. Democracy involves and demands good governance. Good governance must be reflected in every aspect of public life where state agencies are respected and considered as instruments and institutions of service, not as sources of suspicion and fear. One of the best indicators of good governance is the perception of the ordinary person about his state institutions. The failure of any single state institution suggests defects in governance. When the law enforcement agency becomes a failing institution, and there is no credible attempt to address this, the situation is much worse. In India, the institution that is primarily responsible for law enforcement is the state police. There are serious concerns about policing in India — which is not much different from in neighboring countries.

Instances of custodial torture are reported all over from India. It appears that in general, investigation of a crime begins and ends with a confession. In most cases the arrest of a suspect precedes the investigation of a case. The arrest is often followed by a prolonged period of illegal detention during which the detainee is tortured.

Torture is not expressly prohibited in law in India. As of now there are only indirect means through which torture can be addressed in India. For example, the Criminal Procedure Code, 1973 which lays down the rules of arrest, detention and enquiry does not prohibit the use of torture, but only prohibits 'unnecessary use of force'. Section 50 of the Code requires the officer to inform the person arrested of the reason for the arrest, including the alleged offence for which the person is being taken into custody. The statutory requirements have been reiterated by the Supreme Court of India, when it ruled that at the time of arrest, a memo must be prepared by the arresting officer. This memo must contain the alleged crime, the place, date and time of arrest, and also the place to which the person will be taken for detention prior to being produced before a Magistrate.The rules framed by the Supreme Court also require the officers to ask a person to witness the arrest memo. Whatever be the law, when it comes to following it, in spite of dozens of directions from the courts and also recurring orders from the state the police still stick to their habit of torturing the suspect. Often such instances defy human conscience.

The criminal justice dispensation system of India depends much upon the policing and the proactive role played by the judiciary, specially those officers from the lower ranks of the judiciary. Even though scholars and experts argue that the judiciary and the police are two independent institutions responsible for maintaining the rule of law in the country, in practice they are both interdependent and at times, very deficient in their functioning. This interdependency continues all the way through from the very stage of institution of a criminal case to that of the prescribing of punishment if the accused is finally convicted and sentenced for imprisonment or acquitted as the case may be.

It is an alarming trend in India that in an increasing number of cases if the police are certain, according to their 'conviction,' that the suspect in custody was involved in a serious crime, often the suspect is killed, allegedly in an 'encounter.' It appears that the government is increasingly tolerating the misuse of authority by law enforcement agencies. The cases of 'encounter killings' reported from the states of Gujarat, Uttar Pradesh, Karnataka, Chhattisgarh and Andhra Pradesh show a consistent and alarming pattern of tolerance for the use of violence by state agencies.

After each reported 'encounter killing' the government launches a smear campaign against the murdered suspect, justifying the act of the state agencies as if the murder were inevitable and is in fact an achievement. Custodial torture and encounter killings are closely related. State-sponsored interrogation centers — often torture chambers — function in most states in full public view. The suspects are brought in, kept in illegal detention and tortured as part of questioning. Later they are killed and declared as 'killed in an encounter.' Such centers are run under the guise of protecting ordinary citizens from anti-social and anti-national elements. These centers are the Indian version of Guantanamo Bay camps.

In a proceeding in the Supreme Court regarding a case from the state of Gujarat, the state government admitted in court that it was aware of the existence of the interrogation and torture centers. The government also admitted that in several cases the officers might have killed witnesses to an arrest and detention in order to avoid questions at a later stage. The Gujarat experience, while a shocking revelation of the state of policing in that state, is also proof that the public could be forced into silence through fear, if the state so requires. The alleged war against terror — in its Indian version — serves as a good excuse for allowing state agencies to resort to extrajudicial means of punishment.

In this backdrop it is a matter of concern when the judicial officers themselves behave in unwarranted manner, often breaching the procedural laws and mandates set by the Supreme Court. None other than the Chief Justice of India has remarked that about 20% of judges in India are corrupt. The Prevention of Corruption Acts, 1947 and 1988, have not succeeded in checking corruption. A.P. Bharucha as Chief Justice of India admitted that there was corruption in the ranks of the judiciary to some extent, mostly at the lower level.

Even though the use of violence and imparting fear among the populace are considered among the worst methods of crime prevention in many countries, they are widely practiced in India. This is because even today the concept of law and order is based on the principle of imparting fear. The state has neglected the need to modernise and humanise the police. The state police are often under extreme pressure to control crime.

When pushed beyond their capacity and capability, the law enforcement agencies resort to crude forms of policing, which is often the use of brute force. Widespread use of custodial torture in India is not the result of government neglect alone. It is also the result of the lack of seriousness in approaching this issue by the other justice mechanisms in India. Meager compensations awarded after decades long court cases serves no better deterrent than a scarecrow. To punish a law enforcement officer who has engaged in torture, as of now, there is no law in India.

The widespread use of custodial torture has also taken its toll upon the law enforcement agencies and is reflected in the overall state of the rule of law in India. Ordinary people isolate themselves from the law enforcement agencies, not trusting them. The use of torture has considerably reduced the morale of the law enforcement agencies. For example, cases that are brought to court based on evidence gathered by the use of torture often result in acquittal. The loss of morale of the law enforcement agencies is also exploited by corrupt elements in the society.

In spite of all this, neither the government of India nor its state governments have declared a policy of non-tolerance to custodial violence. In the remote villages of India, government means the local police constable. The atrocities committed by these uniformed state agents create a fertile ground for anti-social and anti-state elements to propagate and advocate violence. The increase of violence in society has resulted in the loss of a middle ground for those who do not support violence.

Various state governments in India and their law enforcement agencies have lost control of law and order over considerable parts of their jurisdictions — a backwash of erratic policies. This concern is expressed by various agencies in India like the National Human Rights Commission and the National Police Commission. The state governments are reluctant to free the local police from its political grip. Concerns regarding the political control over policing are not an altogether new issue in India. Even police officers are concerned about this. The directives of the court is intended to setup a temporary arrangement for a balanced and independent policing mechanism in India, free from political influence and to considerably remove the scope of political cronies from being appointed as head of state police service. If the directions are implemented it will free the state police from political clout, provide fixity of tenure for senior police officers, prevent administrative abuse by rampant transfers and also will setup independent mechanisms to investigate into complaints against police officers. The directives of the court is only a temporary arrangement until the central and state governments come up with appropriate legislations and permanent mechanisms to settle the issues regarding policing in India.

The findings of the court is based on reports and recommendations of various commissions constituted during the course of thirty years, to look into matters concerning policing and also on specific concerns aired by the National Human Rights Commission of India. The complete control of the bodies to be constituted to overlook the functioning of the state police is left with the respective state governments.

While several state governments are yet to implement the directives of the court, the state government in Kerala went ahead to partially implement the court's order. An Ordinance was issued by the government, claiming that the government is implementing the directives of the court's directives. However, the Ordinance is a far cry from what the court directed.

Torture is not a crime in India. To convict a law enforcement officer for torture, the act has to qualify all the requirements like any other crimes in the Indian Penal Code, 1890. To prove a crime, meeting all standards, to be punished under the Indian Penal Code, is difficult because of the absence of independent investigating agencies in India. The absence of an independent agency to investigate cases of custodial torture is exploited by the offenders since they know that even if a complaint is made regarding torture it would not be properly investigated.

The widespread use of custodial torture has taken its toll upon the law enforcement agencies in India and is reflected in the overall state of rule of law in India. As of today, the ordinary people have isolated themselves from the law enforcement agencies. The people do not trust the law enforcement agencies. The use of torture has also considerably reduced the morale of the law enforcement agencies. For example cases that are brought to a court based exclusively on the evidence gathered by use of torture often results in acquittal. The loss of morale of the law enforcement agencies is exploited by corrupt elements in the society who would like to use the local police as their militia, paid from the state exchequer. This isolation of the law enforcement agencies from the ordinary people has resulted in increasing number of incidents where people take law into their hands.

In the past few years incidents of violence committed in the name of 'justice' are increasingly reported from India, of which the highest number was reported in 2007. These are acts of violence, is resorted to by either the state agents or the people for executing what they think is justice. Such violence indicates that the public perception of justice in India is rapidly changing - changing for the worse. The people's perception of justice depends upon how the justice dispensation mechanism in a country functions. In theory, India has a reasonably good legislative frame-work within which laws are drafted, debated and implemented. But in practice the drafting and debating of laws remain mostly outside the scope of any public discourse. The acts of the legislature are often dominated by caste, religious and partisan political sentiments as opposed to welfare and betterment of the people.

In addition to the limited scope of people's participation in the legislative process, the justice dispensation organs of the state is also suffering from ineptitude and fatigue due to mismanagement. The delay in court proceedings and a failing policing system are two classic examples. For an ordinary Indian, the courts in India make a mockery of the term 'justice' by delaying proceedings for years. Long periods of delays are often exploited by those who can manipulate the system.

Law enforcement agencies are also exploited and manipulated by the same group of individuals. Instead of serving the general public, the law enforcement agencies in India often tend to serve those who have power and money. It appears that the law enforcing agencies in fact allow themselves to be manipulated so that these agencies could also exploit the resulting opportunity for their benefit. The result is selective justice, often to the detriment of the ordinary people. This situation also facilitates widespread corruption in the society.

For the ordinary person the presence of justice is evident in the functioning of the local police and the local courts. These are the two important institutions in any state structure that provide protection and guarantee to a person's life and property. Due to the proximity of these two institutions to the people and their life, the functioning of these institutions is under the constant scrutiny of the people. When these institutions fail to perform reasonably well, the people will exploit its weakness and will also disregard them. A failing judiciary, inept law enforcement agencies and widespread corruption is the cocktail for disharmony and violence. The convergence of the failing justice mechanisms is the meltdown of the public perception of the justice by the state. When the state fails to provide security and guarantee to its own people, people take law into their own arms. The result is what India is experiencing today.

In spite of all these, the government of India or its state governments have no declared policy of non-tolerance to custodial violence. Instead of preventing the use of torture the attempt by the government is to provide further impunity to the law enforcement agencies by proposing changes in the procedural law. The legislative changes have not been implemented yet, but the proposal by the government is to implement these changes in the recent future.

To remove possible internal resistance in implementing these proposals the government has roped in several non-government organisations under the banner of the UNDP — India office, in an allegedly consultative process on this issue in the name 'Strengthened Access to Justice Programme'. Many organisations in India have inadvertently jointed this lopsided programme, currently executed through the Department of Justice.

The direction towards which India is headed as of now is imminent chaos and lawlessness. The widespread use of violence and the continuing neglect of the government to prevent it have also isolated the ordinary people from the government. In the remote villages of India government means the local police constable. The atrocities committed by these uniformed state agents create a fertile ground for anti-social and anti-state elements to propagate and advocate violence as a means of communication. This has also resulted in the loss of a middle ground for those who do not support violence.

For the central government in Delhi and the mutually opposing state administrations, governance is only an affair of five years. This congenital defect of myopic vision is a shocking feature of all governments in India and is reflected in their policies. A failed policing system and a justice mechanism that depends on such a police is what these governments covet for. Prevention of torture and reformation of law enforcement agencies is the last priority in these circumstances for any government. As of today, various state governments in India and their law enforcement agencies have lost control of law and order within considerable parts of their jurisdictions – a backwash of erratic policies. The spread of anti-state activities covering considerable parts of India must be an alarming wakeup call for the government. This shocking situation of chaos in law and order is certainly the result of the failure of police as an institution in India.

3. Right to Food

The Prime Minister of India in his foreword in the *'Report to The People'* dated May 22, 2007, claimed: *"In this 60th year of independence, the country should have the satisfaction of recording for the fifth year in a succession a rate of economic growth of over 8.5%."* What is not sure however is whether the estimated over 200 million Indians who are presently suffering from malnourishment, and the many more million who have done so during past decades, will be satisfied with this growth. The country's overwhelming population is often given as an excuse to justify poverty and starvation in India.

This theory is applicable only if the State itself is poor and has no means to procure enough food for its people. India is not poor, even though 70% of Indians are. India's projected defense budget for 2007-08 is 24 billion US$ and it plans to spend further on its weapons upgrade programmed. Defense spending of such proportions in a country where a section of the population equivalent to $\frac{2}{3}^{rd}$ the size of that of the United States is undernourished or suffering from malnourishment, is difficult to stomach. The United Nations Special Rapporteur on the Right to Food has highlighted this contradiction of priorities in his report following his mission to India in 2005.

India is a country of contradictions. A country that has a projected 9% development index performs worse than some Sub-Saharan countries with regard to addressing starvation and malnourishment within its territory. The National Minimum Programme promulgated by the Government of India in 2004 speaks about the Rural Employment Guarantee programme, which is also reflected in India's voluntary pledge to the United Nations Human Rights Council. However, millions of Indians in rural villages are not benefiting from this programme and remain unemployed. The programme is not properly implemented and in places where there are possibilities of implementation and thus employment, recruitment to the programme is based on caste bias and nepotism.

Poverty and resultant starvation in India is not limited to the lower caste, although they suffer the most. The lower caste forms only about 20% of the Indian population, whereas starvation and malnourishment affect about 53% of its entire population. Starvation and malnourishment are the direct result of the failing administrative system in India. A malfunctioning administrative system has a direct bearing upon the living conditions of the poor. For example, for the distribution of food to targeted population the government has established the Public Food Distribution System (PDS). However, the management of this system suffers from corruption – particularly black marketing, caste prejudices and the utter failure of various local governments.

The targeted PDS was introduced in India in 1997. The shift from a Universal PDS to a targeted PDS was performed with the intention of avoiding the misuse and wastage of subsidised food materials. However, owing to a lack of proper screening methods and transparency in the procedure, the PDS is still a failure in India. For example, the licensing procedure for running a PDS shop is plagued by corruption. Licenses are awarded by the respective state governments and the authority to issue them is delegated to the district administrations, which are notoriously corrupt. To receive subsidised food a family is required to posses a ration card, which also serves the purpose of determining the family's financial status. This process involves obtaining certificates from the village-head and officers at the district administration. While the village-heads often refuse to issue such certificates, district administration officials demand bribes. This is because the longer the people remain poor and near starvation, the easier it is for the village-head to continue subjecting them to bonded labour.

The continuation of caste-based discrimination is yet another factor that perpetuates poverty and deprivation of food, as was briefly mentioned in the Special Rapporteur's report. 60 years after independence, the prevention of caste-based discrimination remains on paper rather than being enforced in practice. Due to this, caste-based discrimination is widely practiced and discrimination prevents the lower castes from accessing food. Additionally, the lower castes are deprived of landed property and those who have titles to particular pieces of land are frequently prevented from actual possession by local feudal lords.

In addition to this, large-scale land holding still continues in various States, including States that have enacted the land ceiling laws. Holdings of large extents of land (by individuals or families) deprive the poor from having arable lands of their own. However, the poor can still benefit from such large-scale cultivation, by being employed by the landlord, although in reality this tends to be for much less pay than that stipulated in the Minimum Wages Act, 1948. However, when landlords find that agriculture is not profitable for various reasons and sell off their land to property developers, the most affected are the poor landless communities, as this often results in the starvation of the agricultural labourers who depended upon such large-scale cultivations.

In addition to poverty caused by human interference, large-scale poverty exists in remote regions of the country. One such example is the Murshidabad district of West Bengal. This district shares a border with Bangladesh. Land erosion by the river Padma has rendered large numbers of persons landless. Those who could afford to, left well in advance, but the poor had to stay until their land was taken by the river. This situation is exploited by cross-border smugglers based in the state who employ the poor to smuggle articles across the border to Bangladesh.

The smuggling involves crossing the river at night, which often claims peoples' lives, while others are shot and killed by the Border Security Force stationed along the Indian border. Ironically, a major portion of the smuggling involves food – grains collected from PDS shops are smuggled across the border to be sold on the black market. The West Bengal State Government considers the people living along the inter-national border in Murshidabad as being illegal immigrants from Bangladesh and does nothing for their welfare.

The government of India has formulated and is executing several welfare programmes intended to prevent starvation and malnourishment in India. While proper planning and implementation of these programmes are necessary, what has been mostly ignored is the poor state of functioning of the PDS. The system itself, as claimed by the government, covers only 16% of the total population. The actual number of households using the PDS is around 91 million, significantly less than the 160 million being claimed by the government. 78% of these persons are trying to make use of the system - 26% are from urban areas while 52% are rural households. Of these 91 million households an alarming 61% claim that the PDS is plagued by corruption and 49% claim that corruption has increased in the past year. The PDS is viewed as the most corrupt institution in India.

Such corruption exists in the PDS due to the failed criminal justice system in India. Illegal dealing with rationed articles is a crime in India. A crime registered under the relevant domestic law must be tried in a special court constituted in each state. However several states are yet to establish such a court, meaning that cases registered under the law in those states will have to wait for years to be decided through the regular courts. Additionally, states most frequently withdraws from prosecutions related to cases registered under the Essential Commodities Act as compared with other prosecutions. This shows not only the tolerance that various state governments exhibit towards corruption within the PDS, but also the influence of the licensees upon the government.

Even though the Rapporteur expresses his concerns about corruption in the PDS, there are no concrete proposals suggested by the Rapporteur in his report to address this issue. To achieve any improvement in addressing the food security in India, there must be a multi-faceted approach to the issue focusing on: the implementation of welfare schemes; increasing the existing network of the PDS within the country; and taking effective steps to prevent corruption within the PDS.

The prevention of corruption within the PDS cannot happen in a vacuum. It will require equipping the criminal justice mechanism in India to specifically address this problem. In addition to an increase in the number of special courts to try offenses related to the distribution of rationed food articles, a separate and independent mechanism must be constituted to investigate such cases. This must be independent from the local police since the latter is itself corrupt and will therefore fail to effectively investigate crimes related to food distribution. There is also a need to change domestic law, in particular the Essential Commodities Act, 1955.

As a country that has a surplus of food, it is a pity that in India, food that is distributed to the poor does not reach them, but is either spoiled and lost or sold on the black market. To change this, there are no quick-fixes. However, the prevention of corruption within the PDS is a critical starting point. This however requires a consolidated attempt from the state and central government in India which as of today is given the last priority for which there is no excuse.

4. Low Intensity Armed Conflicts

In April 2007 the Chhattisgarh State Police ambushed a 12-member strong brigade of armed Naxalites (a group similar to the Maoists in Nepal) operating near Dhanora village. In the operation, the police arrested two girls, respectively aged 14 and 15 years old, who were wearing school uniforms and were armed with old 303 bore rifles. When questioned, the girls confessed that they had been picked up from school by the Naxalites, and given a few days' training on armed combat, before being sent out in the company of older members to fight against the State Police and the Salwa Judum, a State-sponsored private militia.

Elsewhere, in Chhattisgarh State's capital Raipur, five-year-old Saurabh reports for duty every day at the local police station and works as a boy police constable. Saurabh was employed by the State Police after his father was killed in an ambush by the Naxalites. Saurabh is not the only boy in the State Police. In nearby Korba Police Station, Manish Khoonte, a ten-year-old boy is employed as a police officer. Saurabh and Manish are paid US$ 57 per month by the State Government.

Local human rights organisations, including the National Commission for Women, have expressed concern about the employment of child soldiers in Chhattisgarh by the State and the Naxalites. The Naxalite child soldiers wing is called the Bal Mandal (Child Forum). The members of Salwa Judum are known as 'Special Police Officers' or SPOs.

India ratified the Convention on the Rights of the Child on December 11, 1992. However, protection of the rights of children, particularly for preventing them from being made to fight in armed conflicts, is an area where the country has thus far failed. Children are often forced to take up arms in India after losing a close relative in the conflict.

In Manipur State in the north-east of India, hundreds of children have lost their relatives, including their parents, in the intense armed conflict that has been waged over the past decade. Many children have witnessed atrocities committed against family-members by the members of underground movements as well as by State-agents, including rape, torture and dismemberment and mutilation of bodies. The situation in Manipur and Chhattisgarh is not unique. Child soldiers are used in several parts of the country, in the states of Jammu and Kashmir, Assam, Nagaland, Meghalaya, Tripura, Sikkim, Karnataka and Andhra Pradesh.

Children are often recruited from tribal communities, as these communities are frequently caught up in armed conflicts. A common strategy used by both sides to these conflicts is to recruit children aged around 14, as their age can easily be covered up. The extent to which children are exploited by State-sponsored militias and anti-State militias does not differ much. However, in anti-State militias, girls are reportedly used for the sexual gratification of older cadres. The presence of girls in camps also assists in camouflaging them as being ordinary villages.

Anti-State militias typically falsely claim that children volunteer to justify their recruitment. State-sponsored units recruit children by manipulating their personal and nationalist sentiments. Once recruited, they are trained to use weapons and to manufacture explosives. Those who are not good at using weapons are used for espionage or for passing messages between groups. Children are also used for gathering extortion money for the militia. This practice is more prevalent in the northeastern States.

State-sponsored militias usually recruit children based on the promise of future jobs at the State police department. Forcibly displaced tribal communities in conflict zones are another source of recruits. As the State agencies move in to counter anti-State militia activities, villagers are evacuated and relocated to government schools, forcing the schools to cease functioning normally. Such schools then become military targets for anti-state groups, as these schools will normally be guarded by members of the government-sponsored militias. During this period children, particularly boys, are recruited on the basis of the need for them to protect their parents and sisters from the anti-State groups.

Possession of arms in India is regulated by law. While restrictions are employed for possession of arms and ammunition in India for ordinary persons, the members of State-sponsored private militia groups are given more than one weapon, of which some are provided for use by the child soldiers.

Whenever State-sponsored child soldiers are killed in encounters, the government's claims the child was a member of an anti-State armed group, and the anti-State militia do the same and disown the child. In several cases, child soldiers' bodies have been mutilated in order to hide the possibility of their age and identities being found. Deaths of such children are frequently blamed on having resulted from being caught in the crossfire of an armed encounter.

Child soldiers' living conditions are invariably very poor, regardless of which faction they belong to. They are often denied adequate food. Food is often used as a reward for work. Children are used as scouts and to test the land for anti-personnel mines and other forms of explosives. Using children for these purposes makes troop movement easier for both sides. Even if a child dies or is injured, the loss is considered to be minimal, as a child is considered to be far more expendable than a trained cadre.

India's Naxalite movement and the anti-state sentiments in the north-eastern states are both spreading out, increasing the areas affected by armed conflicts in the country. Child soldiers are considered as being highly expendable pawns in these conflicts.

In Andhra Pradesh, the children's faction of the Naxalite movement is named the Bala Sangam (Children's Group). There were reportedly 75 Bala Sangams groups in the state, including an estimated 800 children in their ranks in 2003. This number has likely increased by 2007, as the Naxalite movement in the State has steadily increased since 2003.

Child soldiers are also used in the mainly Hindu versus Muslim religious conflicts throughout India. Both factions have created their own self-styled armed brigades. The Hindu 'self-defence' groups operate under various banners, such as the RSS, the Bajrang Dal and the Shiv Sena. Similar Muslim factions are known to be operating under the banner of the Jamaat-i-Islami-Hind and the Islamist Sevak Sangh. All these groups have child soldier units. For example, the Viswa Hindu Parisad (VHP) is also reportedly recruiting girls to a group called the Durga Vahini.

Once a child soldier is taken into custody by the State agencies, they are often falsely identified as being adults. Their ages are exaggerated in official records, so that they can be tried in regular courts, instead of juvenile courts. This is possible because in such cases, charges are typically framed without producing the accused in court. Once the charge has been framed, the child will have to wait in custody for a minimum of three to four years for the case to come to trial, by which time the child have often become adults.

Prolonged detention also reduces the prospects of the future rehabilitation of the child, if acquitted. Owing to the non-functioning of the public legal aid service, most cases will be decided without a proper legal defence being provided to the accused resulting in an unfair trial.

There are no existing mechanisms in India to prevent such rights violations from being committed against children, even if the child is fortunate enough to survive a battle and to be produced before a court. Those who dare to complain are targeted by the State police and administration.

There are currently at least 170 of India's 607 districts facing armed anti-state activities. In all of these conflict zones, children are employed by both parties to the conflict. The UN Committee on the Rights of the Child, in its report dated February 26, 2004, urged the Indian government to ensure that thorough and impartial investigations are conducted into allegations of the use of child soldiers in India. However, the reference to child soldiers in the report was limited to the State of Jammu and Kashmir and India's north-eastern states; however the problem of the use of child soldiers is far more widespread than this.

To bring development to these neglected reaches, the government needs to assert control. Private militias like Salwa Judum are the wrong way to go about it. A larger, better-trained police force might help. Eradicating Naxalism, however, is more than a local policing problem. One difficulty has been that, under India's constitution, security is a matter for state governments rather than the centre. So a national policy for dealing with the Naxalites has been inconsistent. In 2004, the government of Andhra Pradesh held abortive peace talks with local Naxalites, while other states continued to fight them.

The spread of Naxalism is causing justifiable alarm. For all their geographical reach, the Maoists' or Naxalite power base remains on the margins of Indian society. They are far from sparking a general insurrection. But, in places such as Chhattisgarh, almost a hole in the map of the Indian polity, it is easy to see how a crude, violent ideology, promising land and liberation, might take root.

Other terrorists attack the Indian state at its strong points—its secularism, its inclusiveness, its democracy. Naxalism attacks where it is weakest: in delivering basic government services to those who need them most. The Naxalites do not threaten the government in Delhi, but they do have the power to deter investment and development in some of India's poorest regions, which also happen to be among the richest in some vital resources – notably iron and coal. So their movement itself has the effect of sharpening inequity, which many see as the biggest danger facing India in the next few years, and which is the Naxalites' recruiting sergeant.

5. Status of Women

"You can tell the condition of a nation by looking at the status of its women" – **Jawaharlal Nehru**

For a country that registers two million cases of female infanticide and nearly 5000 dowry deaths ever year, the less spoken on the status of its women, the better. Looking back we find an ancient Bharat set up on the principles laid down by Manu who saw women as 'worthy of worship'. Even today most of the Hindu deities are female figures that are hailed as 'mata' or 'maa'. But that is about it. Steer away from the altars and come down to the concrete houses to find a very different reality.

The country can boast of a decade of reforms. But of what consequence? Most of these programmes remain limited to the urban population. The rural belts as well as the unskilled urban wage workers go unnoticed and unaffected. The government has proposed and launched a number of programmes for the empowerment of women, including the observance of the year 2001 as the year of women's empowerment. It was said,"Our vision in the new century is of a nation where women are equal partners with men." Many new projects were launched like Swa-Shakti and Stree-Shakti for women's empowerment; Swayamsidha to benefit 1,00,000 women through micro-credit programmes and Balika Samridhi Yojana for the girl child. However, apart from a lot of hoopla and the accompanying verbal diarrhoea, not much was registered. There are those who point to an unfounded development in the social position of women through the achievements of the likes of Indra Nooyi. However, one swallow alone doesn't make a summer. We cannot deny that there have been changes. These changes have been limited to the upper crust of the social order. What we need to realise is that any new programme has to overcome the centuries-old hold of subjugation and marginalisation of women.

There has been an alarming rise in the atrocities committed against women. While the constitution guarantees equal opportunity, patriarchy asserts itself through legal loopholes to consolidate the age-old domination. India has a long history of activism for women's welfare and rights. A range of government programmes have been launched to increase economic opportunity for women, although there appear to be no existing programmes to address the cultural and traditional discrimination against women. Be it education, health care, nutrition, property rights, acknowledgment of labour or life security, women find themselves at the lower rungs of the ladder.

Gender-based violence in the form of rape, domestic violence, honour killing and trafficking exacts a heavy toll on the mental and physical health of affected women. Increasingly, gender-based violence is being recognised as a major public health concern and a serious violation of basic human rights. According to a UN report, on an average, one rape happens every hour in India. Delhi is the sexual-crime capital. The reason for such statistics, according to many is the inefficacy of India's rape laws. Women's rights groups allege that the narrow and conservative outlook of Indian society is responsible for the lackadaisical attitude of authorities and the confidence of wrong doers. Indian families are closed to the concept of sex as a topic of discussion and hence avoid highlighting it in any way and rendering steps towards justice ineffectual. Around 60 to 70 per cent of cases of rape go unreported. Of the few reported cases, convictions are rare.

A 2005 United Nations report said that around two-thirds of married women in India were victims of domestic violence and one incident of violence translates into women losing seven working days in the country. "Discrimination against girl child is so strong in the Punjab State of India that girl child aged two to four die at twice the rate of boys," quotes a 2002 UNIFEM document.

The problem is not only external but intrinsic too. The socio-psychological makeup of most rural and many urban women has been shaped and moulded by more than a century of patriarchal beliefs and a family system where the man (in form of father or husband) is the equivalent of God. The feeling of inferiority has been embedded in their psyche so much so that far from condemning acts of violence against them they are more likely to throttle the voices in favour of them. This is part of the clichéd vicious circle of illiteracy and social backwardness that accounts for all the resultant backwardness of the gender.

Unless social activism groups take these factors into consideration and delve deeper into the social realm of this problem, there is little that can be done. The government, police and the related authorities need to understand the poignancy of their role. Most of all, men and women need to be aware of the much hyped equality of sexes and need to respect the same. Since ours is not a gender-stratified society in the literal sense, both sexes need to learn how to live in co-operation and harmony. The patriarchal heads of society need to answer what the poet PB Shelley asked centuries ago - "Can man be free if woman be a slave?"

6. Status of Children

The report 'Status of Children in India 2008' claims that a vast group of children living in difficult circumstances do not receive even a basic education Thirty-two million children in India under the age of six do not have access to basic education and healthcare, says a recent report released by HAQ: Centre for Child Rights.

The worst affected children in this age-group are those who belong to marginalised sections of society. The report, 'Status of Children in India 2008', reveals that a vast group of children living in difficult circumstances such as children of long-term patients, women prisoners and sex workers, children with special needs, riot-, militancy- and disaster-affected children, refugee and displaced children, and children in orphanages and homes do not receive early childhood education.

Only 13% of children from other backward classes (OBC), eligible to be covered by the Integrated Child Development Scheme (ICDS), are reported to be benefiting from it,the report adds. This figure is lower for scheduled caste (SC) and scheduled tribe (ST) children — 10% each. India has 164 million children in this age-group, of whom 60 million are in the three to six age-group. Only 34 million children in this age-group are covered by pre-schooling schemes, either the ICDS or private initiatives. Nearly, 26 million children have not received any form of intervention.

Children who are not covered are from both rural and urban areas; most belong to vulnerable and marginalised socio-economic groups. In rural areas, the report says, children are located in isolated and remote villages, scheduled caste/tribe habitations, settlements of seasonal migrant roadside workers, construction and quarry workers, or in fishing hamlets. In urban areas, they are the children of construction workers, temporary/seasonal workers, rural migrants, etc, living on pavements, in unauthorised settlements or, at best, in small slums.

Without a major policy shake-up and more efficient implementation of nutrition programmes, India is unlikely to reach the related millennium development goals by 2015. Two of the eight goals set by the United Nations in 2000 relate to children — achieving universal primary education and reducing child mortality. The deadline is 2015. Iinstead of boning up on implementation and universal coverage of the ICDS, policymakers are currently engaged in a frivolous debate over serving biscuits to little children as midday meals, neglecting the nutrition aspect of hot cooked food.

On Aug. 15, 1947, India embarked on a journey toward its independent destiny. Sixty years later, the fate of India as a country is still uncertain. Will it become a democratic, socialist republic or a lawless state? Unfortunately, India in 2010 does not give any indication of becoming a state where all citizens can enjoy their fundamental freedoms and liberties.

Skeptics who would counter the above argument use terms like 'democracy' and 'rule of law' as hallmarks to portray India as a stable nation, but that conclusion depends upon one's definition of democracy and rule of law. If democracy is a means by which criminals retain their authority through elections marred by violence and corruption, this definition is only applicable to a few countries, including India. Today more than 70 per cent of India's politicians have a tainted image. Their names are synonymous with crime, corruption and ineptitude.

As for the rule of law and human rights, it is known in India today more by its absence. Institutions that should protect and preserve the rule of law in the country have a reputation for being its most conspicuous violators. Take, for example, the courts and the prosecution and policing systems. Like their counterparts in the alleged democratic process, those who serve in these institutions have a tainted reputation for corrupt, nepotistic and inefficient practices.

What is left are the people of this huge country. Out of an estimated population of 1.2 billion people, almost 70 per cent still live in conditions that belie a life worth living. The remaining 30 per cent have established their domain over the majority of the population through corrupt and shoddy practices. Moreover, they work to keep India in the same rut which they have created for the country to tread in year after year.

In a functioning democracy the justice system is of great importance. The courts are supposed to be the place where disputes can be decided impartially. In India, however, based on people's experience, the courts are unreliable.

The chief justice of India admitted in a recent statement that there are 25.9 million cases awaiting a decision in the country. Among these, various high courts have 9.8 million cases, and the Supreme Court itself has about 43,000 cases pending. Assuming that not a single new case is filed for the next few years, the Supreme Court itself will take several years to clear this huge backlog. A person thus cannot expect speedy justice. With the administration and law enforcement agencies not functioning properly, it is no wonder that people are increasingly taking up arms, having found that communicating with the government by any other means is meaningless. Thus society is polarised between those who oppose and those who fight back; the only other option is to leave the country. This is the India of today. More than sixty years ago, Indians asked the British to quit India. Now they are doing so themselves. To live with dignity and enjoy relative freedom, one has to quit India! With this massive exodus, what will be left behind a few years from now will be a violently charged and polarized society.

Scheduled Caste and the Scheduled Tribe is estimated to comprise of about ¼ of the total population of India. A discussion about India without referring to such vast a community is never complete. The backbone of rule of law is policing. It calls for a special mention in any human rights report on India. Policing is often the key for promotion and violation of human rights. The state of policing in India is still in doldrums. Consistent calls for attention to improve the state of policing in India within India and outside has been largely ignored by the administration. Even attempts by the Supreme Court regarding this issue have faced a stone-cold response from the government. A large proportion of human rights abuses reported from India are concerning the police.

An empty stomach is no place for any other concern. While India has repeatedly claimed itself to be self-sufficient in food grains and other food stocks, a considerable proportion of Indians live in abject poverty, deprived of daily food. This poorest of the poorest Indians who are deprived of food security are found in rural and urban backdrops. Being exploited by the rich, most commonly as a free form of labour, the poor sections of the society also is a fertile ground for secessionist ideologies. The cases of starvation that are reported from India does not in anyway justify India's great leap forward as a fast developing nation.

Several states of India are facing low intensity conflicts. Of the 607 districts in India about 170 are reportedly affected by armed conflicts. The armed conflicts in these districts are not aimed to break away from the republic, but a response to utter neglect and brutal oppression of the people by feudal landlords or corrupt government agents. It is a shame that in a country like India that has a best justice delivery mechanism in theory fails to address its people's concern in practice and force several of them to take up arms.

The response of the state administration to the armed conflict is presumable. It is neither admirable nor productive. The implementation of draconian laws and the state sponsoring private armed militia has further worsened the situation in these places. The people living in these regions are looked down by the state with suspicion and relative contempt. Such an attitude has not only resulted in further isolating the people from the government, but has resulted in the people developing sympathy towards a violent mode of communication and an affinity towards its carders.

⌘❐⌘

8 Human Rights and Indian Constitution

Enumeration of Rights in the Declaration

The Universal Declaration enumerated the basic postulates and principles of human rights in a most comprehensive manner. It dealt not only with civil or political rights, but with social and economic rights as well.

Civil and Political Rights as per the Declaration

Articles 2 to 21 deal with those civil and political rights, which have been generally recognised throughout the world. These are:

1. Right to life, liberty and security of persons. (Art.3)
2. Freedom from slavery or servitude (Art.4)
3. Prohibition against torture, inhuman or degrading treatment or punishment (Art.5)
4. Recognition as a person before Law (Art.6)
5. Equality before the law and equal protection of the law without any discrimination. (Art.7)
6. Effective remedy before the national tribunals (Art.8)
7. Freedom from arbitrary arrest, detention or exile. (Art.9)
8. Right to a fair and public hearing by an independent and impartial tribunal. (Art.10)
9. Presumption of innocence until proved guilty in a public t.ial with all guarantees necessary for defense in criminal cases. (Art.11-I)
10. Freedom from ex-post facto laws (Art.11-II)
11. Right to privacy, family, home and correspondence. (Art.12)

12. Right to freedom of movement and residence within the borders of a state. (Article 13, I)
13. Right to leave any country, including his own and to return to his country. (Art.13)
14. Right to seek and to enjoy in other countries asylum from persecution (Art.14)
15. Right to a nationality (Art.15)
16. Right to marry and to find a family. (Art.16)
17. Right to own property.(Art.17)
18. Right to freedom of thought, conscience and religion (Art.18)
19. Right to freedom of opinion and expression (Art.19)
20. Right to freedom of peaceful assembly and association (Article 20)
21. Right to participate in the Government of his country (Article 21)

Economic and Social Rights

1. Right to social security (Art.22)
2. Right to work and free choice of employment (Art.23)
3. Right to rest and leisure (Art.24)
4. Right to a standard of living for the health of himself and of his family (Art.25)
5. Right to education (Art.26)
6. Right to participate in cultural life (Art.27)
7. Right to good social and international order (Art.28)

Limitations

Though the rights have been enumerated to safe-guard human rights, the declaration also had laid down under Art.29 certain limitations to these rights and freedoms. By providing that everyone has duties to the community in which, the final and full development of his personality alone is possible. Art.29 Para 2 provides that the rights shall be provided to the individuals, subject to just requirements of morality, public order and the general welfare in a democratic society. Therefore it is to be considered that the rights provided in the Declaration are not absolute.

India and the Universal Declaration

India was a signatory to the Declaration. The Indian constitution adopted by the constituent Assembly on Nov.26, 1949 came into force from Jan 26,

1950 was greatly influenced by the Declaration. A number of fundamental rights guaranteed to individuals in Part III of the Indian constitution are similar to the provisions of the Declaration is clear from the following:

Classifying Human Rights Comparative Table

Name of the Rights:	Universal Declaration	Indian Constitution
1. Equality before law	Art. 7	Art. 14
2. Prohibition of discrimination	Art. 7	Art. 15(1)
3. Equality of opportunity	Art.21(2)	Art. 16(1)
4. Freedom of speech and expression	Art. 19	Art. 19(1)(a)
5. Freedom of peaceful assembly	Art.20(1)	Art.(1)(b)
6. Right to form associations or unions	Art. 23 (4)	Art.19(1)(c)
7. Freedom of movement within the border	Art. 13(1)	Art. 19(1)(d)
8. Protection in respect of conviction for essences	Art. (11)(2)	Art.20(1)
9. Protection of life and personal liberty	Art. 3	Art.21
10. Protection of slavery and forced labour	Art. 4	Art. 23
11. Freedom of conscience and religion	Art. 18	Art.25 (1)
12. Remedy for enforcement of rights	Art. 8	Art. 32

The above-mentioned comparative table shows that the Universal Declaration has provided the model for the Indian Constitution's human rights guarantees.

Human Rights and Constitutional Provisions

Right to Life and Liberty

Art. 21 lays down that no person shall be deprived of his life or personal liberty except according to 'procedure established by law' which means in a simple way that, a person could not be deprived of his life or personal liberty merely by an executive fiat without there being a valid law to support it.

The basic principles of this right are that personal liberty makes for the worth of the human person.

Present View

Right to life includes the right to live with human dignity and all that goes along with it, viz. the bare necessaries of life such as adequate nutrition, clothing reading, writing and expressing oneself in diverse forms, freely moving about and mixing and co-mingling with fellow human beings. Thus it is construed that, the term 'Life' mentioned in Art. 21 of the Indian constitution is not only restricted to the mere animal existence of a person.

Fundamental Right's Growth in India

During the British rule in India, human rights were violated by the rulers on a very wide scale. Therefore, the framers of the Indian constitution, who had suffered long incarceration during the British regime, had a very positive attitude towards their rights.

Secondly, the Indian society is fragmented into many religions, cultural and linguistic groups and it was necessary to declare fundamental rights and to give to the people a sense of security and confidence. Then it was thought necessary that people should have some rights which may be enforced against the government which may become arbitrary at times. Articles 12 to 35 of the constitution pertain to Fundamental Rights of the people. They have been grouped under seven heads as follows:

(i) Right to Equality comprising Articles 14 to 18, of which Art.14 is the most important.

(ii) Right for Freedom comprising Articles 19 to 22 which guarantee several freedoms.

(iii) Right against Exploitation consists of Art.23 & 24.

(iv) Right to Freedom of Religion is guaranteed by Art.25 to 28.

(v) Cultural and Educational Rights are guaranteed by Art.29 & 30.

(vi) Right to constitutional Remedies is secured by Art.32 to 35.

Human Rights of Women and Children

The advancement of women has been a focus of the work of the United Nations since its creation. The General Assembly of the United Nations on November 7, 1967 adopted a Declaration on the Elimination of Discrimination Against Women, and in order to implement the principles set forth in the Declaration, a convention on the Elimination of All forms of Discrimination Against Women was adopted by the General Assembly on December 18, 1979.

Discrimination against Women

Although the International Bill of Human Rights laid down a comprehensive set of rights to which all persons, including women are entitled, additional means for protecting the human rights of women were seen as necessary because the mere fact of their ' humanity ' has not been sufficient to guarantee women the protection of their rights.

The Convention under Art. 1 defines the term discrimination against women as any distinction, exclusion or restriction made on the basis of sex which has the effect or purpose of impairing or nullifying the recognition, enjoyment or exercise by women, irrespective or their marital status, on a basis of equality of men and women of human rights and fundamental freedoms in the political, economic, social, cultural, civil or any other field.

The fields were steps that are to be taken to eliminate discrimination against women are:

(1) Education

The convention under Article 10 provides that women shall be provided same conditions for careers and Vocational guidance as to that of men. They shall be provided same access to studies for the achievement of diplomas in educational establishments of all categories in rural as well as in all types of vocational training. Women shall have access to the same curricula, the same examinations, teaching staff with qualifications of the same standard and school premises and equipment of the same quality as to that of men. Women shall be provided same opportunities as to men in matters relating to scholarship and other study grant. They shall have same opportunities for access to programme of continuing education including adult and functional literacy programmes. They shall have same opportunities to participate actively in sports and physical education.

(2) Employment

The convention under Art.11 provided that states shall take all appropriate measures to eliminate discrimination against woman in the field of employment, in particular (a) the right to work (b) right to same employment opportunities (c) right to free choice of profession and employment (d) right to equal remuneration including benefits and equal treatment in respect or work, of equal value as well as equality of treatment in the education of quality of work (e) the right to social security, particularly in cases of retirement, unemployment, sickness invalidity, old age and other incapacity to work, as well as the right to paid leave (f) right to protection of health and to safety in working conditions. There shall be no discrimination against women on grounds of marriage or maternity.

(3) Health Care

The convention under Art.12 provides that states shall take steps to eliminate discrimination against women in the field of health care, access to health care services, including those related to family planning.

(4) Economic and Social Life

Art.13 of the convention provides that women shall be provided the same rights as to that of men in particular (a) the right to family benefits (b) the right to bank loans mortgages and other forms of financial credit the right to participate in recreational activities, sports and all aspects of cultural life.

(5) Women in Rural Areas

Article 14 provided elimination of discrimination against rural areas. States are required to ensure such women the right to:

(a) Participate in the elaboration and implementation of development planning at all levels;

(b) Have access to adequate health care facilities, including information, counseling and services in family planning;

(c) Benefit directly from social security programmes;

(d) Obtain all types of training and education, formal and non-formal, including, that relating to functional literacy, as well as, inter alia, the benefit of all community and extension services, in order to increase their technical proficiency;

(e) Organize self-help groups and cooperatives in order to obtain equal access to economic opportunities through employment or self-employment;

(f) Participate in all community activities;

(g) Have access to agricultural credit and loans, marketing facilities, appropriate technology and equal treatment in land and agrarian reform as well as in land resettlement schemes; and

(h) Enjoy adequate living conditions.

(6) Equality Before Law

Art 15 of the constitution provides that states shall accord to women equality with men before the law. Women shall have equal rights to conclude contracts and to administer property and states shall treat them equally in all stages of procedure in courts and tribunals. States agree that all contracts and all other private instruments of any kind with a legal capacity of women shall be deemed null and void. States shall accord to men and women the same rights with law relating to the movement of persons and the freedom to choose their residence and domicile.

(7) Marriage and Family Relations

Art.16 provides that states shall take all measures to eliminate discrimination against women in all matters relating to marriage and family relations. Women shall be provided –

(a) The same right to enter into marriage.

(b) The same rights and responsibilities during marriage and at its dissolution

(c) The same rights and responsibilities as parents, in matters relating to their children. In all cases the interests of children shall be paramount.

(d) The same rights to decide freely and responsibly on the number and spacing of their children and to have access to the information, education and means to enable them to exercise their rights.

(e) The same rights and responsibilities with regard to guardianship, wardship, trusteeship and adoption of children.

(f) The same personal rights as husband and wife, including the right to choose a family name a profession and an occupation.

(g) The same rights for both spouses in respect of ownership, acquisition, management, administration, enjoyment and disposition of property whether free of charge or for a valuable consideration.

Status of Women in India

India has given equal status to women. Women in India enjoy right to equality.

Constitutional Safeguards

Indian Constitution under Art.14 provides that "The state shall not deny to any person before the law or the equal protection of the laws within the territory of India". The above provision clearly shows that women in India enjoy right to equality and any discrimination against them shall be violation of equality of right and respect for human dignity.

The Indian Constitution also provides under Art.15 that every female citizen has a right to access to shops, public restaurants, hotels and places of public entertainment and no restriction can be imposed on female citizens with regard to the use of wells, tanks, bathing ghats, roads and places of public resort maintained wholly or partly by state funds.

Art.16 of the constitution provides that there shall be equality of opportunity for all citizens (including women) in matters relating to employment or appointment to any office under the state.

In order to improve the status of women further the constitution provides under art.15 (3) that state may make special provisions for women. Consequently, a number of legal provisions aimed at securing equal status for and removing discrimination against women have been made. For instance, the constitution was amended in 1992 to reserve 33 per cent of the seats in their favour in panchayats and municipalities. The amendment is regarded as a major step for socio economic empowerment of the women in India. The constitution has also cast the duty on every citizen to renounce practices derogatory to the dignity of women.

India and International Convention

India has ratified the convention on the elimination of all forms of discrimination against women on July 9, 1993. Ratification of the convention obliges India to honour the obligations imposed by the convention, which include adapting various measures to uphold human rights with regard to women.

Physical Assault and Harassment of Women

Gender equality is also a basic human right. It could be effectively safeguarded at work places specifically if at all there are said principles and laws for the enforcement of those principles.

The Indian Supreme Court has formulated the guidelines to guarantee the effective implementation of the rights of women against sexual exploitation at work places; in the case Vishaka and others Vs. State of Rajasthan; it is observed that:

(i) Each incident of sexual harassment of women at work places results in violation of fundamental rights of "Gender Equality" and the "Right to life and liberty".

(ii) It shall be the duty of the employer or the responsible persons in work places or other institutions to prevent or deter the commission of acts of sexual harassment and provide the procedures for the resolution, settlement or prosecution of acts of sexual harassment by taking all steps required.

(iii) All employers or persons in charge of work place should take following steps to prevent steps to prevent sexual harassment-

(a) Express prohibition of sexual harassment a defined at the work place should be notified, published and circulated in appropriate ways;

(b) The rules/regulations of Government and public sector bodies relating to conduct and discipline should include rules/regulations prohibiting sexual harassment and provide for appropriate penalties in such rules against the offender.

(c) As regards private employers steps should be taken to include the aforesaid prohibitions in the standing orders under the Industrial Employment (Standing Orders) Act. Appropriate work conditions should be provided in respect of work, leisure, health and hygiene to further ensure that there is no hostile environment.

(iv) Where such conduct amounts to a specified offence under the Indian Penal Code or under any other law, the employer shall initiate appropriate action in accordance with laws. It should ensure that victims, or witnesses are not victimized or discriminated against while dealing with complaints of sexual harassment. The victims of sexual harassment should have the option to seek transfer of the perpetrator or their own transfer.

(v) Appropriate disciplinary action should be initiated by the employer if the conduct amounts to misconduct as per relevant conduct rules.

(vi) An appropriate complaint mechanism should be treated in the employer's organisation for redress of the complaint made by the victim. Such complaint mechanism should ensure time bound treatment of complaints.

(vii) It should be adequate to provide, where necessary, a complaints committee, a special counselor or other support service including the maintenance of confidentiality. The committee should be headed by a woman and not less than half of its members should be women. In order to prevent the probability of any undue pressure or influence from senior levels, such complaints committee should involve a third party, either NGO- Non Governmental Organisation or other body who is familiar with the issue of sexual harassment. The complaints committee must make an annual report to the Government and the action taken by it.

(viii) Employees should be allowed to raise issues of sexual harassment at workmen's meeting and in other appropriate forum and it should be affirmatively discussed in Employer-Employee meeting.

(ix) Awareness of the rights of female employees in this regard should be created in particular by prominently notifying guidelines in a suitable manner.

(x) Where sexual harassment occurs as a result of an act or omission by a third party or outsider, the employer and person in charge will take all steps necessary and reasonable to assist the affected persons in terms of support and preventing action.

(xi) The Central/State Governments are requested to consider adopting suitable measures including legislation to ensure that the guidelines are also observed by the employers in the private sector.

The Supreme Court further stated that the 'above guidelines' and norms would be strictly observed in all work places for the preservation and enforcement of the right to gender equality of the working women.

Human Rights as to Children

The Universal Declaration of Human Rights had stipulated under Art.25 (2) that childhood is entitled to special care and assistance. Following the same, the convention on the rights of the child was adopted by the General Assembly by consensus, on the 30th Anniversary of the Declaration on Nov 20, 1989 which came into force on Sep 2, 1990.

Who is a Child?

The convention under Article 1 states that a child means every human being below the age of 18 years unless under the law applicable to the child, majority is attained earlier.

Rights of the Child

A number of rights have been stipulated in the convention which includes the following:

(i) Right to life (Article 6 (1))

(ii) Right to acquire nationality (Art 7)

(iii) Right to freedom of expression (Art. 13 (1))

(iv) Right to freedom of thought, conscience and religion (Art 14(1))

(v) Right to Freedom of association and to freedom of peaceful assembly (Art 15(1))

(vi) Right to Privacy

(vii) Right to family environment (Art.20)

(viii) Right to education (Art.28 (1))

(ix) Right to benefit from social security (Art.26 (1))

(x) Right to a standard of living adequate for the child's physical, mental, spiritual and social development (Art.27 (1))

(xi) Right to the enjoyment of the highest attainable standard of health and to facilities for the treatment of illness and rehabilitation of health (Art.24 (1)).

(xii) Right to the protection of the law against arbitrary or unlawful interference with his or her privacy family, home or correspondence (Art.16 (1))

(xiii) Right against exploitation of child labour (Art.32)

(xiv) Right against sexual exploitation (Art.34).

(xv) Right against abduction, sale or traffic (Art.35)

(xvi) Right against other forms of exploitation on prejudicial to any aspect ofthe child's welfare.

Child Labour in India

The Indian constitution under Art.24 provides that no child below the age of fourteen years shall be employed in any factory or mine or engaged in any other hazardous employment. The above provision was made in order to protect children from exploitation and to provide them education so that they may develop their personality and may live a dignified life.

Art.45 provides that the state shall endeavour to provide free and compulsory education for all children until they complete the age of 14 years. Despite the above constitutional prohibition on child labour, children are working in a large number in hazardous as well as non-hazardous work.

India has the population of more than 380 million children – the largest population of children in the world. A large number of them are between the age group of 6 to 14 years. It is a difficult task to provide free education to them; similar task is to prevent child labour. It has to be seen that the tender age of children are not abused and that children are not forced by economic necessity to enter avocations unsuited to their age or strength and that children should be given opportunities and facilities to develop in a healthy manner and in conditions of freedom and dignity. Childhood is required to be protected against exploitation and against moral and material abandonment. The only way by which can be prevented is to provide education to the children. Indian Government has estimated that the financial expenditure to implement the free education to child would be nearly forty thousand crore rupees. The Government alone is not responsible to incur such expenditure. It is also the duty of the parents and guardians to provide education to their wards as per Art.51 (A)(k) of the Indian constitution.

Institutions for Implementation of Human Rights

National Human Rights Commission

Constitution

The Constitution of Human Rights commission is dealt with under section 3 of the protection of Human Rights Act. It provides that the commission be constituted by the Central Government as under;

(I) Sitting or retired Judge of the Supreme Court.

(II) Serving or a retired Chief Justice of the High Court.

(III) Two prominent persons having knowledge or practical experience in the sphere of human rights.

(IV) The chairpersons of the National commission for minorities, the scheduled castes and scheduled tribes and women.

The chairperson and the members shall be appointed by the President and they shall hold office for a period of 5 years from the date on which they enter upon their office.

Powers and function of the Commission

Section 12 of the Protection of Human Rights Act deals with the powers:

(i) The commission shall inquire ' suomotto' or on a petition presented to it by a victim or any person on his behalf, into complaints of –

(a) Violation of human rights or abetment thereof.

(b) Negligence in the prevention of such violation by a public servant.

(ii) The commission may intervene in any proceeding involving any allegation of violation of human rights pending before a court with the approval of such court.

(iii) The commission shall visit, under intimation to the state governemrt any jail or any other institution under the control of the state government where persons are detained or lodged for purposes of treatment, reformation or protection to study the living conditions of the inmates and make recommendations thereon.

(iv) The commission shall encourage the efforts of non-governmental organisations and institutions working in the field of human rights.

(v) The commission may perform any other function, as it may consider necessary for the promotion of human rights.

Human Rights Courts

Human Rights Courts are to be established in every district u/s 30 of the Protection of Human Rights Act. These courts ensure the speedy trial of the offences relating to human rights violations.

⌘❐⌘

9 Human Rights Education

Definition

Human rights education (HRE) is an international movement to promote awareness about the rights accorded by the Universal Declaration of Human Rights and related human rights conventions, and the procedures that exist for the redress of violations of these rights (Amnesty International, 2005; Reardon, 1995; Tibbitts, 1996). Decades ago, the United Nations (UN) and its specialized agencies formally recognized the right of citizens to be informed about the rights and freedoms contained in the documents ratified by their countries – the right to human rights education itself (UNGA, 2005). Since then, numerous policy documents developed by UN-affiliated agencies, international policymaking bodies, regional human rights bodies, and national human rights agencies have referenced HRE, proposing specifically that the treatment of human rights themes should be present in schooling (Pearse, 1987).

The U.N. Office of the High Commissioner for Human Rights defines human rights education as 'training, dissemination and information efforts aimed at the building of a universal culture of human rights through the imparting of knowledge and skills and the molding of attitudes directed to:

(a) the strengthening of respect for human rights and fundamental freedoms,

(b) the full development of the human personality and the sense of its dignity,

(c) the promotion of understanding, tolerance, gender equality and friendship among all nations, indigenous peoples and racial, national, ethnic, religious and linguistic groups, and

(d) the enabling of all persons to participate effectively in a free society. (UN, 1996)'

This definition is not specific to the schooling sector and in fact, the United Nations proposes human rights education for all sectors of society as part of a 'lifelong learning' process for individuals (UN, 1996). The 'human rights' to which it refers are broadly defined and include those contained in the Universal Declaration of Human Rights, as well as related treaties and covenants, such as the International Covenant on Economic, Social and Cultural Rights, the International Covenant on Civil and Political Rights, the Convention on the Rights of the Child, and the Convention for the Elimination of All Forms of Discrimination Against Women, among others.

HUMAN RIGHTS EDUCATION declares a commitment to those human rights expressed in the Universal Declaration of Human Rights of 1948, the UN Covenants, and the United States Bill of Rights. It asserts the responsibility to respect, protect, and promote the rights of all people.

HUMAN RIGHTS EDUCATION promotes democratic principles. It examines human rights issues without bias and from diverse perspectives through a variety of educational practices.

HUMAN RIGHTS EDUCATION helps to develop the communication skills and informed critical thinking essential to a democracy. It provides multicultural and historical perspectives on the universal struggle for justice and dignity.

HUMAN RIGHTS EDUCATION engages the heart as well as the mind. It challenges students to ask what human rights mean to them personally and encourages them to translate caring into informed, nonviolent action.

HUMAN RIGHTS EDUCATION affirms the interdependence of the human family. It promotes understanding of the complex global forces that create abuses, as well as the ways in which abuses can be abolished and avoided.

In 1993 the World Conference on Human Rights in Vienna reaffirmed the importance of human rights education, training and public information, declaring it 'essential for the promotion and achievement of stable and harmonious relations among communities and for fostering mutual understanding, tolerance and peace.'

In response to an appeal by this World Conference, the General Assembly proclaimed the period 1995 to 2004 the UN Decade for Human Rights Education.

In proclaiming the United Nations Decade for Human Rights Education in December 1994, the General Assembly defined human rights education as "a life-long process by which people at all levels of development and in all strata of society learn respect for the dignity of others and the means and methods of ensuring that respect in all societies." The Assembly emphasized that the responsibility for human rights education rested with all elements of society—government, nongovernmental organisations, professional associations, and all other sectors of civil society, as well as individuals.

The Plan of Action for the Decade further defines human rights education as 'training, dissemination and information efforts aimed at the building of a universal culture of human rights through the imparting of knowledge and skills and the molding of attitudes which are directed to:

(a) The strengthening of respect for human rights and fundamental freedoms;

(b) The full development of the human personality and the sense of its dignity;

(c) The promotion of understanding, tolerance, gender equality, and friendship among all nations, indigenous peoples and racial, national, ethnic, religious and linguistic groups;

(d) The enabling of all persons to participate effectively in a free society;

(e) The furtherance of the activities of the United Nations for the maintenance of peace.'

Need for Human Rights Education

- Produces changes in values and attitudes
- Produces changes in behavior
- Produces empowerment for social
- Develops attitudes of solidarity across issues and nations
- Develops knowledge and analytical skills
- Produces participatory education.
- Integrates the teaching of human rights standards, values and action skills into the curriculum;
- Promotes knowledge of and respect for the rights contained in the Universal Declaration of Human Rights,
- Creates awareness of human rights violations, and provides tools for action to end violations;
- Teaches the values of human dignity, tolerance, multiculturalism and non-violence, and the skills of critical analysis and civic participation.
- Teaches about the history and current structures of the international human rights system, treaties and declarations;
- Creates awareness and fosters concern about human rights violations and the effects those violations have on people's lives, from denial of free speech, to homelessness, to the oppression of women;
- Promotes understanding and practice of human rights values including respect for human dignity, non-violent conflict resolution, tolerance and multiculturalism;
- Encourages action in response to human rights violations internationally and in local communities.

- Human rights education also teaches important academic and life skills and deepens students' understanding of course material.

Knowledge and skills to be gained from human rights education include

- Critical thinking, analyzing credibility and authenticity of cause-effect relationships, formulating analysis and asking questions;
- Viewing an issue from multiple perspectives and identifying bias in your own and other's opinions;
- Research and data collection, use of statistics, reporting and monitoring techniques, and measuring human rights violations;
- Human rights education also supports the learning of concepts of civic participation and government obligation to its citizens;
- Finally, human rights education stimulates and engages learners, helps them relate emotionally and intellectually to course material, and helps them make connections between their own lives and events happening elsewhere.

Goals of Human Rights Education

- Value your human rights
- Know your human rights
- Be inspired to take action toward realizing human rights for yourself and others

The Expansion Of HRE in Schools

During the 1990s, several important international documents on human rights education were elaborated. These were the World Plan of Action on Education for Human Rights and Democracy (Montreal, 1993), the Declaration and Integrated Frame-work of Action on Education for Peace, Human Rights and Democracy (UNESCO, Paris, 1995), the World Conference on Human Rights (Vienna, 1993), Guidelines for Plans of Action for the United Nations Decade for Human Rights Education 1995-2004 (1995). These refer to the relevant education articles of international treaties and place informal pressure on national governments to co-operate.

Although still a developing field, there is increasing evidence that HRE is emerging in the work of non-governmental organisations at the grassroots level as well as in national systems of education (Buergenthal and Torney, 1976; Claude 1996; Elbers, 2000; HREA, n.d.; IIDH, 2002). The only study focusing on this subject indicated that the number of organisations dedicated to human rights education quadrupled between 1980 and 1995, from 12 to 50 (Ramirez *et al*, 2006). In reality, the numbers are probably much higher since only those organisations that had an Internet presence or were already networked in international circles were documented.

In 2006, an International Bureau of Education (IBE) study that examined the number of times the term 'human rights' was mentioned in official documents found a mean of .70, .82 and .64 for countries within the regions of Sub-Saharan Africa, Eastern Europe and the former USSR, and Latin American and the Caribbean, respectively (Ramirez *et al*, 2006). Interestingly enough, the lowest means were for Asia and Western Europe and North America at .11 (Ramirez *et al*, 2006), although the range of response rates across regions – from 31% to 74% - suggests that these results are approximate at best. A review in 1996 showed that through the co-operative efforts of NGOs and educational authorities, human rights courses and topics had been introduced into the national curricula in Albania, Australia, Brazil, Canada, Denmark, Norway, the UK and Ukraine (Kati & Gjedia, 2003; Tibbitts, 1996). The IBE study and other less formal data suggest that the number of educational systems including human rights in their formal curricula has grown significantly since that time.

During this same period, non-governmental organisations which have traditionally spearheaded human rights education efforts, also gathered to develop human rights education action plans that had an influence on their own work and co-operation with others (Amnesty International, 1996; Netherlands Helsinki Committee, 1996). In the last five years, national and regional HRE networks have been established in many parts of the world (HREA, n.d.). In 2005, with the conclusion of the UN Decade for HRE, the Office of the UN High Commissioner for Human Rights launched an on-going and more focused World Programme with a Plan of Action for Human Rights Education (UNGA 2005), which promises to elicit improved co-operation from governments, as well as cross-cutting support from UN bodies (Amnesty International, 2005). The first phase of the World Programme is focused on promoting human rights education in schools.

Rationales for HRE

The broad normative frame-work of HRE and the wide spectrum of potential learners have resulted in a great deal of variation in the ways in which HRE has been implemented. Although HRE is defined by the universal frame-work of international (and sometimes regional) standards, the specific topics and their applications depends upon local and national contexts.

HRE in post-conflict or post-colonial countries tends to be associated with the rule of law and authorities trying to establish their legitimacy. Among groups that experience a high amount of discrimination, and within countries that are highly repressive and undemocratic, HRE tends to be focused on popular empowerment and resistance in relation to these issues. HRE in countries that are democratic but struggling with development can be oriented towards the infusion of human rights principles within sustainable development (Yeban, 2003). In countries that enjoy strong democratic and economic development, HRE is often focused on issues of discrimination, for example in relation to migrants, minorities, or women. Of course, in any country at any given time, HRE can take on different forms and purposes depending upon the context of the program.

Several explanations have been proposed for the increased presence of HRE in schools since the 1990's. One explanation relates to increased globalization, a term still being defined, but recognized as one emphasizing 'world citizenship and the strong assumption of personal agency required for global citizenship' (Ramirez & Suarez, 2006, p. 36). Moreover, authorities are increasingly calling on schools to promote respect among peoples, democratic governance and viable civil societies.

Democratic citizenship, including HRE, has been seen by regional human rights agencies as a way to 'manage diversity,' with HRE incorporated into processes such as the Graz Stability Pact in South Eastern Europe (Council of Europe, 2001; South House Exchange, 2004). In contemporary Europe, education for democratic citizenship, including HRE, has been seen as a way of promoting young people's active participation in democratic society, in promoting social cohesion and in fighting violence, xenophobia, racism, intolerance, and aggressive nationalism (Froumin, 2003).

In 1978, human rights education was already promoted by UNESCO but linked with disarmament (UNESCO, 1978). In 2005, human rights education has been iinked in inter-governmental circles with a variety of global phenomena, including development and poverty, religious freedom, and globalization in general (UNESCO, 2005). Europe's regional human rights agency, the Council of Europe, is working on developing a 'culture of religion' subject that takes an 'ethics' and 'human rights' based approach to religious teaching. This provides an alternative to governments that currently offer required religion classes that can be a source of division and ethnic nationalism, as in Serbia-Montenegro (Tibbitts, 2003).

Non-governmental organisations from different countries and regions periodically initiate meetings in which they identify strategies for applying the human rights frame-work to global challenges. One such symposium, which took place in South Africa in 2001 in a meeting organised in concert with the World Conference against Racism, identified HRE in schools as a key strategy for combating racism (Flowers, 2001).

THE United Nations General Assembly had declared 1995-2004 to be the Decade on Human Rights Education. At the fag end of this decade it was felt that this Programme is very effective and it was decided to be extended to one more decade *i.e* 2005-2014. Imbibing this spirit a National Action Plan for Human Rights Education had been formulated by government of India which envisages Human Rights Education in Schools, Colleges and Universities. The aims inter alia are to create awareness that the Right to Basic Minimum Education is a Child's Human Right, by a reach-through media advocacy to the deprived the special target group of children. This requires the introduction of human rights issues in the school curricula at both primary and secondary levels as well as preparation of appropriate course materials. For accomplishing the same a plan of action has to be devised for training the teachers in collaboration with State education Departments, State Council for Education and Training (SCERT)/ National Council for Education (NCTE).

Pedagogy Of HRE

Since 1995, further elaborations by the UN and other agencies have clarified that HRE has components of knowledge, skills, and attitudes, which should be consistent with recognized human rights principles and which should empower individuals and groups to address oppression and injustice (Amnesty International, 2007; ARRC, 2003).

Human rights education has both normative and legal dimensions. The legal dimension incorporates sharing content about international human rights standards as embodied in the UDHR and other treaties and covenants to which countries subscribe. These standards encompass civil and political rights, as well as social, economic, and cultural. In recent years, environmental and collective rights have been added to this evolving frame-work. This law-oriented approach recognizes the importance of monitoring and accountability in ensuring that governments uphold the letter and spirit of human rights obligations.

At the same time, HRE is a normative and cultural enterprise. The process of human rights education is intended to be one that provides skills, knowledge, and motivation to individuals to transform their own lives and realities so that they are more consistent with human rights norms and values. For this reason, interactive, learner-centered methods of are widely promoted. The following kinds of pedagogy are representative of those promoted by human rights education advocates. These methods are applicable to all types of HRE but are most comprehensively implemented in adult, popular education learning models.

- Experiential and activity-centered: involving the solicitation of learners' prior knowledge and offering activities that draw out learners' experiences and knowledge;

- Problem-posing: challenging the learners' prior knowledge;
- Participative: encouraging collective efforts in clarifying concepts, analyzing themes and doing the activities;
- Dialectical: requiring learners to compare their knowledge with those from other sources;
- Analytical: asking learners to think about why things are and how they came to be;
- Healing: promoting human rights in intra-personal and inter-personal relations;
- Strategic thinking-oriented: directing learners to set their own goals and to think of strategic ways of achieving them; and
- Goal and action-oriented: allowing learners to plan and organise actions in relation to their goals. (ARRC, 2003)

Human rights education in school settings is adapted to the age of learners and the conditions of national/local educational policies and schools. Developmental and conceptual frame-works for HRE have been developed by the United Nations and several NGOs. These frame-works assist in settings goals for HRE, illustrating both what it shares and what it adds to other educational approaches that address values such as social justice.

TABLE 1: Methodologies: Development and Conceptual Framework For HRE

Levels	**Goals**	**Key Concepts**	**Specific Human Rights Problems**	**Education Standards and Instruments**
Early Childhood **Preschool & Lower primary Ages 3-7**	Respect for self, Respect for parents and teachers, Respect for others,	Self, Community, Responsibility,	Racism, Sexism, Unfairness, Hurting people, (emotionally, physically),	Classroom rules, Family life, Convention on the Rights of the Child,
Later Childhood **Upper primary Ages 8-11**	Social responsibility, Citizenship, Distinguishing wants from needs from rights,	Individual rights, Group rights, Freedom, Equality, Justice, Rule of law, Government,	Discrimination/ prejudice, Poverty/hunger, Injustice, Ethnocentricism, Passivity,	UDHR, History of human rights, Local, national legal systems, Local and national history in

		Security, Democracy,		human rights, terms UNESCO, UNICEF,
Adolescence **Lower secondary Ages 12-14**	Knowledge of specific human rights,	International law World peace, World development, World political economy, World ecology, Legal rights, Moral rights,	Ignorance, Apathy, Cynicism, Political repression, Colonialism/ imperialism, Economic globalization, Environmental degradation,	UN Covenants, Elimination of racism, Elimination of sexism, Regional human rights conventions, UNHCR, NGOs,
Older Adolescents and Adults **Upper secondary Ages 15 and up**	Knowledge of human rights, standards, Integration of human rights into personal awareness and behaviours,	Moral inclusion/ exclusion Moral responsibility/ literacy	Genocide Torture	Geneva Conventions Specialized conventions Evolving human rights standards

Source: (Flowers, 1998)

Human rights themes and content in school curricula can take the form of cross-cultural themes mandated by educational policy or it can be integrated within existing subjects, such as history, civics/citizenship education, social studies and humanities. HRE can also be found in arts programs and non-formal clubs and special events that take place in school settings.

In addition to taking place in schools, HRE is often organised in settings of higher education; in training programs for professionals such as the police, prison officials, the military, and social workers; for potentially vulnerable populations such as women and minorities; as part of community development programs; and in public awareness campaigns.

Reardon Model of Human Rights Education

DEVELOPMENTAL LEVEL	CORE CONCEPTS and VALUES	HUMAN RIGHTS STANDARDS and INSTRUMENTS	ISSUES and PROBLEMS
EARLY CHILDHOOD GRADES K-3	rules, order, respect, fairness diversity, equality, personal responsibility, classroom rules,	Declaration of the Rights of the Child	inequlity, unfairness, harm,
MIDDLE CHILDHOOD GRADES 4-6	citizenship, community, freedom, charter, constitution, law declaration, social responsibility, community standards,	Declaration of Independence, African Freedom Charter, U.S. Bill of Rights, Universal Declaration of Human Rights, Convention on the Rights of the Child,	prejudice, discrimination poverty, injustice,
EARLY ADOLESCENCE GRADES 7-9	justice, equality equity, conventions, covenants, global responsibility,	Regional Human Rights Conventions, U.N. Covenants and Conventions: Elimination of Racism; Discrimination against Women; Civil, Political Rights; and Economic, Social, and Cultural Rights,	ethnocentrism, racism, sexism, authoritarianism, colonialism, hunger,
ADOLESCENCE GRADES 10-12	moral exclusion, moral responsibility, world citizenship, ecological responsibility,	Nuremberg Principles, U.N. Conventions on: Prevention and Punishment,	Defining and developing new standards, ethnocide, genocide, torture,

	of Genocide; Prevention and Elimination of Torture,	political repression, environmental abuse,

* Betty Reardon is a teacher at Columbia University's Teacher College.

The **'National Program for Human Rights Education in Schools'** is now on in the form of human rights education in schools in the following states:

- Andhra Pradesh
- Chattisgarh
- Gujarat
- Karnataka
- Kerala
- Orissa
- Rajasthan
- TamilNadu
- Tripura
- West Bengal
- North east
- Maharastra

The World Conference on Human Rights considers human rights education is essential for the promotion and achievement of stable and harmonious relations among communities and for fostering mutual understanding, tolerance and peace. The **'National Program for Human Rights Education in Schools'** is implemented in different states in consonance with the objectives of the World Programme for Human Rights Education.

The Introduction of Human Rights Education in schools is the result of a deep reflection that the value of rights can be firmly established only when we instill into the tender minds of children this value as a social virtue, as a value to be safeguarded and protected as something stable and indestructible.

Developments and the Future of HRE

The HRE field shows signs of continuing development and evolution. At the international level, UN agencies continue to encourage governments to develop formal plans of action for HRE and provide reports on its internal HRE activities as part of regular treaty-based reports. International and national networks of educators, institutes and organisations continue to dialogue and share resources on the content, standards, and methodology of HRE and learning. Research in the field, although currently sparse, is beginning to increase.

Within the educational sector, the human rights normative system is increasingly being proposed as the ethical framework for cultural globalization. Within the human rights sector, the 'human rights based approach' that the United Nations has advocated for all development programming has begun to trickle down to the education sector. Thus HRE, which has primarily focused on teaching and learning, may eventually seen as part of an overall 'human rights based approach' to schooling, which calls attention to overall school culture, policies, and practices related to human rights values.

Arguments Made for Teaching and Learning about Human Rights in the Schools

1. To know about basic rights and fundamental freedoms is part of the birthright, and should be part of the entitlement curriculum of all young people. For students in the Council of Europe's Member States, where human rights are not just claims and assertions but part of the legal framework, human rights are part of the students' law related education.
2. Human rights cases and issues are **human** and can interest and encourage the humanity of students.
3. Human rights offer a value frame-work suitable for modern society which, typically, is multi-cultural and multi-faith, and part of an interdependent world. Human Rights are, thus, an essential element in education for modern citizenship.
4. Human rights offer to young people something positive to believe in and support.
5. No man or woman is an island. We are all our brother's and sister's keepers and helpers.
6. Young people have rights and responsibilities, and developing an awareness of them is a proper part of education in citizenship.
7. Important organizations — such as the United Nations, the Council of Europe, and some national human rights commissions — support the teaching of human rights in the schools.
8. The facilitation of non-violent change is the most urgent task today — both within societies and between societies.
9. Teaching and learning about human rights can contribute to a political education which is over and above party politics.

10. Teaching about human rights affords students opportunities of active learning, working on non-partisan projects—such as when they work for Amnesty International and conduct campaigns on behalf of political prisoners or raise funds for famine relief.

Arguments Made against Teaching and Learning about Human Rights in the Schools

1. Human rights are too complex for immature minds (an argument also made about other activates — such as political education and economics).
2. Human rights over-stress **rights** and under-stress **responsibilities.**
3. To teach human rights is a form of indoctrination, in which the teacher becomes a preacher (albeit of a secular religion).
4. Human rights teachers are usually more interested in social change (or in subversion) than in maintaining the fabric of society.
5. Human rights is a culture-bound conception, born in Western Europe and North America, foisted on the world in 1948.
6. There is no consensus about what it is 'to have a right', and no consensus about human rights in general. Schools should teach only those things about which consensus exists.
7. Human are too individualistic and private. Group rights, collective rights and the importance of public domain are under-represented.
8. If we arrogate to ourselves the right to pass judgement upon, and seek to interfere with, the internal administration of justice in other countries, we are in effect according the same right of judgement and interference in our own. There is no good so great that it is worth purchasing it at the price of national independence (Extract from a letter by a politician to a schoolteacher who had invited the politician to make a statement in support of a human rights exhibition mounted by students in a comprehensive school).
9. Human rights issues are complex, long-term, and often intractable. Teaching about them can give students a feeling of impotence, rather than enable them to act upon issues and affect their outcomes.
10. Teachers of human go too far. They are not satisfied with teaching about human rights. They want to teach for human rights. They want 'human rights schools' and 'human rights classrooms'. They assert women's rights, children's rights, and animal rights. Some even talk of the 'rights of trees'. Ordinary citizens will not support this.

⌘❒⌘

10 Education for Human Rights – Methods and Techniques

Every teacher aspires to be an effective and successful teacher. In order to excel a teacher needs to provide successful learning experience to her students. She will require knowing the strategies supporting a successful learning experience. Good teaching is time consuming. It takes time to create clear, structured, and meaningful assignments. It takes time to provide constructive and specific feedback. And it takes time to be available and approachable for students. But the rewards are hopefully well worth the effort.

Creating a Safe and Secure Classroom

1. Present any factual information in an inviting way. Try to avoid lecture unless it is absolutely necessary. Keep it simple and short.
2. Know your subject area. Students will have very specific questions especially about areas of great interest such as the laws of search and seizure.
3. Use participatory activities such as case studies, mock trials, moot courts, role plays, and simulations. Students will not become bored, and therefore potential disciplinary problems, and they will learn much more than if they simply sit and listen.
4. Know your audience. Avoid legal terms unless you define them. Ask the age of the group, how many, extent of knowledge of the subject area so that you can adjust your lesson.
5. The teacher should remain in the classroom to deal with administrative issues and discipline problems.
6. Prepare an agenda for yourself, the more detailed the better. Break it down into minutes if possible. However, be prepared to vary from it and remember that in most cases your are limited to a specific amount of time and will not be able to go beyond that time. Never 'wing it.'

7. Don't underestimate the knowledge of your audience. Everyone watches law programs on T.V. Be prepared to address some common misconceptions. Anticipate questions.
8. Try to "'uncover,' 'discover,' instead of 'cover.'
9. Encourage students to ask questions when they think of them. Asking students to wait until the end of your comments results in their confusion and 'dropping out.'
10. Be realistic. Present situations as they really happen. Students will know when you are explaining the ideal or 'the way it is supposed to happen.'
11. Avoid placing yourself in the middle of a controversy. If the information you are going to present will flag questionable behavior by school administrators, prepare for that by first talking to the teacher or administrator if possible.
12. Understand your power as an outside resource person. You are an expert and you are a new face in the classroom. The students will probably listen carefully and repeat much of what you say. They might also adopt your attitudes.
13. Present balanced information. This is especially important when teaching current events as they have unfolded in the media.
14. Be enthusiastic and have fun! Move around the room. Vary your voice. Your enthusiasm will be contagious.

A resourceful teacher should possess an array of teaching methods and strategies at her disposal. She can make a choice of the method depending on the content and the student level.

[1] Role-play

What is it and why do it?

A role-play is a short drama played by the members of the group. It is mostly improvised. It aims to bring to life circumstances or events which are unfamiliar to participants. Role-plays can improve understanding of a situation and encourage empathy. In a robbery role play for example, members, by acting the part of the victim, can gain insight into what it is like to be the victim of crime.

How to do it?

With the group members

Identify the issue, which the role-play will illustrate. For example, the right to property (Article 17 of the UDHR).Decide on the situation, the problem, and who the characters are. For example, if the group is studying the right to property, they could think of a situation where someone might be deprived of their apartment, maybe because of their ethnic origin, or the lack of fair laws. With the group, decide how many people will do the role-play, how many will be observers, whether to do the role-play simultaneously in small groups, or all together as a whole group. Encourage all individuals to be involved, especially those who might be shy. Also, decide how the role-play will work. For example, it could be:

- told as a story, where a narrator sets the scene and other members tell the rest of the event from the point of view of 'their' character;
- a drama, where the characters interact, inventing dialogue on the spot;
- a mock trial, where the participants pretend to be witnesses testifying in a court.

Now allow a couple of minutes for people to think about the situation and their roles. If the furniture needs to be re-arranged to make space, do it now.

The role-play is performed.

During the role-play, it might be useful to stop the action at a critical point to ask the participants and the observers about what is happening. For example, in a role-play about violence, ask the group members if they can think of a way that the situation could be resolved peacefully. Then ask the participants to play out those possible endings. After the role-play, it is important that participants think about what just took place, so that it is not just an activity, but is also a learning experience. When planning the role play, be sure to leave time at the end to reinforce the purpose and learning points of the activity. For example, if the role-play was a mock trial with witnesses, ask for the verdict, and then discuss how it was reached. End by summarizing the main learning points.

If the role-play was unsuccessful, ask the group members how it could have been improved. If it went well, maybe it could be performed for other members of the youth club or parents, with an explanation of the subject it illustrates.

Remember

Because role-plays imitate real life, they may raise questions to which there is no simple answer. For example, about the right or wrong behaviour of a character. Do not give the impression that there is one answer for every question if there isn't. It is very important that everyone accepts different points of view as a natural, normal situation. Peer group leaders should not impose their view on controversial matters or try to get consensus at any price. However, you can summarize the points where agreement seems to have been reached, and leave open other points which are debatable.

Role-plays need to be used with sensitivity. The leader needs to respect the feelings of individuals. For example, a role-play about ethnic minorities needs careful handling if there are ethnic minorities in the group, so that people will not feel exposed or marginalised.

[2] Pairs and Small Groups

What is it and why do it?

Dividing the group into pairs or smaller groups gives members more opportunities for participating and co-operating. Pairs and small groups can be useful to generate a lot of ideas very quickly, or to help people think about an abstract concept in terms of their own experience. For example, if you were studying the right to life, you could give pairs or small groups five minutes to decide 'Is it ever right to kill someone?', before returning to the whole-group for further discussion.

How to do it?

When organising the small groups, ask yourself how you would like to divide the large group, e.g. by age, sex, experience etc. Sometimes groups can be chosen at random. For example, by birth date, or by the first letter of their name, or other non-obvious criteria. If a group will be together for more than a few minutes, it might be necessary to have a chairperson and someone to write notes. The group would need to decide who will do these jobs.

Organising the activity: Explain the task clearly. Make sure everyone can see each other. Tell the participants how long they have for the task. ?When the pairs or groups are working:

- Stand back, but be available.
- Do not interrupt, unless a group has misunderstood what it is supposed to be doing.
- Spread your attention between groups.
- Allow group and pair discussions to flow, only intervene if asked to by the group.
- Groups often need encouragement to get them going.
- A pair is more likely to stop work when you approach.

Reporting back: It might be necessary for small groups to report their work to the whole group. This might involve reporting a decision, summarizing a discussion, or giving information about how the group functioned. This sort of debriefing can be very useful for both the peer group leader and the members for improving group-work technique. If the small groups will need to report back, they need to know this at the start so that they can select someone for this task.

Evaluation

Ask participants whether the activity was useful, and what they learned. If there is a negative response, ask them how the activity could have been improved. Make note of their ideas for the future.

[3] Brainstorming

What is it and why do it?

Brainstorming is a way to encourage creativity and to generate a lot of ideas very quickly. It can be used for solving a specific problem or answering a question. For example, the group could start a study of the right to citizenship by brainstorming answers to the question 'what reasons do you think a government might use for taking away someone's citizenship?' Some ideas for when to use it might be:

To find a solution to a problem. For example, after an 'incident' involving conflict between young people, ask the group to brainstorm all pertinent conflict resolution alternatives. To introduce a new subject. Brainstorm everything that the members already know about the subject. This is a good way to arouse their interest and find out what they already know. As a quick creative exercise. For example, brainstorm possible endings for an unfinished story.

How to do it?

Decide on the issue you want to brainstorm. Formulate a question which will have a variety of possible answers. Write the question where everyone can see it. For example: 'In what ways can we improve our group meeting place?'

Ask members to contribute their ideas. Write the ideas where everyone can see them. These should be single words or short phrases.

Tell the participants that in a brainstorm they can't comment on each other's ideas until the end, or repeat ideas which have already been said.

Encourage everyone to contribute, but do **NOT** move around the group in a circle, or force people to think of an idea - this is likely to discourage creativity.

Don't judge the ideas as you write them down. If possible, ask someone else to write them. Only give your own ideas if it is necessary to encourage others.

If a suggestion is unclear, ask the person to clarify it, or suggest a clarification *and check that they agree with it.*

Write down **EVERY** new suggestion. Often, the most creative or outrageous suggestions are the most useful and interesting!

Stop the brainstorm when ideas have run out. **NOW**, you can go through the suggestions, asking for comments.

Remind peers that constructive criticism is welcome so long as it is done with consideration of others feelings.

[4] Whole Group Discussion

What is it and why do it?

Discussions are a good way for the peer leader and the group members to discover what their attitudes are about human rights issues. This is very important for human rights education, because as well as knowing the facts, young people also need to explore and analyze issues for themselves. Discussions are also an opportunity to practice listening, speaking in turn and other group skills which are important for respecting other people's rights. In order to have an open discussion, it is important to have an atmosphere of trust and mutual respect and understanding. One way to help create a 'safe' environment is to develop 'Rules for Discussion'. This is best done at the beginning of the education programme, when standards of behavior are normally being established, but these rules can be created at any time.

How to do it?

Ask the group members if they want to feel free to express themselves and to learn through discussion with each other. (This subject might come up naturally following a difficult discussion.)

Suggest that it might be possible for the group to reach a common understanding of the best ways for listening and speaking.

Ask for some principles for discussion which they think everyone should follow. Write all of these suggestions where everyone can see them.

After the members have brainstormed for a while, look and see if there are any suggestions which could be combined, and invite discussion or comment. If they have not been suggested by the group, you might want to suggest some of the following principles:

- listen to the person who is speaking
- only one person speaks at a time
- raise your hand to be recognized if you want to say something

- don't interrupt when someone is speaking
- when you disagree with someone, make sure that you differentiate between criticizing someone's idea and the person themselves
- do not laugh when someone is speaking (unless they make a joke!)
- encourage everyone to participate

Brainstorm possible consequences associated with rule breaking. Write these consequences down.

Suggest that the group agree by consensus to follow the rules that they have listed. They are then responsible for applying the rules to themselves and to other members of the group. If serious violations of the rules occur, the identified consequences will follow.

Write the list up neatly on a large piece of paper and keep it for the rest of the human rights education programme, to be referred to, added to or altered as necessary.

[5] Questioning

What is it and why do it?

Of course, questions are used all the time in education activities, but what sort of questions? Often, they are questions such as 'what did I just say?', which are used to by some teachers to control a class or to ensure student attentiveness. Other questions which are used a lot are so-called 'closed' questions. They have only one correct answer and are used to test knowledge. Many of the activities in this manual use discussions to explore human rights issues. In these discussions, the questions you ask are very important for encouraging participation and analysis and higher level thinking.

Here are some examples of 'open' questions which you could use. If you practice using them, they will become easier. The key point to remember is: "What do I want from this discussion? Yes and no answers, or an open, interesting debate?"

Hypothetical questions: 'What would you do/think if...?' These help people to imagine situations and stimulate thought.

Speculating: 'How might we help to solve this problem?'

Encouraging/supporting: 'That's interesting, what happened next?' These draw out individuals' own experience and views.

Opinion seeking: 'What do you think or feel about...?' This tells others that their opinion is important and interesting to you.

Probing: 'Why do you think that?' If asked in a non-aggressive way, this can help participants to think deeply and justify/analyse their opinions.

Clarifying/summarising: 'Am I right to say that you think...?' Summarising what a person said and checking if you understand it will help others to think whether they agree with what is being said.

Identifying agreement: 'Do most of us agree that...?' This can provoke discussion or can come at the end, where, by using a question like 'Have we finished that part...?', you can agree to move on to the next topic.

Finally, try to remember to avoid leading or trick questions such as 'X is correct, isn't it?'. These discourage participation. Asking too many questions at once or asking questions that are unclear should also be avoided. Always give participants sufficient time to formulate an opinion or thought before asking for a response.

And remember, an occasional nod, a smile or even just sitting on the same level as the participants, will improve the responses you get!

[6] Projects

What is it and why do it?

Projects are the independent investigation of topics by participants over an extended period, ending in a final product. Projects are useful for human rights education because they:

Help people to see links between separate subjects and between their school studies and the outside world.

Give young people practice at organising themselves for action, planning their own time and following a schedule.

Allow participants to take control of their own learning, with the guidance of the peer leader.

Create opportunities for young people to interact with each other and with diverse people in the community outside the peer group.

Give group members practice at presenting and defending their own findings and opinions in public - an important skill for promoting human rights.

How to do it?

Projects have distinct stages. Throughout, the emphasis is on allowing young people to take responsibility for their own study.

The topic or problem

These can be identified by the peer group leader, and presented to the group as choices, or chosen directly by the members of the group. You may want to begin with a brainstorming session. It is good to have a direct question on an issue of interest to young people. For example, 'Are foreign refugees in our town treated well?' or 'What do local parents fear most about young people and drugs?' The question needs to be specific to avoid group members getting 'lost' in the subject.

Alternatively, your starting point might be a particular sort of activity or equipment which you want group members to use during their project. For example, an audio tape machine.

Planning

Peer leaders and members need to decide when the project will begin, how long it will take, what resources will be used, where these can be found, whether members will work alone or in groups, on the same or different topics, and so on. People who are not used to doing research might find it easier to work in groups. It is very important to discuss at this stage how the project will be carried out (see below for more ideas about this).

Research/action

Project work builds a lot of skills very quickly. For example, an investigative project about local health care might involve visits, interviews, reading, taking photographs, collecting statistics, and analysing data. A creative project might involve technical knowledge, such as how to work a video camera, and artistic skill, such as banner-making. The best projects combine academic, social and creative skills to involve all the participants' abilities. The peer leader can help during this stage by answering questions or offering advice, but the young adults are responsible for doing the work.

The product

This might be a report, a film, an exhibition, an audio tape, a lecture, a painting, a poem.....It is a good idea if the product records not only the participants' findings but also the different stages of the project and the participants' own feelings about the topic being studied. For example, students making a poster campaign about alcohol abuse in their town could take photographs of themselves at work and write about how they chose and created their designs.

The product can be presented to the group, or to a wider audience. For example, a project about poverty in your area might interest the local newspaper or the municipal authorities might want to know the results of a project about environmental damage.

Evaluation

The group should review the projects undertaken, e.g. what did members learn from them?

[7] Buzz Session

What is it and why do it?

A "buzz session" can be used to change the pace of a human rights education activity. For example, after a long presentation by the peer leader. It is an opportunity to talk in pairs or threes.

How to do it?

Tell group members that for five minutes they can react to what has just been said or shown. They can say how they feel, what they think or ask each other questions about things they didn't understand. After the buzz session groups or pairs may be invited to share ideas or questions with the group.

[8] Pictures and Photographs

What is it and why do it?

Although the message behind a pictures or photograph may seem obvious, it can be open to interpretation. Photographs can be an extremely effective tool for learning. Seeing the physical realities of human right abuses may prompt a more pro-active attempt by group members to end such atrocities.

How to do it?

Give participants in pairs a picture to look at. Give the pairs five minutes to write down all the questions they have about it. Ask them to choose the four most important questions. The picture could be related to a topic which you are focusing on at the time.

Now ask each pair to show their picture and their four most important questions to the pair beside them. Give them ten minutes to work together to find answers to all of their questions.

Ask them to make two lists:

1. Questions they can't find an answer to.
2. Questions with a possible answer.

For the questions with a possible answer it is important that they write down **WHY** they chose this answer. For example, if they think that a child in a picture is from a cold country, what clues were there in the picture which helped them to decide this?

Make a display of all the pictures, questions and answers. Ask the group members to look at everyone else's picture, questions and answers, and make further comments where necessary.

Leave a space where other people can also comment and contribute their own ideas about the pictures.

[9] Cartoons and Comics

What is it and why do it?

Cartoons and comics can have a powerful influence on young people. They can entertain and inform or encourage prejudices and stereotypes. They can be used in human rights education in many different ways. In preparation, for example, for a discussion about violence in the media ask group members to count how many episodes of violence occur in cartoons and comics in a single week. Cartoons drawn by the young people themselves can also be used as a way to communicate human rights issues to the rest of the community.

How to do it?

Take cartoons/strips from newspapers, magazines, comics and adverts which relate to the subject being studied. For example, violence, intolerance, or racism. Ask participants to discuss them in groups. Then ask:

- What is your first emotional response?
- What is the message of the cartoon or comic story?
- Are the images effective in telling the story, expressing the point of view, or making people think about the issues?
- Does it criticize an idea, or a group of people?
- Does it include stereotypes or prejudices towards a particular group of people, such as women, ethnic groups, refugees, people with disabilities?
- Is it serious, humorous or ironic? How does this contribute to the message?

or

Ask participants to choose a human rights issue and draw a cartoon or comic strip about it. Ask them to try to present this topic in the most powerful way, so that the pictures will make people think about the issues.

Display the results.

[10] Video

Organisations like the Council of Europe and Amnesty International have produced video cassettes for use in human rights education. Parts of the TV programmes, News or a documentary can also be useful. Here are some suggestions to remember when using videos:

- Begin by previewing the video
- Create a series of questions based on the video which will help focus your discussion
- Share the questions with the group prior to watching the video
- Discuss upon completion
- If people process the information received from videos, they are more likely to remember it. For example, they could use their imagination to write a diary from the point of view of a character seen in the video. See the other methods in this part of the manual for ideas.

[11] Newspapers

What is it and why do it?

The media is an essential tool which enables the circulation of information in a democratic society. However sometimes we find reporting which is biased or one-sided and which uses stereotypes and prejudices. Identifying and analysing prejudice in newspapers prepares young people to become much more media literate in a media driven world. This sort of activity also improves members' communication skills.

How to do it?

Choose a current rights issue which receives a lot of media coverage in your country, for example, the treatment of minorities. Alternatively, choose a trend which lies behind several different stories, such as intolerance.

Divide the whole group into smaller groups of four or five.

Give each small group at least one story from local or national newspapers about the chosen topic.

If necessary, the same report can be used by all the groups. Reports from different newspapers about the same event are good for comparison.

Each group should read the article and identify the main arguments, opinions, facts.

The following questions can be considered:

- What was the article's main argument?
- Were there enough facts given to support arguments raised? What were they?
- What sources were cited? Were the sources credible ones?
- Were both sides of the issue adequately addressed?
- Was the article mainly opinion based? Is this a problem? Why or why not?
- Is the article biased? Explain.
- Ask each group to also discuss some questions from the following list. Select questions appropriate to the reports being used, or invent others:
- Does the title of the report suggest its view on the issue?
- What is your first impression of the situation described? Does anyone seem to be at fault? If so, who?
- Is someone being accused of having done something wrong?
- How much of the report criticizes someone?
- How much supports or defends them?
- Are there any direct quotes from the people who are being criticized?
- Which words do you think are the most important in creating your impression of the report?
- What impressions, if any, are given of ordinary people's views on the issue?
- What is the attitude of people in authority? For example, social workers, police, officials and so on.

This sort of analysis can be followed up in many ways. For example, through a wider discussion, or participants writing their own newspaper-style reports or comparing newspaper coverage of an issue with that on TV/radio.

You could also ask members to bring in interesting articles or stories they have found in newspapers. In this way, a collection can be formed, which can be used as a basis for group discussions.

[12] Word Association

What is it and why do it?

This method can be used with a class at the beginning of a topic to find out how much they already know about it, and at the end to find out how much they learned.

How to do it?

- Take a key word related to the issue being studied.
- Ask the students to quickly write down other words which they think of when they hear this word. This is a very short exercise, a minute or two is enough time.
- Make it clear that writing nothing at all is quite acceptable. The result is a 'snapshot' of the range of vocabulary which the students associate with the original trigger-word.
- To evaluate the learning process, 'before' and 'after' results can be compared. This can help you to evaluate your teaching, and your students can see the progress they are making.
- Alternatively, at the end of a topic, ask each student to say in one word what they think or feel about that topic. Or, ask for a word which relates to the topic. Go round the class gathering words. Ask one or two students to make a list of these words.

[13] Re-creating information

What is it and why do it?

A good way to internalise and understand information is to re-create it in another form. For example, to listen to a story and then tell it in pictures. Students will have to identify the most important part of the information and decide how to re-create it. The student has to decide, 'I'm going to do it this way because...'.

This technique helps to develop the imagination, as well as skills of observation, selection and reasoning.

How to do it?

- With the students, choose a source such as a story, a picture, a poem, a cartoon or a film. For example, if the class is studying the right to be with one's family, a picture of a refugee child could be used.
- Students read, look at or listen carefully to the original version.
- They decide which parts of the story to transfer to the new medium, and explain their choices. If you are using a picture, then they will need to imagine the story behind the picture.
- If they want to add things that were not in the original, they need to explain why.
- Students produce the new version.

Ideas for re-creation media

- a 'radio play', recorded on tape.
- a written short story.
- a story in comic strip form.
- a narrative poem.
- a painting
- a story told to the class, or to the rest of the school.
- a display for the classroom.

There is no single technique of teaching that works well with all the people for all the topics at all times. If there is one thing that always works, it is the attitude of the teacher towards the subject of human rights. A teacher with the right attitude puts students' learning as the ultimate goal and will mix and match all the available tools and techniques to suit the teaching-learning process unique to a given human right concept/issue. This is because teaching is not a job but an inspired profession or passion.

⌘❒⌘

11 Education for Human Rights – Activities

Teacher can design her own human rights education activities by keeping in mind the following points —

1. Select a general topic or theme. The topic could be from a current event (such as a local election), a theme that is of interest to students (tolerance) or an issue required in the formal curriculum.
2. Decide which **SKILLS, KNOWLEDGE** and **ATTITUDES** the students need to develop around this topic. Write these down.
3. Choose the most appropriate **METHOD** of teaching or the materials on which you want to base the lesson. It might help to focus on a core activity, around which the lesson will be built. This activity might involve conventional activities such as students reading text and responding to it in discussion and essays, or less conventional activities such as a research project, the use of newspapers, the organisation of a debate, or the writing of a poem.
4. Write an outline of the different stages which you would like to have in the lesson. Most activities in this chapter have the following structure:
   - warm-up, motivation exercise (such as open-ended questions)
   - concrete task (done individually or in small groups)
   - whole group discussion (following presentation of small group work, if appropriate)
   - ending and follow-up assignments
5. Now think what previous knowledge the students will need. Also, think how you will evaluate the activity. Remember to estimate the time for each part of the activity.
6. Now return to your original list of goals. Have you covered them all in your preparation? Think about having an overall balance between discussion, thought and action in the classroom.

[1] Starting up – Introductory Activities

Because several of the activities in this chapter refer to the Universal Declaration of Human Rights, here are two activities to help familiarize the group with it.

Activities should be chosen or adapted to suit the needs of your group.

The Imaginary Country

(This activity is based on ideas from Ed OBrien and Nancy Flowers)

This activity is appropriate for ages 14-18 and 18 plus.

Aim

This activity introduces participants to the idea of rights based on needs, and familiarizes them with the Universal Declaration of Human Rights. It raises ideas of how we value rights, and that the 'Choices' we make give options for establishing more permanent 'group rights'.

Learning points

- Human Rights documents are based on our own inherent needs.
- We value some rights more highly depending on our own situation, but every right is important to someone.

What you need?

- Simplified Version of the Universal Declaration of Human Rights.

Time

About an hour and a quarter for the basic activity.

How to do it?

Form into small groups of five or six.

Read out the following scenario:

"Imagine that you have discovered a new country, where no one has lived before and where there are no laws and no rules. You and the other members of your group will be the settlers in this new land. You do not know what social position you will have in the new country." ? Each participant should individuall / list three rights which they think should be guaranteed for everyone in this new country. Now ask the participants to share and discuss their lists within the group, and select a list of 10 rights which their whole group thinks are important.

Now, ask each group to give their country a name and to write their 10 chosen rights on a large piece of paper or on a blackboard where everyone can see them. Each group presents their list to the whole group. As they do this, make a 'master list' which should include all of the different rights from the group lists. Some rights will be mentioned several times. Write them on the master list once, and tick them each time they are repeated. When all the groups have presented their lists, identify rights on the master list which overlap or contradict one another. Can the list be rationalized? Can some similar rights be grouped together? When the master list is completed, compare the Simplified Version of the Universal Declaration of Human Rights. What are the differences/similarities between your list and the UDHR?

Use the following questions to draw out the learning points. The choices below give options for extending the activity.

Questions

- Did your ideas about which rights were most important change during this activity?
- How would life be if we excluded some of these rights?
- Are there any rights which you now want to add to the final list?
- Did anyone list a right themselves which was not included in any of the lists?
- Why is it useful for us to make such a list?

Choices

If you have time, ask participants to put a mark next to the three rights on the master list which they personally think are most important, or which they think we could not live without. (This could be done during a group break.)

This activity has been used in many different countries. In countries were war is a problem, students value the right to life most highly, while in those with economic problems the right to work comes first. You can explore this issue with the participants by asking question such as: Do you think the situation in our country has affected your choices of rights? Why? Why not?

This activity can be adapted into a project format. Participants make a list of 'group rights' which they think would improve their school environment. For example, the right to work in peace, the right to have your point of view respected the right to privacy for your personal property.... Be open to their suggestions, but emphasize that all rights have corresponding responsibilities. This living document could be displayed and updated as necessary. Ask the group, what do you think should happen if someone violates these rights?

[2] Rights in the News

(Based on a demonstration by Nancy Flowers)

This activity is appropriate for ages 14-18 and 18 plus.

Aim

This activity is a good introduction for people who might already have some understanding of what human rights are. It helps them to recognize rights and to place everyday situations in a human rights frame-work.

Learning point

Rights on paper relate to everyday situations.

What you need?

Old newspapers and magazines of all kinds, enough for small groups to have at least one each, Blackboard or large piece of paper and pens, Universal Declaration of Human Rights and the Simplified Version of the Universal Declaration of Human Rights **(given at the end of the chapter)**.

Time: One hour.

How to do it?

Read the following text to the group:

In our modern world, we all have access to more information than ever before. For most of us, this information comes through the media, and especially via the news. Everyday, TV screens and newspapers are filled with situations and stories which are hopeful, tragic, happy, sad, simple or complex. Usually, we look at the terrible news stories and feel powerless. However, by looking again, using the ideas of human rights, we can see patterns of success, where rights are protected and acted upon, and patterns of problems, where rights are denied.

Form small groups of four.

Distribute the newspapers and magazines randomly.

Using the whole of the blackboard/large paper draw a large circle. On the circumference of the circle write the following three phrases in such a way that they are as far away from each other as possible. (This allows lots of room for newspaper cuttings to be stuck up later).

Three phrases:

- Rights denied
- Rights protected
- Rights in action

Ask the groups to look through their newspapers and magazines to find things which illustrate each of the three phrases. Encourage the participants to use all parts of the magazines and newspapers, including advertisements, classified adverts and other items.

Offer the participants the following examples:

Rights denied

This could be an article complaining that a municipal health clinic has been closed without consulting the local community. This would illustrate the denial of the right to health or even life.

Rights protected

This could be a story about children who have been rescued from people who were mistreating them.

Rights in action

This could be a picture of a footballer scoring a goal, illustrating the rights to leisure, health, freedom of association, or even travel (if it is an international match.)

When the task has been completed (usually after about 10 minutes) ask the participants to look at the Universal Declaration of Human Rights or its Simplified Version (**given at the end of the chapter**). to find the article or articles which relate to the stories or pictures which they have found in the newspapers. Allow another 10 minutes for this part of the activity.

Now, ask each group in turn to stick up the findings on the blackboard/large paper. As they do this, they should explain why they chose that example and which specific UDHR articles it relates to. Some of the selected examples will involve situations where the same right or rights are denied, protected, and in action all at the same time! Use the questions below to help the group to analyze these situations.

Questions

- Was it easy to find examples to illustrate rights denied, rights protected and rights in action?

- Was one phrase more difficult to illustrate? Why?
- Were there any newspaper articles or other examples where all three phrases could be said to be relevant? Which? Why?
- Were there any examples where one person or a group had their rights protected and this resulted in someone else's rights being denied? Could the concept that my rights end where yours begin and *vice versa* be useful in such a situation? Would using this concept give a better result for all concerned? Why? Why not?

Choices

As a project peer group members could examine international efforts to protect the rights of civilians in conflict situations, or the defence of the rights of a vulnerable group in your local area.

(**Note:** Although young people need to know that rights are often denied, it is important for them to develop knowledge of how they are protected if they are to feel that the defence of human rights is possible.)

[3] Living Together – Activities about Respect

These activities emphasize that the way we choose to interact with others on an every day basis has a direct effect on respect for human rights. A game with rules raises questions about how laws are made, and an activity about listening focuses on the right to an opinion and the responsibility to respect the opinions of others.

Activities should be chosen or adapted to suit the needs of your group.

Camping Out

(Adapted from an idea in Understand the Law 1994, The Citizenship Foundation)

This activity is appropriate for 14-18 year olds.

Aim

This game helps young people understand how communities develop rules and laws to protect people's rights.

Learning points

Rules of conduct prevent conflict and protect rights.

Such rules are best made democratically.

What you need?

A copy of the 'situations' from the next few pages for each group.

Time: About one and a half hours.

How to do it?

Form into small groups of five or six.

Tell the group:

"Imagine that you are going on a camping trip with a group of friends. Someone has told you about a wonderful location for a camp, a clearing in the woods near a lake, far from civilization. You have been planning together for several weeks, and finally the weekend arrives. After a long journey, you arrive at the clearing. You have brought everything you need for your holiday, including one large tent for all of you to sleep in. There is a well nearby with good water, and you have permission to cut wood and make fires. There are no other facilities, no rules, and no adults or camp administrator. You set up camp, swim, and prepare for a week of fun!

However, by the end of the first day at the campsite, there have already been some disagreements about how the camp should be run. You all realize that it would be better if you could agree on ways to make your holiday easier. You hold a meeting."

Ask the participants in their groups to see if they can think of four or five problems that their group might face. Ask them to decide how each problem could be solved.

Ask the participants to consider the following questions:

- How did they make their decisions?
- Did anyone disagree?
- Did everyone have an equal say? Why or why not?
- What was the most difficult decision made? Why?

Now, read the following text to the participants:

"After the meeting, all goes well and things are much better. However, after a couple of days, more problems arise, which together you have to sort out to prevent them from happening again." If you are able to copy the 'situations', distribute a set of them to each group. In their groups the participants should place all the 'situations' face down on the table and take them up one at a time. They should try to reach a decision about what to do in each 'situation.' If possible they should try to agree. (If you were unable to hand-copy or photocopy the 'situations', read them out one by one, and try to reach a decision as a group, although this will be more difficult).?If some groups finish the game more quickly than others, ask them to think about the discussion questions below.

When all the groups have finished playing the game, go through the 'situations' asking the whole group what decisions they made. Don't ask every group to comment on every 'situation' – that would take too long.

Follow the activity with a discussion using the questions below:

Questions

In this activity you used rules to protect the rights of everyone in the camp. What would have happened if you were unable to agree on rules or if everyone ignored the rules?

What makes a rule appropriate or not?

What about laws? Should you always obey laws, even if they are unfair or bad?

Some rules and laws are unwritten, for example, 'moral' or religious laws. Why do groups of people obey these rules/laws, even though they don't have to?

Rules and laws are usually enforced by a punishment or sanction. You probably decided to use sanctions against people who broke the rules in the camp. What is the aim of sanctions? What sort of sanctions are most effective? Can sanctions be counter-productive?

Choices

This activity could be the starting-point for making a set of group rules, which are agreed by the peer group members and the peer leader in a participatory way. In many countries, execution is the punishment for all sorts of 'crimes', from murder to offences such as trading on the black market. This activity can be a starting-point for a discussion about whether or not execution is a real deterrent for crime.

Situation Cards for "Camping Out" Activity

Situation One

Someone has to sleep near the door of the tent, which doesn't close properly. By the morning, this person's belongings have usually spilled out of the opening onto the wet grass. He or she complains that their belongings will be damaged. What do you do?

Situation Two

You all agreed at the meeting how the camp should be run. Now, one of you takes no notice of what was decided. How can you enforce the rules?

Situation Three

Someone left the kettle boiling on the fire and went away to swim. The kettle fell into the fire and sparks set fire to a corner of your tent. You all realise that you have a safety problem. There may be others. What do you do?

Situation Four

Getting water from the well is a very boring job. Everyone would prefer to go swimming than fetch water. However, one of you strains your arm while swimming and can not carry water anymore. This means that the rest of you will each have to spend more time carrying water. What do you do?

Situation Five

Two of you are smokers, the others are not. The non-smokers strongly object to the smell of smoke in the tent but the smokers feel they should be able to smoke while they are relaxing. What do you do?

Situation Six

One of you has brought a radio and plays loud music early in the morning. This makes everyone angry. What do you do?

Situation Seven

You all share one tent, but cannot agree about keeping it tidy. Some like the tent to be neat all the time, the others do not. The arguments are affecting the atmosphere in the camp. What do you do?

Situation Eight

Someone damages an expensive guitar belonging to someone else. She or he refuses to pay for the repairs. What do you do?

Situation Nine

A friend of yours joins you for a couple of days. She or he has brought their own tent, but ignores the rules which everyone else has agreed upon. What do you do?

Situation Ten

Two of you feel that the camp should have a rule about alcohol and drinking. You ask for a meeting to discuss the matter. Most of you are against a complete ban. What do you do?

[4] Active Listening

This activity is appropriate for 14-18 year olds.

Aim

This listening activity helps young people to improve their listening and to think about what results in effective and ineffective listening skills.

Learning points

Listening is an important skill for respecting each others right to an opinion. (See Article 12 of the Convention on the Rights of the Child, and Article 19 of the Universal Declaration of Human Rights).

We can improve our listening skills by practice.

What you need?

The boxes what helps us to listen? What prevents us from listening?

Time: About 30 minutes.

How to do it?

A group member is asked to volunteer to lead the exercise.

This individual is given a sheet of paper with rectangles drawn in different directions on the sheet. All of the rectangles are attached in one way or another. There are no independent or free standing rectangles. The rectangles can be horizontal, diagonal, or vertical. The task of this individual is to describe the image only using words, and without using hand gestures. The Group members are asked to draw the image, but are **not** allowed to ask questions. The volunteer describes the image a second time and the group members draw the image again. This time group members are encouraged to ask one question at a time.

This activity should give way to the importance of clear, concise, communication, and the obstacles that prevent the transmission of an effective message.

Questions

- What difficulties did you experience the first time in drawing the image?
- What would have improved your ability to draw the image effectively?
- What has this taught you about communication?
- When and where could this be useful to you?

Listening is an important skill for respecting and protecting human rights, it is especially important for Article 12 of the Convention on the Rights of the Child, and Article 19 of the Universal Declaration of Human Rights, but also for all of the other Articles. Why is this so? What do we gain from listening to each other? Have you ever been in a situation where no-one would listen to you? How do we feel when our opinion is ignored? Do you agree with the idea that we can improve our listening skills by practice?

Choices

It can be fun to repeat the game, making it harder every time, over several days or weeks, so that group members can see their listening improve.

What prevents us from listening?

On-off Listening

People think faster than they talk. This means that when you listen to someone, you have a lot of spare time for thinking. Often, we use this time to think about lunch, or what we did last night, instead of thinking about what the other person is saying!

Prejudice Listening

In every part of the world, there are words or phrases which cause people to stop listening. Words like 'capitalist', 'communist', 'fundamentalist.' When people hear these words, they stop listening and start to plan their defence, or a counter-attack.

Closed Mind Listening

Sometimes, we decide quickly that the person (or the subject) is boring, wrong, or not relevant, or that we know what they are going to say. Then, we stop listening.

Distracted Listening

Noise, lights, temperature, other things in the room, or what you ate for breakfast can all prevent us from listening to what people are saying. However, with practice, we can still listen well under these circumstances.

What helps us to listen?

We listen with our bodies as well as with our minds...

- face the speaker
- have good eye contact
- have an open posture (don't fold your arms, turn your back......)
- lean towards the speaker
- relax

Listen to what is being said...

- listen for the central theme, not just the 'facts'
- keep an open mind
- think ahead
- analyze and evaluate
- don't interrupt

Listen to how it is being said...

- non-verbal signs (for example face expressions, body posture)
- tone of voice

Listening is important because...

- It shows people that you value their experiences and what they are say
- It encourages people to talk honestly and freely
- It can help you to identify areas where people agree or disagree, and helps you to think of solutions to these disagreements

[5] Who, me? – Activities about Responsibility

These activities emphasize personal responsibility. A real-life moral dilemma is used to raise questions about honesty and everyday responsibility. Another activity about censorship looks at the responsible use of power. The overall aim of these activities is to show that rights have corresponding responsibilities.

Activities should be chosen or adapted to suit the needs of your group.

Rights and Responsibilities

This activity is appropriate for ages 14-18 and 18 plus.

Aim

This short listing and discussion activity helps young people to understand the connection between rights and responsibilities.

Learning point

Every right has a corresponding responsibility.

What you need?

Simplified Version of the Universal Declaration of Human Rights. **(given at the end of the chapter).**

Information about Rights and Responsibilities (see next page).

Time: Forty-five minutes.

How to do it?

Ask the group to form into pairs. Each person should write down five important rights which they think they should have in the group and five important rights which they think they should have at home, for example, the right to their own space. (This could be done as a reflection exercise which recalls previous work on human rights.) Ask each person to swop their list with their partner. Each participant should think of the responsibilities which correspond with each right that their partner listed, for example, the responsibility to respect the space of the people they live with. Every pair reports to the rest of the group two rights and their corresponding responsibilities from their lists. The peer leader should write the rights and responsibilities on the wall. Ask the participants to read the Information about Rights and Responsibilities. Start a discussion using the following questions:

Questions

- Was it easy or hard to think of each right's corresponding responsibility?
- In the example about seatbelts (see Information about Rights and Responsibilities), who do you think is right, the government or the people who refuse to wear seatbelts?
- What if someone you knew was injured because a driver refused to wear a seatbelt? How might this happen? How would you feel? ?What if a sick

child died because the doctor was too busy helping a driver who had refused to wear a seatbelt and was injured? Look at the Simplified Version of the Universal Declaration of Human Rights. Which rights are involved in this example? Can you think of similar examples where other rights and responsibilities conflict?

Choices

Because issues of rights and responsibilities affect everyone (for example the right to give your views and the responsibility to respect the views of others) this activity can be the basis for using the language of rights and responsibility in everyday situations. As an action, the group can keep the list of rights and equivalent responsibilities on the wall. When conflicts occur, or when other rights issues come up, anyone is free to add to the list. For example, if some group members have been borrowing other people's possessions without permission, one person might decide to add to the list. I have the right to privacy and security for my belongings/and I also have the responsibility to respect the privacy and security of my group members. It might be useful to write at the top of the list: We all have the right to add to this list/and we have the responsibility not to write things which violate the rights of others.

To help clarify rights and responsibilities, group members could read the following information on 'Negative' and 'Positive' rights, then go through the Universal Declaration of Human Rights identifying 'Negative' and 'Positive' rights (they will find that many rights consist equally of 'negative' (responsibility) and 'positive' (right) elements.

Information about Rights and Responsibilities

Every right has a corresponding responsibility. For example, your right to freedom of speech is limited by your responsibility not to say untrue things which will degrade another person and abuse their right to dignity and good reputation. The balance of our rights and our responsibilities to respect the rights of other people means that we usually have to exercise our rights within certain restraints. There are many situations where rights and responsibilities of different people conflict, for example, some countries have laws making the wearing of seatbelts compulsory in cars. Many people oppose these laws, arguing that it is a restriction of their right to act freely. The governments of these countries argue that people in cars have a responsibility to the hospitals, doctors, and the rest of society to do everything possible to avoid getting injured while they are driving. It is argued that if people do not wear seatbelts and are injured, they take time, money and hospital space away from people with illnesses, and therefore restrict the right of sick people to proper health care.

Information on "Negative" and "Positive" Rights:

The term "negative right" is used to describe a right which stops something harmful or unpleasant being done to us. Examples of negative rights are the right not to be killed or badly treated or to have your possessions stolen. These are negative rights because they say NO to someone who might want to hurt you.

The term "positive right" is used to describe a right which declares our freedom to do something, for example, the right to be paid for your work is a positive right. These are positive rights because they tell you that **YES** you have this right, and they tell other people that **YES** they must support your right. For example, your employer has a responsibility to pay you.

[6] Sample Lesson on Stereotyping

Aims/Learning Points

(**Note:** you can think about these in terms of skills, knowledge and attitudes if you like.)

Knowledge

Participants will distinguish between generalizations and stereotypes.

Skill

They will identify examples of stereotypes in their local media.

Understanding

They will develop sensitivities for those groups that are negatively stereotyped.

Knowledge the participants should already have

Some general understanding of culture, generalizations and stereotypes.

What you will need?

Blackboard or large sheets of paper.

Newspapers and magazines.

Time: 45 minutes.

How to do it?

Introduction (10 minutes)

The peer leader writes down certain categories of people (old person, girl, boy, handicapped person) and asks group members to suggest descriptive words which define these groups. These are written so that everyone can see them.

The leader summarizes these views, looking for links within categories, and decides with the members if the attributes mentioned are positive, negative or neutral.

He or she explains the difference between a generalization and a stereotype.

The leader asks the members: 'Where do you think you got these views?' 'From your own experience, or from mass media, or from family and friends?'

Group work (10 minutes)

Participants break into groups of five or six. Each group can be given a newspaper and magazine, or groups can consider different mass media, including popular television programmes or books. Participants go through the materials, looking for representations of certain groups - both in the text and in the pictures. The groups could be the ones used at the start of the introduction, but also other groups known to be discriminated against in your society. Stereotypes could be positive, negative or neutral in nature.

Groups make their presentations to the larger group (10 minutes).

Discussion (10 minutes)

Ask the group as a whole to answer the following questions:

'What similarities did you find between the groups that were positively stereotyped?' 'What about those that were negatively stereotyped?'

The leader might take the opportunity to point out that:

generalizations about certain groups are negative, and these can be called prejudices

negative generalizations about whole groups of people are often not based on actual, personal contact with the group

Conclusion (5 minutes)

- 'What are the sources of these stereotypes?'
- 'What conclusions can be drawn about generalizations and stereotypes, based on this activity?'

(For example, that generalizations and stereotypes are found in many parts of the culture, in mass media, in the opinions of friends and family. That negative stereotypes are based on fear, and positive ones on envy.)

Follow-up

Participants might write something short about an occasion when they felt that they were stereotyped in either a positive or negative way. How did this make them feel?

Evaluation

Your evaluation criteria for this activity could be:

- how did individuals contribute to group discussion
- how did individual members participate/co-operate in group work
- result of group work (group mark)
- written follow-up

Adapting your session

Be somewhat flexible in how you do your activities. Some parts of a session will excite group members more than others and you might be surprised to discover certain discussions or stages of the activity are particularly useful to young people and therefore take longer. An activity should be designed as an 'accordion', with individual parts able to be expanded or contracted depending upon the response of the participants. After trying the activity, make notes for yourself so that you can adjust it next time.

[7] Thief?

(Adapted from p.82 of Understand the Law 1993, The Citizenship Foundation)

This activity is appropriate for ages 14-18 and 18 plus.

Aim

This case study uses a moral dilemma to introduce young people to ideas of responsibility in society. Although the person in the case study is accidentally overpaid a large amount, many young people will have been given the wrong change in a shop and had to make a similar choice.

Learning point

Every right has a corresponding responsibility, for example, the right to be judged equally by the law has the corresponding responsibility to respect the law.

What you need?

The Simplified Version of the Universal Declaration of Human Rights. **(given at the end of the chapter).**

Time: At least one hour.

How to do it?

Form into small groups of five or six.

Read the following text to the group:

"Every month Alexander puts a small part of his wages into his account at the local bank. It's not a lot, but it is the only way he can save enough for a holiday with his children. Each month the bank sends Alexander a statement telling him how much he has in his account. This month Alexander sees that he has much more money than he thought. There must be a mistake. He writes to the bank to say it has given him $2,000 more than it should have. 'No,' says the bank, 'there has been no mistake. The money is yours.' Alexander writes again. 'We have double checked,' says the bank, 'we have not made a mistake.' Alexander still isn't happy. He writes for a third time, and the bank tells him again that the money is his. After this, Alexander doesn't think he has anything to lose. He starts to spend the money on things he and his family need. He buys some new furniture, redecorates his flat and goes away on a week's holiday with his family. A little later, the people at the bank realize that they have made a mistake. The $2,000 that Alexander has been given belongs to another customer who has the same name. The bank asks Alexander for the money back. He gives them what he has left, but he has spent more than $1,000. Alexander is charged with theft".

If Alexander is to be found legally guilty of theft, it must be proved in court that he:

- behaved dishonestly
- took or kept something belonging to someone else
- intended to keep it permanently.

Ask the participants to decide in groups

Whether Alexander should be found guilty of theft? To answer this; they need to ask three questions:

- Did Alexander behave dishonestly?
- Did Alexander take something from someone else?
- Did Alexander intend to keep it?

If the answer to all three questions is **yes**, then Alexander is guilty in law.

If the participants answered **no** to one or more questions then he is not guilty.

If the participants decide that Alexander is guilty under the law of theft, what punishment do they think he should be given?

If the participants decide that Alexander is not guilty, would they make him pay back the money that he spent on his family and his home?

Now, explain to the group what actually happened to Alexander:

"After a three day trial, the jury found Alexander not guilty of theft. Juries don't have to give reasons for their verdict, but we can presume that Alexander's attempts to draw the error to the attention of the bank convinced the jury that he had not behaved with dishonest intent.

Although Alexander was found not guilty of theft, there still remained the question of whether he should return the money that he had already spent. It was not within the power of the court to deal with this and the bank needed to bring a new case through a different court to reclaim the money."

Questions

- What would you have done if you were Alexander? Why?
- Who was responsible for correcting the bank's mistake - Alexander or the bank? Why?
- Would it make a difference to your answer if the amount of money was smaller/larger?
- What about other cases? For example, is it the responsibility of a car owner to lock her or his car or the responsibility of everyone else not to steal it if it is unlocked?
- Imagine you were a friend of Alexander's. Would you report him to the police?
- Who is responsible for enforcing the law?
- Look at the Simplified Version of the Universal Declaration of Human Rights (given at the end of the chapter).
- Which rights are involved in this case?

Choices

As a project, the group could find out about the legal system in your country. Many courtrooms accept visitors. The project could result in a mock trial of a case involving rights and responsibilities.

[8] Let Me Speak!

This activity is appropriate for ages 14-18 and 18 plus.

Aim

This letter-writing activity examines the rights and responsibilities of the individual and the state regarding freedom of expression. Because it depends a lot on trust between the peer group members and the peer leader, it is better to use it only when the group has already had experience of other activities in human rights education. Make sure that group members are aware that some might feel uncomfortable doing this exercise and that they do not have to participate if they do not want to.

Learning points

Every right has a corresponding responsibility.

For example, the right to freedom of expression has the corresponding responsibility to respect the opinion of others.

Time: An hour and a half.

What you need?

The Simplified Version of the Universal Declaration of Human Rights. **(given at the end of the chapter).**

The Information on Censorship from the next page.

How to do it?

Ask the group members to imagine that they are each writing to the local newspaper. (If your area does not have a local newspaper, you can invent one with the group, including the title, the frequency it is printed, etc). Ask them to write a short letter about something which they do not like at all in their local area. Explain that these letters will not be seen by anyone outside the group. Make sure that they are not.

After the participants have written their letters, form the group into pairs. Ask each pair to exchange their letters. Now ask them to imagine that they are all editors of the local newspaper. They have received this letter which they are worried will upset the local authorities and the Mayor. Ask them to cross out (censor) the parts of the letter which they think are dangerous. They are allowed to change the letter in any way they like.

Return all the letters to those who wrote them. Either as a whole group, or in smaller groups, discuss the questions below. After the discussion, go through the Information on Censorship and ask the group to think of a scenario to illustrate each of the points, for example, under 'WHAT is being censored' the information lists,'artists'. Ask the participants why they think someone would want to censor an artist. If your country has censorship now or in the past, refer to that, giving specific examples.

Questions

- Did you use some self-censorship before you wrote your letter? Why/ Why not?
- Did you use polite or offensive language?
- If you wrote a polite letter, was it because you felt responsible toward the feelings of others or was it because you were afraid of possible punishment?
- Were you thinking more about how to improve the situation or did you just want to show your anger?
- How did you feel when your letter was censored?
- How did your letter look after censorship?
- How did you choose what to cross out on your friend's letter?
- How do you think you would react if you were a local official who received a letter of complaint?
- What if the letter attacked your personality or used offensive language?
- Do you think a government has a responsibility to listen to all complaints, even if they are –
- 'dangerous'? Why/ Why not?
- Was your letter 'dangerous'?
- Why do you think we did this activity?

Choices

As a project ask the group to monitor newspapers over a period of time. They could choose one news item and compare how different newspapers write about the same issue according to their bias. If members feel strongly about an issue which they see in the newspapers, they could write a polite letter to the media as a group to express their point of view.

[9] Information about Censorship

Freedom of expression is a human right set out in the Universal Declaration of Human Rights.

Many people believe that it is the heart of a democratic society. Others say that too much freedom of expression can be dangerous. In many countries, free speech is controlled when it causes violence by inciting riots, calling on people to revolt, or when it is racist or bigoted. In some countries, criticism of the government is also censored.

Who is doing the censoring?

- official censors
- the government
- the law
- the media
- civil servants
- employers
- unions
- pressure groups

What is being censored?

- information
- access to information
- expression
- collective action
- attacks upon accepted values
- artists
- writers
- political opposition
- critics of society

WHY censorship is carried out?

- to cover up incompetence and/or information - to defend status quo
- to protect government policy - to protect privilege
- to defend the vulnerable, for example, juveniles - to preserve power

How censorship is carried out?

- by stopping something from being carried out (preemptive censorship)
- by punishment after the event (punitive censorship)

When censorship is carried out?

- Before an election
- At a time of rapid social change
- During a period of national/international crisis
- When a government is weak and under threat

What would you do?

This activity is appropriate for ages 14-18 and 18 plus.

Aim

This case study about a political killing encourages participants to discuss the responsibilities of the state and of the individual.

Learning point

Every right has a corresponding responsibility. For example, the right to personal security has a corresponding responsibility to defend this right for other people.

What you need?

Case Study: Luis Diaz

Information about political killings

Text: What happened?

Time: About one hour.

How to do it?

Read, or ask the group members to read the Case of Luis Diaz. Tell them that deaths like Luis's are called extrajudicial executions or political killings. Read, or ask each person to read, the Information about Political Killings from next page.

Luis's family wants to bring the people responsible for his death to justice. The army doesn't want this to happen. Ask participants to discuss in groups of four or five why the family and the army have these points of view. Here are some questions to help the government, Luis, the soldier who shot him?

- How would it affect other members of the security forces if the guilty soldiers were punished?

- If the guilty soldiers are punished, would the power of the government, security forces and army increase or decrease? What about their image?
- What if they are not punished? Will the army lose the trust of the people?
- Does it matter if the army loses the trust of the people?
- Do you think it is all right to say that soldiers cannot be prosecuted for killing anyone, even under these circumstances?

If the soldiers are not punished, what effect will this have on the public's perception of the legal system (courts, judges, etc.)? Ask the participants to imagine that they were hiding nearby when Luis was killed. They saw the face of the soldier who shot him, but were not seen themselves. What would you do in this situation? Would you:

- go home and forget all about it? Would this be possible?
- go to a police station and report it?
- tell Luis' family or someone else what you saw?
- do something else? What? Why?

At the end of this activity, you can read the text *What happened?* (on the next page).

Choices

Ask the group to imagine that they are friends, family, or colleagues of someone who has been extrajudicially executed. Ask them to write a poem or a story or paint a picture to show how these people might feel. As a project ask the participants in groups to pretend that one of them is a journalist who has come to ask Luis Diaz's family about his death. Each group should prepare a small drama about the meeting with the journalist.

Some questions to think about are:

- Do they want to talk to the journalist? Is it dangerous? Can they trust him/her?
- What does the journalist want? What is his/her point of view about the killing?
- Can the journalist help to publicise the killing? Do the relatives/friends/colleagues of Luis want this?

Each group can present their drama for the others.

The Case of Luis Diaz

On 17 September 1992 Luis Enrique Landa Díaz, a 21 year old medical student at Carabobo State University in Aragua, Venezuela, was celebrating the medical school's 17th anniversary with fellow students and staff. According to witnesses, there was a verbal disagreement- at a distance – between some of the students and the National Guards who were patrolling the area. Twenty members of the National Guard began firing teargas at the students.

At 2.30 per minute the guards started to shoot live ammunition in the direction of the students. The whole incident was recorded on video. Luis Landa was killed by a bullet a few minutes later.

An official investigation was opened into the killing and a member of the National Guard was identified as a suspect. Proceedings were opened by the military and civilian courts. However, in March 1993 the military courts requested exclusive jurisdiction (power) over the case.

In the past, the military courts have repeatedly exonerated members of the security forces accused of human rights violations. (They were not convicted of any crime). Luis Landa's family, who sought publicity for his killing, were the target of systematic harassment.

They received threatening phone calls and shots were fired at their house. In December 1992, Luis Landa's father was shot in the knee by a group of armed men in a car.

Information about Political Killings

The term 'extrajudicial execution' describes an unlawful deliberate killing carried out on the orders of a government or with its knowledge. If the authorities refuse to investigate an unjustifiable killing by the security forces or bring those who have committed the crime to justice, then it is an extrajudical execution for which the government is responsible. The term 'political killing' can also be used as it is more easily understood and includes deliberate killings by armed political groups. Political killings are different from killings which occur within a legally justifiable context. If someone is killed as the result of soldiers acting in self-defence, or by police during a riot, then the killing may be legally justifiable. Also, when someone is executed after being found guilty in a fair trial, the state responsible will argue that the killing is legally justifiable. Also, if a soldier kills for personal reasons and is punished like any other murderer, the killing he committed is not an extrajudical execution. Also, killing enemy soldiers during fighting is legal. Many governments who use political killings are bound by treaties pledging them to respect human rights. Some governments do not try to justify their actions. Some use methods of murder which conceal the crime. Killings are carried out at night, when the victims are alone. Bodies are mutilated and hidden to avoid recognition. But most governments lie or play down the facts. In June 1989, tanks of the Chinese army massacred pro-democracy protesters in Tiananmen Square, Beijing. Television cameras recorded it and it was headline news around the world. Thousands of people witnessed it. Hundreds of bodies were traced in morgues and hospitals. Nevertheless, the government initially said no one had been killed. This version was later changed: the government said 200 civilians had been killed in Beijing in clashes between soldiers and demonstrators, a gross underestimate of the reality. Some governments make the excuse that violence is everywhere in their societies, or results from ethnic tensions. Violence will be in any society where human rights are violated. Intercommunal violence is therefore, not the inevitable product of ethnic or religious tensions. It often starts or is made worse because of official policies.

What happened?

Luis' case was taken up by the human rights organisation Amnesty International. As part of the Amnesty International campaign on the case, ordinary people from all over the world wrote letters to the government of Venezuela asking for action on Luis' death and for an end to the harassment of his family. In July 1995, the National Guardsman who shot Luis was sentenced by a civilian court to eighteen years imprisonment, pending appeal. Luis' father said that this was: ...thanks to international pressure... I had already lost hope....The threats and attacks had nearly finished me off. That all changed with your campaign.

[10] Rights for Life – Activities about the Universality of Rights

These activities help young people to understand that all human beings have the same rights.

Our rights can be violated, but they cannot be taken away from us. We are born with them and die with them.

Activities should be chosen or adapted to suit the needs of your group.

Wheel rights

(Adapted from Human Rights Education Workshop on Women's Human Rights and Gender Equality, presented by the Croatian NGO B.a.B.e, Sljeme, Croatia, March 1996)

This activity is appropriate for ages 14-18 and 18 plus.

Aim

This activity uses life experience as a basis for thinking about how we defend our own rights and the rights of others.

Learning point

Throughout our lives we have all in one way or another defended our rights and the rights of others, even if we did not use the language of rights.The recognition of the need to uphold these rights is the main objective.

What you need?

Blackboard or large piece of paper and pens.

Time: About one hour.

How to do it?

This is an activity for groups of about six people. With a large group, do the activity first with a small group (maybe before the large group meets). These group members can then act as the facilitators of small groups.

Divide into groups of about six people, with a facilitator for each group.

The facilitator asks each person in the group to remember a time when they stood up for their rights or the rights of other people. (For example, members might remember a time when they were unfairly accused of something as a child). If they wish, the members of the group can describe their memory to a neighbour. At the end of five minutes, every person in the group should have the following information ready:

- A time when I stood up for rights
- What happened?
- Where it happened?
- The motive. Why I stood up?
- Who or what were my sources of support?

While they are thinking, the facilitator draws a large wheel with spokes.

The facilitator of each group now asks each member of the group to tell their story, keeping closely to the five points listed above. As each group member tells their story, the facilitator writes where each incident happened at the end of one of the spokes, and writes the motive and the sources of support along the spoke. (To make writing easier, the facilitator can summarize what is said, if the group member agrees.) When everyone has told their story, the facilitator can use the questions below to draw out the learning points.

Questions

- Were your experiences similar/different? For example, did they happen in public/private, at home/work?
- Were certain places or persons both positive and negative?
- Did anyone mention the law or authorities as a source of support? Why? Why not?
- How did you feel when you remembered standing up for your rights or the rights of others?

- Were these positive experiences? Why? Why not?
- Did many of us experience support or solidarity from our friends/ colleagues/family? Why do?
- you think this sort of support is useful when we stand up for human rights?

Choices

This activity is very flexible. It can be used for analyzing any sort of past experience with any age group. It is particularly useful for showing that we share many experiences. Participants can look at the human rights documents to see which rights might have been relevant in their stories. As a project, ask each person to monitor the media and their own experiences over a weekend. How many examples can they find of people standing up for their rights?

[11] "Mignonette"

(Adapted from p.11 of Understand the Law 1994, The Citizenship Foundation)

This activity is appropriate for ages 14-18 and 18 plus.

Aim

This morally complex story about the right to life will help young people to think about how rights work in practice. It also links well with activities about conflict.

Learning points

Everyone has the right to life.

There is a concept of natural rights.

Time: About one hour.

What you need?

The Simplified Version of the Universal Declaration of Human Rights.

How to do it?

Show the group article three of the Universal Declaration of Human Rights which sets out the right to life:

'Article 3. Everyone has the right to life, liberty and security of person.'

Form into small groups of five or six.

Read the following story:

"On 19 May 1884, four men set sail for Australia from England in a yacht called the *Mignonette*. They were Captain Thomas Dudley, First-mate Edwin Stephens, Seamen Ned Brooks and Richard Parker, the 17-year-old cabin boy. On 5 July, a huge wave smashed into the side of the yacht. It started to sink. The men had time only to grab two tins of food and to get into an open boat before the *Mignonette* sank. The four unlucky sailors found themselves in the middle of the Atlantic Ocean, 1,600 miles from land, with only a few tinned vegetables to keep them alive. After three days, the hungry men managed to catch a turtle. This provided them with food and drink, but nine days later that was all gone. Still 1,000 miles from land, with no food and only the occasional drop of rainwater to drink, the sailors became desperate. The Captain wrote in a letter to his wife that, if no ship should come, 'we must soon die... I am sorry I ever started such a trip...' There was, however, one chance of survival, at least for three of the crew, for a few more days. Someone would have to become food for the others. The Captain suggested that they draw lots to decide which of them should be killed, but Stephens and Brooks objected. 'if we are to die,' they said, 'we should all die together'. Young Richard Parker, lying hardly conscious in the bottom of the boat, said nothing. After two more days without food and water, the Captain convinced Stephens that one of them ought to be sacrificed to save the others, and that the obvious candidate was Richard Parker. He was an orphan, had no wife or family, and was already on the brink of death. He woke from his coma only occasionally to drink sea-water which was making him even more ill. They knew their little boat was drifting towards the shipping lanes. They might sight a ship any day - or they might not. They agreed that if no help came to them by the next day, then they would kill the boy. None came. Seamen Brooks wanted no part in the killing. While he covered himself with a jacket at the end of the boat, Dudley and Stephens knelt over the unconscious Parker.

'Richard, my boy,' whispered the Captain, 'your time has come. Stephens stood ready to hold the boy's feet but there was no need. He was too ill to struggle as the Captain took out a pocket-knife and plunged it into the boy's neck, killing him instantly. All three men drank the blood and ate Richard's heart and liver for the next three days. On the fourth day, they were sighted by a German ship, the *Montezuma*. The three men were very weak. The First-mate and Captain needed to be hauled on board by rope. The men landed in England on 7 September. Dudley, Stephens and Brooks went straight to the authorities and explained the reasons for the death of the boy."

Ask the participants in their groups to answer the following questions:

- Do you think the three men did anything wrong?
- Should they have been charged with a crime?
- Should they all be charged with the same crime?

Now, read the next part of the story to the group:

"Incidents like this had happened before, and so Dudley, Stephens and Brooks were very surprised when they were immediately charged with murder - although the charge against Seaman Brooks was later dropped. There was a lot of public interest in the story as it was reported in detail by the newspapers. Money was collected to pay for lawyers to defend the men in court. At the trial, everyone agreed about the facts of the case, but the jury were faced with a difficult task. They sympathised with the three men, and would have liked to agree that it was not wrong for someone to kill another to save his or her own life. But they did recognize that to kill someone intentionally who was not threatening your own life must be murder. The judge offered the jury a way out of this problem by allowing them to take the unusual step of a 'special verdict'. In this, the jury stated the facts of the case, but left a panel of five judges to decide whether Dudley and Stephens were guilty of murder."

Ask the participants in their groups to answer the following questions:

If you were one of the five judges, would you find Dudley and Stephens guilty or not guilty of murder?

- Why?
- If they are guilty, how should they be punished?

Now, explain what happened:

"The court passed a verdict of murder on Dudley and Stephens. The sentence for murder was death, but in this case it was changed to six months imprisonment. By the standards of the time, and compared with the treatment given to other sailors in a similar position, this was still thought by many to be severe."

Questions

- Richard Parker's right to life was violated. What about the right to life of the other men in the boat?
- What would you have done? Would you die rather than kill someone else?
- This story happened 64 years before the Universal Declaration of Human Rights was made. Does this make any difference to Richard Parker's right to life?

- Some people argue that there are 'natural' laws and rights which have always existed, and which are common-sense and fair. For example, the right to be free would be a 'natural' right. Do you agree that with this idea?
- What other things, apart from life itself, do you think we might have a 'natural' right to?
- Make a list and compare it with the rights in the Universal Declaration of Human Rights.

Choices

What if the men had not told the authorities that they killed the boy? Ask participants to make a play, stories, poems, or imaginary letters in which they imagine that they are the three men ten years after the story. How would they feel about what they did? Would they feel guilty? Why/Why not?

How would you react if you were a friend of Richard Parker?

As a project, group members to survey their friends and family, asking:

What do you think are your natural rights? The resulting data could be collated and used for discussion.

[12] What's Fair? – Activities about Justice

These activities about justice use the discrimination faced by women and minorities as a way to examine everyday injustice.

The aim is to show that large numbers of people are unfairly denied their human rights in everyday situations, and that this should be opposed and overcome.

Activities should be chosen or adapted to suit the needs of your group.

Vesna's Story

(Adapted from p.16 of Understand the Law 1995, The Citizenship Foundation)

This activity is appropriate for ages 14-18 and 18 plus.

Aim

This case study about racial discrimination aims to explore issues of justice and human rights.

Learning point

Discrimination, including racial discrimination, is a violation of human rights.

Time: About an hour and a half.

What you need?

A copy of the Simplified Version of the Universal Declaration of Human Rights for each group.

How to do it?

Form into small groups of five or six.

Explain that many countries have laws against unfair discrimination on the grounds of race or sex. Also the Universal Declaration of Human Rights contains articles against discrimination.

Ask the participants in their groups to identify which articles in the Universal Declaration of Human Rights are relevant to discrimination. (They may wish to consult the simplified version of the Universal Declaration of Human Rights.) **Note:** Almost every article is relevant in some way. Ask them to justify their choice to the whole group by giving a practical example of how that article counters discrimination.

Read out Vesna's Story:

Vesna is a Roma woman. This is her story.

"I saw a job for a sales assistant advertised in the window of a clothes shop. They wanted someone between 18 and 23. I'm 19, so I went in and asked about the job but was told by the manageress to come back in two days because not enough people had applied. I returned twice, and was always told the same thing. Nearly a week later I went back to the shop. The job advertisement was still in the window. The manageress was too busy to see me, but I was told that the vacancy had been filled. After I left the shop, I was so upset that I asked a non-Roma friend if she would go in and ask about the job. When she came out she said that she had been asked to come for an interview on Monday."

Now read out the manageress's response:

"I felt that Vesna would find it difficult to work here, because of the distance that she would have to travel in to work each day. It would be an eight-mile journey on two buses. It makes it very difficult to run the shop if staff are always late. I'd much prefer to appoint someone from this area. The person to whom I offered the job seemed just right."

Ask participants in their groups to decide:

- Do you think Vesna was discriminated against? Why?
- If so, what do you think the shop should have to do?
- What could Vesna do about this situation? Do you think her non-Roma friends should help her to get justice? How?

Now, explain what happened:

Vesna took her case to a special European court which enforces the law about discrimination. The court agreed that she had been discriminated against. Several other people who lived far away from the shop had been interviewed. The girl who got the job was only 16, white, and lived the same distance from the shop as Vesna. The shop had to give Vesna some money for the injury to her feelings."

Questions

- Vesna was unfairly discriminated against because of her ethnicity. The manageress didn't really know anything about her. Which groups of people are discriminated against in your country? Why? Do you agree with this discrimination?
- Do you know anything about these groups? Do you think this knowledge is accurate?
- "Ignorance encourages prejudice and makes discrimination possible". Do you agree with this statement?

Choices

As an action, ask the group to write stories, poems, a play or make cartoons/pictures about a time when they felt unfairly discriminated against, for example, because of their sex or age. What would it be like to be discriminated against all the time? If everyone agrees, display these. As a project the group could find out about a group in your country which is discriminated against, focusing on the question, Is this discrimination justified? What could be done to change the circumstance? Present your information to the group and work on a plan towards rectifying the problem.

[13] She Doesn't Work

This activity is appropriate for ages 14-18 and 18 plus.

Aim

This project activity aims to draw attention to discrimination against women and to encourage them to challenge it.

Learning point

Discrimination against women is a violation of human rights.

What you need?

Simplified Version of the Universal Declaration of Human Rights. **(given at the end of the chapter).**

Text "She doesn't work".

Blackboard or large piece of paper.

Time: Two sessions.

How to do it?

Read, or ask a group member to read the text "She doesn't work".

With the whole group, make a quick list of all the jobs which a wife does.

Now brainstorm reasons why the husband doesn't think his wife 'works'. Encourage participants to think of as many reasons as possible why the husband might think like this, for example, it might be because she is unpaid, or because he thinks his work is harder. Spend about five minutes on this part. Now, brainstorm reasons why the wife's responsibilities are work, for example, her longer working day. Spend about five minutes on this part.

Explain that Articles 1 and 2 of the Universal Declaration of Human Rights, or it's summary, specifically mention sexual equality. Read these articles - either the full or simplified versions.

Ask the group to form pairs. Each pair should make a list of all the work which has to be done in and around **their** home. After five minutes, go around the pairs, asking for one item from each pair's list until there are no more suggestions. Write all the suggestions up on the wall.

Form groups of four or five. Ask each group to write their own questionnaire about household work. The aim of the questionnaires is to find out about housework in their own area. They will need to phrase the questions in such a way as to find out as much as possible about the subject from the people they interview. They could include questions such as:

- Who makes the meals in your house?
- Do men and children help around your house?
- How long does housework take?
- Do the women have other jobs to do in addition?

Each questionnaire will probably be different. Alternatively, the group could work together to make one questionnaire. Allow a week for participants to make a survey about house-work in the community, using their questionnaires. Remind them to question both men and women!

After the survey has been done, have a report-back session, where each group member is allowed to contribute one thing that they discovered through the survey. During or after the report-back, use the following questions to help participants to analyze their results.

Questions

- Did you discover anything surprising?
- How did you feel about what you found?
- Did your discoveries change the way you think about the work women do? Why/ Why not?
- Did you discover any tasks which could only be done by men?
- Did you discover any tasks which could only be done by women?
- Would the young men like to do all the work that women do? Why/ Why not?
- Is it right for women to have to do all this work?
- What can we do in our schools, the workplace, in our homes, and in society at large, to treat each other more equally? Which tasks could be done by men or women? Which tasks could be done together?
- Has the role of men and women in your county changed in recent years? Discuss.
- What can we attribute this change to?
- What kind of changes need to be made in the future? How can these changes be brought about?
- What role can you play in bringing about such change?

Choices

As a project, ask the group to write an article for the local newspaper which outlines the findings of their research. Some members of the group could take responsibility for meeting with the editor and discussing any changes which might have to be made so that the article can be published.

She doesn't work

"Have you many children?" the Doctor asked.

"Sixteen born, but only nine live," he answered.

"Does your wife work?"

"No, she stays at home."

"I see. How does she spend her day?"

"Well, she gets up at four in the morning, fetches water and wood, makes the fire and cooks breakfast. Then she goes to the river and washes clothes. After that she goes to town to get corn ground and buy what we need in the market. Then she cooks the midday meal."

"You come home at mid-day?"

"No, no. She brings the meal to me in the fields, about three kilometres from home."

"And after that?"

"Well she takes care of hens and pigs. And of course she looks after the children all day. Then she prepares supper so that it is ready when I come home."

"Does she go to bed after supper?"

"No, I do. She has things to do around the house until nine o'clock."

"But you say your wife doesn't work?"

"No. I told you. She stays at home."

Advantages and disadvantages

(Adapted from Amnesty International USA HRE Resource Notebook: Women's rights)

This activity is appropriate for ages 14-18 and 18 plus.

Aim

This activity helps young people to examine their own attitudes and perceptions about the differences between the way men and women are treated in society.

Learning point

Discrimination against women is a violation of human rights.

What you need?

The Simplified Version of the Universal Declaration of Human Rights. **(given at the end of the chapter).**

Pens and paper.

Time: One hour.

How to do it?

Form small groups of males and females. Ideally, there will be an equal number of male and female groups. Explain that each group will be asked to make a list and that this will be used for a discussion. Ask each group of **males** to make a list of the advantages and disadvantages of being **female**. Females do the same for males. Allow ten minutes for this. The lists should have an equal number of advantages and disadvantages. Now pair each group of males with a group of females. Each female group reports its list to a male group and responds to the male group's reactions. Now each male group reports its list to a female group and responds to the female group's reactions. Discuss how this exercise and your findings relates to the simplified version of the United Declaration of Human Rights.

If necessary, use the following questions to start a discussion.

Questions

- Was it easy to think of the advantages and disadvantages of being a male or female? Why? Why not?
- Did you find yourselves listing things which could be called sexist?
- Do you thing those sorts of generalizations about people are realistic? Do they apply to the people you know?
- Was it a useful activity? Why? Did you learn anything that you didn't know before?
- What have you learned about gender stereotyping and the value of all work?

Choices

This activity can also be used to examine other differences apart from gender, such as class or religion.

[14] My Rights/Your Rights – A Situation Where Rights Conflict

These activities use imaginary situations to help young people to understand that where one persons' rights end and the rights of the next person begin, conflicts can occur. In the game 'What now', participants must cooperate to find solutions to these situations where rights conflict. Activities should be chosen or adapted to suit the needs of your group.

Refugee role-plays

Aim

This activity uses a role-play where refugees and border officials express different points of view on the rights of refugees. This role-play is designed to increase young peoples' knowledge about refugee rights.

Learning point

Refugees are a specially vulnerable group who have specific rights.

What you need?

Immigration officers arguments and options.

Refugees arguments and options.

Information about refugees.

Time: One hour.

How to do it?

Start by brainstorming to find out what group members think about refugees. Write the word 'refugee' on the wall, and ask the participants to say the first things which the word makes them tink of.

Read the Information about refugees to the group to introduce the subject.

Consulting the advice on using role-play in Part Two, help the class to play the following role-play.

Read out the following scenario (if you wish, you can invent imaginary names for countries X and Y):

"It is a dark, cold and wet night on the border between X and Y. A column of refugees has arrived, fleeing from the war in X. They want to cross into Y. They are hungry, tired and cold. They have no money, and no documents except their passports. The immigration officials from country Y have different points of view - some want to allow the refugees to cross, but others don't. The refugees are desperate, and use several arguments to try to persuade the immigration officials.

Ask one third of the participants to imagine that they are the immigration officers from country Y. Give this group the Immigrations officers' arguments and options. Ask another third to imagine that they are refugees. Give this group the Refugees arguments and options.Tell the players that they can use the arguments on their cards and any other relevant arguments they can think of. If it helps, draw a line along the floor to symbolise the border. Tell them that when the role-play begins, they have ten minutes to reach some sort of conclusion, which may be one of the options listed, or another solution. It is up to you and the participants to decide whether the refugees and the immigration officers will put their arguments as a group, or whether they will individually take responsibility for raising individual arguments. Ask the remaining third of the people to act as observers. (Half can monitor the 'immigration officers', and half can monitor the 'refugees'.) Give the refugees and the immigration officers a few minutes before the roleplay to read through their arguments and options and to decide on tactics. Start the role-play. Use your own judgement about when to stop. After the role-play, discuss what occurred, using the following questions. This is important to draw out the points which have been learned.

Questions

- How did the situation work out? What happened?
- How did it feel to be a refugee?
- How did it feel to be an immigration officer?
- Refugees have a right to protection under the 1951 Convention Relating to the Status of Refugees. Were these refugees given their right to protection? Why/why not?
- Do you think that a country should have the right to turn away refugees?
- Would you do this yourself? What if you knew they faced death in their own country?

Choices

If there is time, play the role-play again, but the participants who were immigration officers must now be refugees. The Office of the United Nations High Commissioner for Refugees (UNHCR) is responsible for protecting the rights of refugees. Ask the participants in groups to pretend that they are an official team sent by UNHCR to help the refugees from country X. Ask them to write an official report including the following issues:

- What arguments could you use to persuade the immigration officers to let the refugees in?
- Are the immigration officers doing anything wrong?
- Are any of the articles of the Human Rights Documents relevant?
- What could be done with this report to make country Y protect the rights of the refugees?

As a project, refugees in your country could be useful resources for your group to find out more about the problems of securing rights as a refugee.

Check the newspapers for local refugee case studies and discuss with the group.

As an action, students could gather essential items and deliver them to refugees who are sheltering in your country.

Immigration officers' arguments and options

You can use these arguments and any others you can think of:

They are desperate, we can't send them back.

If we will send them back we will be responsible if they are arrested, tortured or killed.

We have legal obligations to accept refugees.

They have no money, and will need state support. Our country cannot afford that.

Can they prove that they are genuine refugees? Maybe they are just here to look for a better standard of living? Our country is a military and business partner of country X. We can't be seen to be protecting them. Maybe they have skills which we need? There are enough refugees in our country. We need to take care of our own people. They should go to the richer countries. If we let them in, others will also demand entry. They don't speak our language, they have a different religion and they eat different food. They won't integrate. They will bring political trouble.

Before the role-play, think about the following options:

- What is your responsibility as an immigration official?
- Will you let all of the refugees across the border?
- What will you base your decision upon? Will these decisions be based on fixed principles or international legislation, or will there be some degree of subjectivity?
- Will you let some across the border?
- Will you split them up by age, profession, wealth?
- Will you do something else instead?

'Refugees' arguments and options

You can use these arguments and any others you can think of:

- It is our right to receive asylum.
- Our children are hungry, you have a moral responsibility to help us.

- We will be killed if we go back.
- We have no money.
- We can't go anywhere else.
- I was a doctor in my home town.
- We only want shelter until it is safe to return.

Other refugees have been allowed into your country.

Before the role-play, think about the following options:

- Will you split up if the immigration officers ask you to?
- Will you go home if they try to send you back?
- Are there international laws which protect you as a refugee and guarantee you a safe haven?

Information about Refugees

Every year tens of thousands of people leave their homes and often their countries because of persecution or war. These people become refugees. They nearly always have to move suddenly, leaving their possessions behind, tearing families apart. Many are never able to return to their homes. In 1992, there were almost 19 million refugees in the world. The numbers grow every year. Most refugees seek safety in a neighbouring country. Others have to travel great distances to find safety. Refugees often arrive at airports and sea ports far from their native land, asking for entry. In 1951, the United Nations adopted the Convention Relating to the Status of Refugees. More than half of the countries in the world have agreed with the Convention. They give protection to refugees and agree not to force them to return to their country to risk persecution or death. Article 33 of the Convention says: "No Contracting State shall expel or return a refugee in any manner whatsoever to the frontiers of territories where his/her life or freedom would be threatened on account of his race, religion, nationality, membership in a particular social group or political opinion."

This also applies if a government wants to send a refugee to another country from which the refugee might be sent home. Governments must hear the claim of a refugee who wants to find safety (seek asylum) in their country. This principle applies to all states, whether or not they are party to the 1951 Convention. According to the Convention, a refugee is someone who has left their country and is unable to return because of a real fear of being persecuted because of their race, religion, nationality, membership of a particular social group, or political opinion.

The 1951 Convention also says that refugees should be free from discrimination and should receive their full rights in the country where they are seeking asylum or safety. There are many articles of the Universal Declaration of

Human Rights protect refugees. Often however, countries disagree about who is a 'genuine' refugee. The media and politicians often demand limits on the number of refugees, saying that they cause racial tension, and shortages of housing and jobs. In recent years the governments of many of the world's richest countries have reduced the number of refugees they allow in, for two reasons. First, air travel has become cheaper, meaning that more refugees from developing countries want to enter developed countries. Second, the world economic downturn has reduced the need for large workforces. This means that refugees who used to come as migrant workers now have to apply for refugee status. To justify restrictions on refugees, rich countries often say that refugees are not victims of oppression, but just want a better standard of living. They call them "economic migrants". To protect the rights of refugees the **Office of the United Nations High Commissioner for Refugees (UNHCR)** based in Geneva, was established by the UN General Assembly on 14 December 1950. Governments often argue that refugee's fears are exaggerated or untrue. Refugees are protected from this argument by organisations who use evidence of human rights violations in the refugee's country to persuade the government to let them apply for asylum.

Action! – A Practical Guide to Human Rights Activism

These activities help young people to think of human rights as something which they are able to defend and fight for, wherever they live. There are also suggestions for action in the Choices parts of many of the activities in the preceding pages. This section offers practical hands on advice on how to organise for action by establishing campaigns, which relate to your education work. Different campaign techniques are described such as letter writing, petitions and lobbying.

[15] The Power of Action

This activity is appropriate for ages 14-18 and 18 plus.

Aim

This case study about a famous human rights campaigner aims to show the power of action by giving an example of someone who acted successfully to obtain their rights.

Learning point

Individuals, and especially groups, can act to successfully oppose human rights violations.

What you need?

Mahatma Gandhi's Story from the next page.

Time: About half an hour.

How to do it?

Read, or ask the group members to read, Gandhi's story.

Use the questions below to start a discussion.

Questions

- What do you think prompted Gandhi to take action?
- The Indian people protested without violence. Why do you think this was?
- If they had protested violently, for example, by killing British soldiers, what do you think the British would have done? Do you think many Indian people would have died too?
- Gandhi asked for "world sympathy in this battle of Right against Might." Do you think that the other people of the world would have been so sympathetic if the Indians had attacked the British? Why? Do you think that peaceful protest was the right choice in this case? What about other cases? For example, in your own country? ??What are some examples of peaceful protest that have occurred in your community or around the world? Have these types of protest been successful? Why or why not? What are the advantages associated with peaceful social protest?

Choices

Give the group an example of a person or a group from your own country who acted to obtain their rights. As a project the group could research this person or group and make a poster picture, story or play to show what they found out. As a group, brainstorm how you would set up an organisation to deal with a pressing local issue. Cons'der putting into action.

Mahatma Gandhi's Story

The Mahatma (Great Soul) gave a new meaning to non-violence. He said that anything gained through violence was not worth having. Born Mohandas Karamchand Gandhi in Gujarat, India in 1869, he qualified as a lawyer in England before practising in South Africa. There he experienced racial discrimination for the first time. There were laws to stop people without white skin from doing many things, such as becoming a lawyer or travelling in the first class compartments of trains. Gandhi saw that many black people in South Africa were poor and they were treated badly by the whites. He organised protests and went to prison fighting against injustice. From the beginning of his life as a protester Gandhi was directed by his deep religious convictions. He believed that violence was always wrong. Gandhi returned to India in 1915. There was a great poverty among the Indian people too. The British were ruling India harshly, taking taxes that the people could not afford, preventing Indian people from ruling their own country, discouraging their industry and using force to control the people.

In 1930 Gandhi began to protest the salt tax, which initially was seen as of little concern to the British. During this time salt was collected from the oceans, processed, and sold by British government who made money from it. Gandhi said that the salt belonged to India and that he would break this law. First, he asked to discuss the issue with the head of the British government in India the Viceroy. The Viceroy refused, thinking it was unimportant. Then, on 12 March 1930, when he was sixty years old, Gandhi set out with his followers to march 322 kilometres from his home to the sea to make salt. For twenty-four days the people of India and the rest of the world followed his progress. The anticipation was intense. On 6 April, with thousands of onlookers Gandhi walked into the sea and picked up a handful of salt. This act of defiance was a signal to the nation. All along the coast of India people made salt illegally. He wrote, "I want world sympathy in this battle of Right against Might." A month later Gandhi was arrested and tens of thousands had been put in prison. Gandhi and the people of India spent many years protesting before the British finally left. They continued to march, to refuse to co-operate, and to stretch British resources by allowing themselves to be imprisoned. Finally, India achieved success in 1947 when the British gave up their rule and India became independent.

[16] Action Role-plays

This activity is appropriate for ages 14-18 .

Aim

This roleplay activity aims to encourage young people to apply their rights in real situations.

Learning point

Human rights violations occur in everyday situations and can be opposed by everyday people.

What you need?

Simplified version of the Universal Declaration of Human Rights, (enough for one copy per four or five students - these can be hand-copied).

Role-play situations given below.

Time: One and a half hours.

How to do it?

Divide into small groups of three or four. Read out roleplay One and ask the group to identify the articles of the Universal Declaration of Human Rights which are relevant to it. Below are some likely answers, but this list is not exhaustive. Allow five to ten minutes for this.

Repeat for roleplays Two and Three.

In roleplay One, the most relevant articles are:

- Article two, articles six and seven, and article thirteen.

In roleplay Two, the most relevant articles are:

- Article twenty and article twenty-three.

In roleplay Three, the most relevant articles are:

- Articles nineteen and twenty, and article twenty-four.

Now re-arrange into three groups, and give each group one of the role-play situations. Ask each group to roleplay their situation, with their own ending. They will need to decide who will play each role, and how to play the end of the situation. Ask each small group in turn to play their roleplay for the whole group. After each roleplay performance, ask the players how it felt, then ask the participants to think of other possible endings. Encourage them to think about ways in which the people in the situations could prevent their rights being violated.

Choice

If the group is small, or there is a lack of time, a few members could perform one role play for the whole group.

Role-plays

One

Ida wants to cross the border into the neighbouring country to visit her daughter, who has married someone from that country. The border officials refuse to let her in. They say that she is too poor to pay for a hotel in their country.

Two

Ivan is a cleaner in car wash company. In the winter his hands are hurt by pieces of ice. His boss said he will not buy gloves for Ivan because they are very expensive. Ivan can't afford to buy them for himself. He asks his Union to help. When his boss finds out, Ivan loses his job.

Three

The last park in town is going to be made into a car park. Ten people from the neighbourhood demonstrate peacefully in the park, saying they need a place to relax and for their children to play in. The Police come and say that they are not allowed to demonstrate and that they should go home. The demonstrators sit down on the ground and refuse to move. The police move them by force, hurting some of them.

[17] Campaigning and Education

What is it, and why do it?

Campaigning focuses on selecting a specific course of action in order to achieve identified objectives. Approaches to strategic campaigning may include, letter writing, lobbying, demonstrations, and generating public awareness. The action component of human rights education is very important. Campaigning allows group members to become active for human rights.

How to do it?

Begin by deciding what strengths, weaknesses, and what external factors could inhibit or enhance the quality of your work. You may want to harness the support of the media, or a special interest group. Decide how you will deal with such forces, if at all.

Deciding what problem or issue you would like to address. Consider the following questions:

- What is the human rights situation in the target country?
- Are torture and ill treatment ofprisoners or disappearances wide-spread?
- What is your specific objective? What do you want to achieve?
- Who specifically is responsible for the human right situation you are concerned about?
- Who indirectly can be held responsible for the situation in question? Are they politicians, police or prison officials?

- Who can influence those responsible? Doctors, politicians, religious organisations, journalists, etc. What other information do you need to encourage support of your campaign? How can you develop awareness of this and related human rights issues to compliment your action?

Chose a specific campaign approach, lobbying, petitions, educational campaign, etc.

Create an action plan! Decide what you need to do, who will do it, when, and how much it will cost. Put your plan into action! Remember to periodically evaluate your progress and modify your plans in order to ensure success.

Remember!

Always give people information about the human rights situation they are campaigning on.

[18] Letter-Writing

What is it, and why do it?

Letter writing is the writing and sending of numerous letters to influential individuals in order to end human right abuses and violations. The advantages of letter writing campaigns include:

- They are easy to organise
- They are a low cost means by which to influence governments
- They take advantage of the way bureaucratic systems work

How to do it?

Decide who your target group will be, for example, government officials, military commanders, editors of newspapers, embassies, human rights and non-governmental organisations or even the family of the prisoners in questions. Decide as a group the objective of the campaign and the type of information that will appear in your letters. What information will you need to give people that they understand the issue? How will you present this? ?You may chose to write individual personal letters or generate several standard letters in which the text may be slightly modified. The disadvantage with the standard letter is that although the initial letter may have a substantial impact, a higher volume of letters needs to be produced in order to have the same response as a smaller volume of personalized letters. You may want to set up a stand in a high traffic area, with letters, and stamped envelopes or postcards to encourage people outside of your group to support your cause. Remember to ask such individuals to include their personal return address. Asking for donations to help cover the cost of postage would also be appropriate during this time.

[19] Petitions

What is it, and why do it?

A petition is a short and simple statement which is made by a group. Members of the pubic are encourage to sign the petition which in turn will be delivered to a particular government official or minister. Generating a petition is a simple, fast and easy way for the general public to show their support for a specific issue. The more names you collect the more impact your petition is likely to have.

How to do it?

Decide what your objective will be, and to whom it will be sent.

Create a **SHORT** and **SIMPLE** statement outlining your objective. The longer the statement the less likely a passerby will be to stop to read and sign your petition. Each page of your petition should include:

- the contact information for your particular organisation
- the statement
- space for names, addresses and signatures
- and a column for additional comments

Consider where you will set up your stand in order to get the maximum number of individuals to sign your petition. Decide how you will deliver the petition, for example, by way of a personal meeting with a government official or via the mail. Consider calling the media to be present during your signing campaign and when you deliver your petition, this will ensure maximum impact. It is also an opportunity for public raising awareness of human rights in general. Your petition can take on numerous forms, for example, a large scroll, or even a banner. Be creative!

Choices

Why not use your petition to lobby a government minister about the issue.

You could hold a public meeting and invite a speaker who knows about the issue to speak. This will develop public awareness and generate support for your campaigning.

[20] Lobbying

How to do it?

You could hold a peaceful public protest outside of your government's legislature.

Successful lobbying is the product of a clear focus, well defined objectives, the credibility of the group or organisation, the use of reliable information, access to target groups, professionalism, and above all timing. Successful lobbying takes time, so don't be disappointed if your initial efforts are not met with much success- be patient and persistent and success is sure to follow.

[21] Word Search

Levels

Grade 11 & 12.

Task

Individually or in small groups, your students will complete the rights and freedom word search.

Expectations

The student will:

- Engage in learning terminology and meaning of human rights.
- Appreciate the wide spread nature of Human Rights violation around the world.
- Synthesize information on a world issue and share their opinions with classmates.

Timeframe: 75 Minutes.

Achivement Categories

- Knowledge/Understanding
- Thinking/Inquiry
- Communication
- Application/Making Connections

Materials

Rights and Freedom word search

Pen or pencil

Vocabulary

- Assembly,
- Free press,

- Equality,
- Right to Food,
- Vote

Procedure

- Explain to your students that they will be filling a Rights and Freedoms Word Search. Each student will receive a copy of the word search (See Student Activity Work-sheet 1).
- They must find out 35 words (or combinations of words – e.g. "health care") that have to do with our rights and freedoms hidden in various directions – horizontal, vertical, diagonal, backwards, etc.
- There are no extra letters, so when all of the words are found the grid will be filled with lines.
- When the students have completed their word search, ask them to form groups of 3 or 4 students.
- Ask each group to choose 5 words from the Word Search. Ask them to define these words in relation to human rights and to illustrate each word with a real life example. Make sure each word is only defined by one group.
- Each group must present to the class their definitions and examples with a view to encourage class discussion and exchange. (Use flipchart paper and markers if you wish).
- Once the presentations are over, ask the same groups of students to prepare short skits illustrating two human rights violation in India. Remind the students to use and integrate the words. assign to words they have defined.
- Finally, encourage class discussion after the presentation of the skits from each group.

Student Work-sheet 1

Name: ________________

RIGHTS & FREEDOMS WORD SEARCH

Instructions

There are 35 words (or combinations of words – e.g. 'health care') that have to do with our rights and freedoms hidden below in various directions – horizontal, vertical, diagonal, backwards, etc. There are no extra letters, so when all of the words are found the grid will be filled with lines.

Student Work-sheet 1

Name: ____________________

RIGHTS & FREEDOMS WORD SEARCH

Instructions

There are 35 words (or combinations of words – e.g. "health care") that have to do with our rights and freedoms hidden below in various directions—horizontal, vertical, diagonal, backwards, etc. There are no extra letters, so when all of the words are found the grid will be filled with lines.

OUR RIGHTS&FREEDOMS:

P	F	R	O	M	D	I	S	C	R	I	M	I	N	A	T	I	O	N	the
E	O	P	I	N	I	O	N	H	E	A	L	T	H	C	A	R	E	C	u
A	O	T	n	Y	i	v	O	O	E	D	U	C	A	T	I	O	N	I	F
C	D	N	e	T	r	M	a	I	s	L	A	N	G	U	A	G	E	T	A
E	Y	E	D	E	E	l	d	C	U	L	T	U	R	E	S	T	e	A	I
F	C	M	I	F	V	O	T	E	X	P	R	E	S	S	I	O	N	I	R
U	A	E	G	A	W	G	N	I	V	I	L	c	R	E	S	P	E	C	T
L	V	V	N	S	l	a	r	Y	T	I	L	A	U	Q	E	a	t	O	R
P	I	O	I	M	A	R	R	Y	G	F	R	E	E	P	R	E	S	S	I
R	R	M	T	i	o	C	H	I	L	D	H	O	O	D	n	of	h	S	A
O	P	u	Y	M	I	N	O	R	I	T	Y	L	B	M	E	S	S	A	L
T	R	E	T	A	W	N	A	E	L	C	m	J	U	S	T	I	C	E	I
E	S	E	L	F	D	E	T	E	R	M	I	N	A	T	I	O	N	a	F
S	n	ri	ght	N	O	I	T	A	T	N	E	S	E	R	P	E	R	s	E
T	N	E	M	Y	O	L	P	M	E	L	U	F	G	N	I	N	A	E	M

Some words that have to do with our rights and freedoms include:

... assembly; association; childhood; choice; clean water, culture, dignity; education; equality; expression; fair trial; food; free press; from discrimination; health care; home; justice; language; life; living wage; marry, meaningful employment; minority; movement; opinion; peaceful protest; privacy; religion; representation; Respect; rest; safety; self-determination; shelter; vote ..

[22] An International Criminal Court

For higher grade teacher can introduce the working of International Criminal Court. Teacher can distribute in small groups the following case study-

At the international military tria's held in 1945-1946 in Nuremberg and Tokyo, the victorious Allies prosecuted individual German and Japanese officials for 'crimes against peace', 'war crimes' and 'crimes against humanity' committed in connection with the Second World War. Since that time, such crimes and massive human rights violations have been committed in many other armed conflicts. In Cambodia, the Khmer Rouge killed an estimated 2 million people during the 1970s. Thousands of civilians, including horrifying numbers of unarmed women and children, lost their lives in armed conflicts in Mozambique, Liberia, El Salvador and other countries. However, international agreement to establish international courts to deal with such atrocities could not be reached until the 1990's, when the conflict in the former Yugoslavia erupted and war crimes, crimes against humanity and genocide – in the guise of 'ethnic cleansing' – once again commanded international attention. In 1993, the United Nations Security Council established the *ad hoc* International Criminal Tribunal for the former Yugoslavia, to prosecute and punish individuals for those systematic and massive human rights violations. Similarly, following the end of the civil war that raged in Rwanda from April to July 1994, in which some 1 million unarmed civilians were massacred, the Security Council established the International Criminal Tribunal for Rwanda. History has shown that without the enforcement mechanism of an international criminal court to deal with individual responsibility, acts of genocide and egregious human rights violations often go unpunished. Such a court could provide a complementary means by which to ensure that individuals can be prosecuted for genocide, war crimes and crimes against humanity when the country in which such crimes are perpetrated is unable or unwilling to prosecute. Also, such an institution could deter grave crimes under international law from being perpetrated in future. Accordingly, in 1998 government representatives met at a diplomatic conference in Rome to formulate a statute for a permanent international criminal court. On 17 July 1998, the Statute of the International Criminal Court was adopted: 120 Governments voted in favour, 7 against and 21 abstained. The Statute entered into force in July 2002, having been ratified by at least 60 States, and the International Criminal Court has now been set up in The Hague (Netherlands). The establishment of the International Criminal Court raises several important issues and provides opportunities for student research and activity:

- Why is such a Court needed? Can it be effective?
- By what authority can the international community intervene in a country's internal matters, such as how a Government treats its own citizens? Is this interference in domestic affairs? (A class activity could be developed to discuss whether and when an international body has the right to intervene in a country's domestic affairs.)
- Find out more about the International Criminal Court (e.g. its rules of procedure, the kind of cases it will deal with, etc. – the official web site of the Court is http://www.icc.org). What will be the obligations of each Government to co-operate with the International Criminal Court?

- For the International Criminal Court to be set up, its Statute had to be ratified by at least 60 countries. Find out which countries have ratified it so far. If your own country has not yet ratified, hold a debate about the pros and cons of ratification. Send letters or petitions to your country's legislators urging your position(s) on ratification.
- Survey world history for examples of situations that might have been taken to an international criminal court, if such a court had existed at the time.

[23] Human Rights Club

A direct experience of working together for something worth-while may be achieved from having the class form a club to promote human rights. The teacher can initiate a number of relevant tasks aimed at establishing such a club

- Define the purpose of the Human Rights Club in more detail;
- Hold a competition for a club symbol;
- Make individual membership cards that carry this logo;
- Organise office-holders;
- Put up a special notice board for Human Rights Club activities;
- Find out about national and international human rights networks and organisations with which the club can liaise; ask for their publications and display these where people can use them;
- Begin holding meetings – the first could discuss the right to freedom of association itself: 'Why organise? Why it is important to take part in public affairs, locally, nationally and beyond?'
- Invite guest speakers (e.g. local politicians, issue specialists, area specialists) to give short talks and hold discussions;
- Set up sub-committees to meet and to research particular tasks;
- Commemorate International Human Rights Day, 10 December; find out about other International Days related to human rights and commemorate them. A group could approach other classes with offers to speak to them about particular human rights issues/areas, explaining why the club was formed and what it does, and offering associate membership; where resources permit, the club could also publish a regular newsletter.

How can human rights be part of the curriculum?

Ideally, human rights should be a part of all school subjects, and should permeate the students' whole learning experience. However, because circumstances are different in each country and region, teachers have used many different tactics for fitting human rights into their school curriculum. These tactics can be placed in two broad categories:

- Starting to teach human rights at a 'grassroots' level in whichever way you can, with the permission of the Principal or local-level officials.
- Persuading the local or national educational authorities to change the system from the top to make funding and time available for human rights teaching.

Often, teachers have combined these tactics by beginning with their 'grassroots' teaching then using their successes as evidence to persuade the educational authorities to change the system.

Primary Curricula

In primary schools, because there is less exam pressure on children and staff, and because teachers usually teach several subjects to one class, teachers have often found it quite easy to get the Principals' permission to teach human rights in a way which involves many subjects. Teachers in describe their teaching about rights as a 'line' running through all subjects, which they have used to help children to understand that different subjects, different people, and the world around them are inter-connected..

Secondary Curricula

Introducing teaching for human rights at this level can be more difficult. A lot depends on the attitude of the Principal and the educational authorities, who are often worried about the already-overcrowded timetable and the students' need to prepare for major examinations (especially in the last grades of school). The subject specialisation of secondary school teachers also means that co-operation between staff is needed to integrate human rights teaching across the curriculum.

However, many teachers have successfully introduced teaching human rights at this level in the following ways:

- As an optional, separate subject after school or in weekly class 'free time'. This approach gives teachers and students the freedom to explore teaching human rights without pressure, but has the disadvantage that students sometimes do not take seriously subjects which are not essential for examinations.
- Some teachers have started teaching human rights within their own specialist subject. There are ideas for how to do this on the next few pages. In particular, human rights teaching fits well with Civics and Law, although teachers who have used this approach stress that it is important to avoid presenting human rights as an academic subject unrelated to real life.

- Teachers have also planned jointly with colleagues to involve students in project work which involves several core subjects. This avoids the danger that students might see human rights as one, academic subject, and helps them to see the relevance of school subjects to the real world around them.

Ideas for teaching human rights in core subjects.

History

When teaching history, human rights can be introduced around traditional subject matter. Here are some examples.

- Documents: Magna Carta (1215 England)
  US Declaration of Independence (1776 USA)
  The Declaration of the Rights of Man (1789 France)
- Major events: War, slavery, colonialism, imperialism and Nazism, can all be studied with special attention to their violation of human rights. More recent history, for example apartheid, political oppression in Latin America, or under Stalinism, also provides lots of material about human rights.
- The growth of human rights through history: For example, the origins and growth of democratic thinking and organisation, the development of the United Nations, the growth of trade unions.
- Historical Figures: Anne Frank (Netherlands)
  Mahatma Gandhi (India)
  Martin Luther King (USA)
  Andrei Sakharov (USSR)
  Rigoberta Menchú (Guatemala)

Study of well known figures can lead on to study of 'unknown' people who have had their rights violated or who have fought for human rights and peace. For example, slaves throughout history, or ordinary people, such as students' relatives who have had their rights violated by war in this century.

Geography

Urban geography can include problems of poverty in tower block estates, and how this affects the human rights of poor people. Economic geography can study the effect of investment and trade on standards of living, or the link between environmental degradation and ill health. Population studies could include examination of how famine and poverty are created, and how racism, colonialism and the treatment of minorities and women has affected the rights of populations.

Law

This subject is an opportunity to teach students about the responsibilities, as well as the rights, which living in peace involves. For example, studies of the structure and processes of their government can emphasise the role of individual citizens. Teaching from a human rights perspective can be especially useful if this part of the curriculum has previously focussed on obedience to the state. The duty of the nation and its citizens to uphold national and international laws against religious, gender and racial discrimination could also be studied. The way in which human rights are developed, recognised, and made into laws could also be examined here. For example, students could examine the process through which women have gradually gained the right to vote.

Sociology

In this subject, social inequalities and their causes can be examined. For example, xenophobia, poverty, racial and religious discrimination, and all the mechanisms and social structures which combat these injustices. Also the functions and responsibilities of the police, trade unions, education and mass media can be studied. A study of how societies deal with dissent can be particularly useful for bringing up issues of human rights.

Literature

Books and poems are excellent resources for vivid accounts of human rights violated or defended. Historical literature is an opportunity for History and Literature teachers to work together to make human rights vivid for students.

Some useful books might be:

- Animal Farm/Nineteen Eighty-Four (George Orwell)
- Brave New World (Aldous Huxley)
- Cry, The Beloved Country (Alan Paton)
- The Diary of a Young Girl (Anne Frank)
- One Day in the Life of Ivan Denisovitch (Aleksandr Solzhenitsyn)
- Role of Thunder/Hear my Cry (Mildred D. Taylor)

Science

Health issues are a good way to introduce human rights in this subject. For example, students have a right to health care, but also the responsibility to respect their own and other people's health. There are great opportunities for cross-departmental teaching. For example, a biology lesson examining myths about racial superiority can inform students to make better judgements in a parallel study of racism in history.

Mathematics

Statistics can be used to hide or reveal human rights abuses. The maths teacher can also show students how to critically interpret figures which appear in newspapers.

Foreign Language

Language skills can be used to study interesting current themes from other countries. For example, a short text about action against racism in England could be used to teach English vocabulary. The aim would be to give students an understanding of the human rights issues facing people in all countries, as well as knowledge of a foreign language. If available, foreign language press or literature is helpful for this teaching style, but not essential.

Foreign language classes are opportunities for students to talk and discuss. They will be most motivated to discuss when the topic is one on which there are different opinions. Questions of discrimination or of gender equality make good discussion topics. Students can also enjoy role-play. Foreign language classes are also a chance for students to correspond with students in other countries. They could ask about political systems, current social questions, the treatment of minorities and any other questions relating to human rights.

Evaluating your Human Rights Education Activities

Depending on how you introduce human rights education to your peer group, evaluation may be something which you have to do or which you want to do. Whatever your motive, there are many good reasons to do it:

It is a chance to prove to yourself that your efforts are working and are worth-while (or to see why they are not working and how to change them).

It gives your efforts credibility.

It gives the group members the opportunity to monitor their own progress.

It can be part of the process of improving members' personal responsibility for their learning.

Below are some ideas about evaluating human rights education.

(This advice is based on the essay Lesson Evaluation in the Human Rights Classroom by Felisa Tibbitts)

Academic evaluation methods (such as marking essays on factual accuracy), are more suited to formal education settings. Although useful for evaluating the **KNOWLEDGE** part of human rights education, such methods are not so useful for evaluating **SKILLS** and **ATTITUDES**. It is quite difficult to monitor the development of skills and attitudes among peer group participants, particularly if they are working in small groups. Some peer group leaders may feel nervous about the challenge. Human rights educators, and especially peer group leaders, tend to use new evaluation techniques which can be used in consultation with the peer group members. Such methods are designed to assess the effectiveness of the skills and attitudes aspects of the human rights education programme and to involve peer group members in the evaluation.

Evaluating Human Rights Education Activities

The evaluation of any activities can be done:

- Formally through the distribution of a questionnaire, or the creation of a suggestion box.
- Informally through discussions when an activity is finished.
- Personally through individual self evaluation of your lesson plans.

Formal and Informal Evaluation Questions

You may want to include some of the following questions in either your formal questionnaire or informal discussion with group members:

- The type of sessions I like best are .... Discuss.
- The type of activities I like best are .... Discuss.
- The type of sessions I like least are.... Discuss.
- The type of activities I like least are .... Discuss.
- The two things that should stay the same are.... Discuss.
- What I like most about the way our group works.... Discuss.
- What I like least about the way our group works.... Discuss.

In formal questionnaires participants should not be made to identify who they are, unless they want to.

Self Evaluation

You may want to get into the habit of evaluating the success of your lessons upon completion.

Making note of any kind of changes you want to make will ensure that your lessons are fine tuned for future use. Questions you may want to consider:

- Did the participants seem eager to participate?
- Were there certain aspects of the session that seemed more engaging?
- Would a break have been useful to help maintain group attention and interest?

- Did I use a variety of techniques to ensure group interest?
- Which ones were better received?
- How could this lesson have been improved?

Simplified Version of the Universal Declaration of Human Right

1. Everyone is free and we should all be treated in the same way.
2. Everyone is equal despite differences in skin colour, sex, religion, language for example.
3. Everyone has the right to life and to live in freedom and safety.
4. No one has the right to treat you as a slave nor should you make anyone your slave.
5. No one has the right to hurt you or to torture you.
6. Everyone has the right to be treated equally by the law.
7. The law is the same for everyone, it should be applied in the same way to all.
8. Everyone has the right to ask for legal help when their rights are not respected.
9. No one has the right to imprison you unjustly or expel you from your own country.
10. Everyone has the right to a fair and public trial.
11. Everyone should be considered innocent until guilt is proved.
12. Every one has the right to ask for help if someone tries to harm you, but no one can enter your home, open your letters or bother you or your family without a good reason.
13. Everyone has the right to travel as they wish.
14. Everyone has the right to go to another country and ask for protection, if they are being persecuted or are in danger of being persecuted.
15. Everyone has the right to belong to a country. No one has the right to prevent you from belonging to another country if you wish to.
16. Everyone has the right to marry and have a family.
17. Everyone has the right to own property and possessions.
18. Everyone has the right to practise and observe all aspects of their own religion and change their religion if they want to.
19. Everyone has the right to say what they think and to give and receive information.
20. Everyone has the right to take part in meetings and to join associations in a peaceful way.

21. Everyone has the right to help choose and take part in the government of their country.
22. Everyone has the right to social security and to opportunities to develop their skills.
23. Everyone has the right to work for a fair wage in a safe environment and to join a trade union.
24. Everyone has the right to rest and leisure.
25. Everyone has the right to an adequate standard of living and medical help if they are ill.
26. Everyone has the right to go to school.
27. Everyone has the right to share in their community's cultural-life.
28. Everyone must respect the 'social order' that is necessary for all these rights to be available.
29. Everyone must respect the rights of others, the community and public property.
30. No one has the right to take away any of the rights in this declaration.

⌘❑⌘

12 Human Rights Based Approach to Development

The origins of a human rights-based approach (HRBA) trace back to the convergence between the human rights and the human development discourses over the past decade. It is also being promoted in the context of the UN Reform. Operationally, a HRBA involves the application of certain tools (human rights) in development analysis and planning.

A HRBA is based on two types of rationale: normative and instrumental. The normative justification of a HRBA high-lights human rights as norms that should be respected by States as well as by UN agencies in conformity with the UN Charter. The instrumental rationale considers a HRBA can serve to: (a) reduce abuses of power and violent conflict, and to (b) progress in the achievement of targets and goals, minimizing the risk of set-backs. A human rights approach to development is a response to the limitations of previous approaches (such as basic needs and sustainable livelihoods) to address the influence of power inequalities in the development process. However, a human rights approach does not discard previous development approaches, but builds on them.

Definition of a Human Rights Approach to Development

A **human rights approach** may be defined as a ***frame-work*** *for the pursuit of* ***human development*** *that is normatively based on, and operationally directed to, the development of* ***capacities to realise human rights.***

This implies that:

(1) The objective of a human rights approach is human development.

Human rights provide a detailed guide towards generic human development goals (such as health, education, good governance, etc). In other words, human rights can act as a 'roadmap' towards human development objectives. For instance, under a human rights framework the objective of 'health' includes affordability, accessibility and quality of health services, and embraces the underlying determinants of health (such as clean water and a healthy environment). A human rights approach can also go beyond the human rights frame-work - it may require expanding human rights to better achieve human development goals. For instance, free legal counsel is a human right only with regard to criminal cases, although poverty reduction requires that free legal counsel be extended *as a matter of right* to other cases too (e.g. land ownership, labour relations)

(2) The approach seeks to ground human development on human rights for instrumental reasons (reducing poverty and violent conflict), although there are also normative considerations: human rights are norms to which both States and the United Nations should abide to.

(3) The two main causes preventing the realisation of human rights are lack of political will and insufficient capacities. Whereas 'human rights monitoring' seeks to foster political will, a human rights approach to development seeks to develop capacities accordingly. The UN system performs different functions in the field of human rights, a major objective of the United Nations Organisation. These functions are carried out by different structures within the system. Some bodies (such as the General Assembly), set human rights standards. Other mechanisms (such as treaty bodies or the UN Commission on Human Rights) monitor their implementation. UN specialized agencies (UNDP, UNFPA, UNICEF, WHO, etc) focus on capacity development.

(4) The realization of human rights requires capacities at two levels:

a. **Capacities for empowerment**: right-holders need to strengthen their capacities to claim and exercise their rights effectively.

b. **Capacities for accountability**: duty-bearers need to strengthen their capacities to fulfil human rights obligations.

Why are Human Rights Needed in Development Practice?

Instrumental Rationale for the Use of a Human Rights Approach in Development Strategies

The human rights approach seeks to respond to two interrelated problems facing poverty reduction efforts today: 'capture' of economic and political benefits by the better-off, and growing violent conflicts.

(1) The problem of 'elite capture'

It is now generally accepted that over the past decades the poorest members of society have become poorer, whereas the richest are richer now than they have ever been in the course of history. Income inequality has been rising in many developed, developing and transitional countries. As high-lighted by recent studies, a high-inequality growth pattern makes it difficult to achieve poverty alleviation, and it is hardly politically sustainable over the long-term. Income is not the only aspect that may be affected by inequality.

Public policies in fundamental issues such as education and health often neglect poor people and favour the wealthy. The Human Development Reports 2002 and 2003 present important findings in this regard – to the extent that some 'development gains' are in jeopardy, and some development indicators have already suffered setbacks. In other words, the expected 'trickle down' effects of economic and political development have not reached the bottom. This failure has a lot to do with the fact that most of these benefits have been 'captured' by the better off – that is, the already powerful and wealthy and those who are relatively less poor. Elite capture may be defined as the process by which powerful elites skim resources intended for the bottom, and/or define policies in a way that protects their own interests. Elites may be economic, ethnic, national, gender-based, etc. Capture may occur at national and international levels.

Although elite capture may not be completely eliminated, human rights are brought to the development process in order to set certain limits, and to guarantee basic human conditions for those who suffer the consequences. Even the grievances of the poor may be manipulated by political actors who just seek to pursue their own personal or organisational goals. Human Rights are established by legal norms in order to avoid that any of the parties can define its obligations or entitlements for its own vested interests at the expense of others.

Human Rights create entitlements and obligations that are universal – that is, they apply to all human beings, including the most disadvantaged, and they must be respected by all, including the most powerful. Because of their universality, human rights represent a useful frame-work to prevent abuses of power and ensure there is no discrimination against most disadvantaged groups.

(2) The problem of violent conflict

Another problem facing poverty reduction efforts today is the spread of violent conflict, a phenomena that is partly related to the growing impact of capture. Conflicts are natural in human interaction, but they may produce positive change as well as damaging destruction. A human rights approach seeks to manage existing conflicts so that they do not turn into violence (by establishing limitations on abusive capture, and redress mechanisms when abuses occur). Hence Human rights are useful to prevent and overcome violent conflicts.

A human rights approach brings two main contributions to conflict transformation:

(1) **A human rights approach helps to reduce the risk of violence, by detecting growing conflicts and providing a framework of entitlements and obligations to manage them –** As human rights are naturally conflictive, a human rights approach helps to reveal existing conflicts within the society, some of which may be hidden within social and political structures. This 'early warning' mechanism is coupled by a framework of entitlements and obligations, which can be applied by the parties for managing the conflict in nonviolent forms.

(2) **A human rights approach helps to overcome persistent violent conflicts: Not only it deals with the problem of greed (through setting limits for abusive capture), but also establishes the obligation to redress grievances (the so-called 'right of a remedy and reparation')** – Although poverty is at the root of many violent conflicts, conflict studies highlight that the 'triggers' of violence are usually related to two elements: 'greed' and 'grievances'. Regarding the later, people may resort to violence when they perceive they are suffering grievances to which they cannot find appropriate redress within the system. Indeed, history shows violent conflicts cannot be fully overcome unless appropriate redress to human rights grievances is eventually given.

HOW TO APPLY A HUMAN RIGHTS APPROACH IN DEVELOPMENT PROGRAMMING?

A human rights approach uses the human rights framework in analyzing development problems and designing and implementing strategies. The objectives are to (a) ensure minimum conditions of well-being for poor and marginalized people (b) reduce the risks of set-backs and (c) minimise violence risks.

The operationalization of a Human Rights approach is called, **Human Rights based Programming (HRBP).** It consist of the **integration of human rights principles and standards into all stages in the programming process** – *assessment and analysis, objective setting, design of capacity development strategies, implementation, and monitoring and evaluation.* As a technical tool, HRBP draws heavily on basic elements of the so-called 'good programming'.

More specifically, rights-based programming involves:

(a) Identifying what specific results should be pursued in line with a human rights frame-work, and who are the claim-holders and duty-bearers in that particular situation.

(b) Identifying their specific claims and obligations.

(c) Identifying specific capacity problems they face to exercise those claims or fulfil those obligations.

(d) Designing capacity development strategies accordingly.

(e) Ensuring the process respects basic human rights principles.

Rights-based programming uses human rights principles and standards.

Human Rights principles provide the frame-work for the *process* of development. Human rights standards help to define the type of *results* pursued in the development process.

Applying human rights principles in development practice.

A human rights approach states that the process of development is as important as the outcome, and that indeed the process largely determines the type of outcomes resulting from development activities. Rights-based programming applies guiding principles to ensure an adequate development process.

The two major principles are **ACCOUNTABILITY** and **NON-DISCRIMINATION**, although a simple acronym (PANEL) is often used to clarify the implications of rights-based programming. The acronym **PANEL** stands for:

- Participation
- Accountability
- Non-discrimination, Equality and Attention to vulnerable groups
- Empowerment
- Linkages to human rights standards, progressive realisation of rights and non-retrogression.

Although some of them are not new to development practice, the value of a human rights-approach is that these principles become **mandatory**. This is important, given that those whom these principles protect the most (that is, poor and marginalized groups), are not generally in a position to claim them.

(1) Participation

Participation means involving claim-holders and major duty-bearers in the assessment, decision-making and implementation of development strategies. Rights-based programming pays special attention to **creating channels of participation for poor and disadvantaged people**, as the ones whose claims are most affected. Also, a human rights approach qualifies the scope of 'participation' as **active, free and meaningful**. The approach seeks a specific type of participation, not participation at any cost. Participation is not consultation: it must shape and determine development decisions. This requires adequate access to information, adequate organisational capacities, absence of threats, etc. Therefore, rights-based programming should **devote time and resources to create capacities for participation** if the later is to be meaningful, as 'participatory' approaches are vulnerable to be used simply to legitimise pre-existing decisions.

(2) Accountability

Good programming stresses that **in order for results to be achieved, clear accountabilities must be set**. That is also the reason why for all human rights, there are corresponding duties. The value of a human rights approach for understanding 'accountability' in development activities is that it sets *specific* entitlements and obligations. It ensures that accountabilities with respect to the results and the process of development are not defined exclusively by those who take the decisions, thus lessening the probability that such a definition would help to protect their own interests at the expense of those of most disadvantaged groups. To ensure accountability, rights-based programming starts by assessing specific obstacles that duty-bearers face to exercise their obligations. This analysis sets a baseline to formulate development strategies to remove them. A human rights approach uses a **'capacity development perspective'**: in other words, it aims to build on claim-holders and duty-bearers' **existing strengths and solutions**, rather than substituting them. Defining clear accountabilities, and developing capacities accordingly, may however be insufficient. For accountability to be effective, it needs to be demanded. Therefore, rights-based programming calls for the **inclusion of civil society oversight elements** in programme design and implementation. Lastly, a fundamental implication of accountability from a rights-based perspective is the need to strengthen **risk analysis** in development programming. As empowering disadvantaged people is likely to face resistance by some groups, such an analysis should include assessing the conflict potential of development activities, and establishing strategies to manage it.

(3) Non-discrimination, equality and attention to vulnerable groups

The principles of non-discrimination and equality require paying special attention to those who are more discriminated against, or those who are more negatively affected by the unequal distribution of economic, social and political resources. These groups involve not just 'poor people', but also the most vulnerable people among the poor – e.g. women, the elderly, members of low-castes, internally displaced persons, persons living with HIV/AIDs, etc. Rights-based programming seeks to **identify different vulnerable groups among the claim-holders, in order to target them explicitly**. This requires an adequate level of data disaggregation – for which usually investments at early programming stages will need to be made, as available data may be inadequate to reflect distinct situations among the poor.

(4) Empowerment

Empowerment is **the process by which the capacities of people to claim and exercise rights grow**. People are 'empowered' when they are able to claim and exercise their rights more effectively. Empowerment is a key principle to guide development strategies. Rights-based programming starts by analysing **what specific capacities are needed** to claim and exercise rights in a particular situation. These are the capacities that HRBA programs seek to focus on. **Participation is linked to empowerment** in the sense that, when participation is active, free and meaningful, the mere fact of being able to take and implement decisions is an indicator of empowerment.

(5) Linkages to human rights standards – progressive realisation and non-retrogression

A defining feature of a human rights approach is its explicit linkage to human rights standards. **Human rights standards** are an *objective* 'roadmap' to human development goals that **prevent 'capture'** of the development agenda, **and set minimum guarantees** for poor and disadvantaged groups. They also **help to identify where problems exist, and what are the capacities and functions required to address them**. For instance, if the problem is one of access to information, a human rights approach would include in the analysis not onlv availability of information, but also related standards of the right to information such as transparency affordability, physical reach, adequacy and non-discrimination. The picture of the problem (and of the strategy), becomes comprehensive, as it includes multiple dimensions affecting the entitlements of poor and vulnerable people. Human rights standards exist in many fields; most of them are 'legal obligations', some of them are politically binding. As an instrumental 'roadmap', however, all human rights standards are equally useful. In the programming process, they can **help to define a comprehensive but targeted scope for development strategies** – and they provide a rationale of cost-effectiveness. Human rights standards can also help **to set results based outcomes and outputs**. Human rights standards should be respected for all, although this may require **progressive realisation** within limited resources. Human Rights Standards may be found in both treaties and declarations, and in the so-called, "General Comments" of the Human Rights treaty bodies (providing detailed explanation of the standards contained in particular rights). allow for progressive realisation, although they set clear limits on the possibility for setbacks. The principle of **non-retrogression** means that duty bearers should at least protect the human rights gains already made, when factors beyond their control prevent these gains to grow further.

Globalisation raises important challenges in this regard. Co-operation among States is necessary to progressively ensure human rights standards for all, and also to sustain the gains. International target-setting, such as the Millennium Development Goals (MDGs) is a major step forward. Strengthening capacities to implement human rights safeguards can reduce the risk of setbacks – from which the MDGs are not exempted, as revealed by the Human Development Report 2003.

⌘❐⌘

Bibliography

1. Amnesty International. (1996). Human rights education strategy. Accessible at http://www.amnesty.org/ailib/aipub/1996.
2. Amnesty International. (2007). What is human rights education? Accessible at www.amnesty.org.
3. ARRC [Asia-Pacific Regional Resource Center for Human Rights Education]. (2003). What is human rights education. In Human rights education pack. Bangkok, Thailand: ARRC.
4. Baas de Gaay Fortman, 'Rights-Based Approaches: Any New Thing Under the Sun?', IDEA Newsletter, December 2000, accessible at http://www.carleton.ca/idea/newsletter.
5. Buergenthal, T. and Torney, J.V. (1976). International human rights and international education. Washington, D.C.: U.S. National Commission for UNESCO. .
6. Claude, R. P. (1996). Educating for human rights: The Philippines and beyond. Quezon City, Philippines: University of the Philippines Press.
7. Council of Europe. (n.d.). Council of Europe. Accessible at http://www.coe.int/.
8. Dey A. K – 'Environmental Chemistry' New Delhi – Vile Dasaus Ltd.,
9. Daniel Langenkamp, 'The Human Rights Overlap', accessible at http://fletcher.tufts.edu/humansecurity/pdf/Langenkamp.pdf.
10. Elbers, F. (Ed.). (2000). Human rights education resource book. Cambridge, MA: Human Rights Education Associates.
11. Flowers, N. (Ed.) (1998). Human rights here and now: Celebrating the Universal Declaration of Human Rights. Minneapolis, MN: Amnesty International USA and University of Minnesota Human Rights Resource Center.

12. Flowers, N. (2001, August). Report. Unpublished report presented at the Human Rights Education Symposium, Durban, South Africa.
13. HREA.(n.d.) Human Rights Education Association. Accessible at http://www.hrea.org/.
14. Hugo Slim, 'Making Moral Low Ground: Rights as the Struggle for Justice and the Abolition of Development', accessible at http://fletcher.tufts.edu/praxis/xvii/Slim.pdf.
15. Human Development Report 2000: Human Rights and Human Development, UNDP, accessible at http://hdr.undp.org/.
16. Human Rights: Questions and Answers by Leah Levin, illustrated by Plantu.
17. IDEA Newsletter, December 2000: 'Human Rights and Human Development: Seven Commentaries on the Human Development Report 2000', accessible at http://www.carleton.ca/idea/newsletter.
18. IIDH [Inter-American Institute of Human Rights]. (2002). Inter-American report on human rights education, a study of 19 countries: Normative development. San Jose, CA: Inter-American Institute of Human Rights.
19. Inter-Agency Workshop Report on Implementing a Human Rights-based Approach in the Context of UN Reform, (Stamford, USA, 5-7 May, 2003).
20. Kati, K. and Gjedia, R. (2003). Educating the next generation: Incorporation human rights education in the public school system. Minneapolis, MN: New Tactics in Human Rights Project.
21. Manual for Human Rights Education An educational manual for primary and secondary levels. OHCHR.
22. Netherlands Helsinki Committee. (1995, October). Human rights education: Planning for the future. Soesterberg, The Netherlands.
23. OHCHR, Human Rights and Development: Documents accessible at http://www.unhchr.ch/development/mainstreaming-01.html.
24. Patrick Van Weerelt, 'The Application of a Human Rights-based Approach to Development Programming: What is the added value?', UNDP 2000 and 'A Human Rights-based Approach to Development Programming in UNDP: Adding the Missing Link', UNDP 2001, accessible at http://www.undp.org/governance/hurist.htm.
25. Peter Uvin, 'On High Moral Ground: The Incorporation of Human Rights by the Development Enterprise', accessible at http://fletcher.tufts.edu/praxis/xvii/Uvin.pdf.
26. Pearse, S. (1987). European teachers' seminar on 'human rights education in a global perspective'. Strasbourg, Austria: Council of Europe.
27. Ramirez, F.O., Suarez, D. and Meyer, J.W. (2006). The worldwide rise of human rights education. In A. Benavot and C. Braslavsky (Eds.), School

knowledge in comparative and historical perspective: Changing curricula in primary and secondary education. Hong Kong, Hong Kong: Comparative Education Research Centre (CERC) and Springer.

28. Rights and Livelihood Approaches: Exploring Policy Dimensions, Tim Conway, Caroline Moser, AndyNorton & John Farrington, ODI Natural Resource Perspectives, May 2002, accessible at www.gtz-asiaonline.org/HDP/Lib.nsf/0/a7fd15937750a10447256c2f0028cd9f?OpenDocument.
29. 'Rights, Claims and Capture: Understanding the Politics of Pro-Poor Policy', Craig Johnson and Daniel.
30. Richard A. Falk, 'Human Rights Horizons: The Pursuit of Justice in a Globalised World', New York,Routledge Press 2000.
31. Ruhela S. P – 'Human Value and Education' New Delhi –Sterling publishers.
32. South House Exchange (2004). Education for peace, human rights, democracy, international understanding and tolerance. Report of Canada. Prepared for The Council of Ministers of Education, Canada in collaboration with the Canadian Commission for UNESCO.
33. OHCHR,[2004] Teaching Human Rights Practical activities for primary and secondary schools, United Nations New York and Geneva, 2004.
34. UNESCO, Section for Humanistic, Cultural and International Education.
35. Start May 2001, Overseas Development Institute (ODI), Working Paper 145, accessible at www.odi.org.uk/pppg/activities/concepts_analysis/rightsinaction/Publications/WP145_RightsClaimsCapture.pdf.
36. Tibbitts, F. (1996). On human dignity: A renewed call for human rights education. Social Education, 60(7), 428-431.
37. Tibbitts, F. (2003). Report from the United Nations Office of the High Commissioner sub-regional meeting on human rights education in south-eastern Europe. Skopje, Macedonia, 7-8 July 2003.
38. To Claim our Rights: Livelihood Security, HR & Sustainable Development, Caroline Moser & Andy Norton with Tim Conway, Claire Ferguson, Polly Vizard, ODI, 2001, accessible at www.odi.org.uk/pppg/activities/concepts_analysis/rights inaction/Publications/To Claim Our Rights.html.
39. UN. (1996). International plan of action for the decade of human rights education. Geneva, Switzerland: United Nations (1996). Report of the United Nations High Commissioner for Human Rights on the implementation of the Plan of Action for the United Nations Decade for Human Rights. Accessible at http://www.unhchr.ch/huridocda/huridoca.nsf/(Symbol)/A.51.506.Add.1.En?OpenDocument.

40. UNDP Capacity for Development: New Solutions to Old Problems, Ed.: S. Fukuda-Parr, C. Lopes and K. Mali, Executive Summary, accessible at http://capacity.undp.org/books/Summary_en.pdf.

41. UNESCO. (1978). Final document: International Congress on the Teaching of Human Rights. SS-78/Conf.401/Col.29. Vienna, Austria. (2005). The plan for action for 2005-2009 in brief, the World Programme for Human Rights Education. Accessible at http://www.ohchr.org/english/issues/education/training/docs/PlanofActioninbrief_en.pdf.

42. UNDP Policy on Integrating Human Rights with Sustainable Human Development, 1998, accessible at www.undp.org/governance/docshurist/rightsapproach.doc.

43. UNGA. (2005). Draft plan of action for the first phase (2005-2007) of the proposed World Programme for Human Rights Education. A/59/525.

44. Yeban, F. (2003). Building a culture of human rights: Challenge to human rights education in 21st century. In Human rights education pack. Bangkok, Thailand: ARRC.